Language Study

LANGUAGE STUDY

STUDY
*The School
and the Community*

Peter Doughty, Geoffrey Thornton,
and Anne Doughty

ELSEVIER

NEW YORK   OXFORD   AMSTERDAM

ELSEVIER NORTH-HOLLAND, INC.
52 Vanderbilt Avenue, New York, NY 10017

First published 1973, 1974
by Edward Arnold (Publishers) Ltd.

Elsevier North-Holland edition
published in 1977

Calligraphy in cover design adapted from
Calligraphy by Arthur Baker. © 1973 by Arthur Baker.
Published by Dover Publications, Inc.

Library of Congress Cataloging in Publication Data

Doughty, Peter Symonds.
  Language study: the school and the community

  Comprises 3 previously published essays: Language study,
the teacher and the learner, by P. Doughty and
G. Thornton; Language, experience and school, by
G. Thornton; and Language and community, by
A. and P. Doughty
  Includes bibliographies.
  1. English language—Study and teaching.
2. Children—Language. 3. Community and school.
I. Thornton, Geoffrey, joint author. II. Doughty,
Anne, joint author. III. Doughty, Peter Symonds.
Language study, the teacher and the learner. 1977.
IV. Thornton, Geoffrey. Language, experience and
school. 1977. V. Doughty, Anne. Language and
community. 1977. VI. Title.
LB1576.D643   1977   407'.1   76-30410
ISBN 0-444-00202-2

Printed in the United States of America

Contents

Publisher's Introduction

This volume comprises three previously published essays in the *Explorations in Language Study Series* published in Great Britain by Edward Arnold Limited under the general editorship of Peter Doughty and Geoffrey Thornton. We are reprinting selected essays from this series because of the importance and relevance of the material to American educators. In addition to this volume, two other books in the series are now available for sale from Elsevier, *Explorations in the Functions of Language* and *Learning How to Mean,* both by M.A.K. Halliday. Additional volumes in *Explorations in Language Study* will be forthcoming.

Foreword

In the course of our efforts to develop a linguistic focus for work in English language, now published as 'Language in Use', we came to realise the extent of the growing interest in what we would call a linguistic approach to language. Lecturers in Colleges and Departments of Education see the relevance of such an approach in the education of teachers. Many teachers in schools and in colleges of Further Education see themselves that 'Educational failure is primarily linguistic failure', and have turned to Linguistic Science for some kind of exploration and practical guidance. Many of those now exploring the problems of relationships, community or society from a sociological or psychological point of view wish to make use of a linguistic approach to the language in so far as it is relevant to those problems.

We were conscious of the wide divergence between the aims of the linguist, primarily interested in language as a system for organising 'meanings', and the needs of those who now wanted to gain access to the insights that resulted from that interest. In particular, we were aware of the wide gap that separated the literature of academic Linguistics from the majority of those who wished to find out what Linguistic Science might have to say about language and the use of language.

Out of this experience emerged our own view of that much-used term, 'Language Study', developed initially in the chapters of 'Exploring Language', and now given expression in this series. Language Study is not a subject but a process, which is why the series is to be called 'Explorations in Language Study'. Each exploration is focused upon a meeting point between the insights of Linguistic Science, often in conjunction with other social sciences, and the linguistic questions raised by the study of a particular aspect of individual behaviour or human society.

Initially, the volumes in this series have a particular relevance to the role of language in teaching and learning. The editors intend that they should make a basic contribution to the literature of Language Study, doing justice equally to the findings of the academic disciplines involved and the practical needs of those who now want to take a linguistic view of their own particular problems of language and the use of language.

Peter Doughty
Geoffrey Thornton

LANGUAGE STUDY, THE TEACHER AND THE LEARNER

Peter Doughty and Geoffrey Thornton

Part I
The Concept
of Language Study
by Peter Doughty

1 The nature of the need

1. A new focus on language

In the summer of 1971, over seven hundred teachers, academics, advisers, inspectors and educational administrators gathered together at the University of York, England. They had come from the United States, Canada and Great Britain to take part in an international conference on the teaching and learning of English. It might seem to many teachers that a major gathering of people concerned with one single subject could have very little relevance for those who teach any other subject. This was not the case, however. Interest and discussion moved away from a narrow concern with the practice of 'English' and took up a new focus, the part played by *language*, not just in 'English', but in all teaching and learning. As the conference went on, moreover, it proved impossible to focus upon language in teaching and learning without considering, at the same time, the part played by language in shaping the lives of men and the fabric of their societies.

The people who met at York brought with them an enormous diversity of educational experience, which ranged from the nursery group to the post-graduate seminar, with learners of all ages and levels of ability. They combined a similarly wide range of experience in the area of organization and administration, from the problems of running a small department to the complexities of planning educational policy for a large state. Above all, they were people who had come to the conference because their individual experience had led them to ask questions about many aspects of what is now done in the name of education. They met to talk about the practice of their trade as teachers of 'English' and discovered in the process that it only made sense to do so as long as they were willing to focus upon all learners as, first and foremost,

5

users of language. By reaching this conclusion, they recognized the inescapable fact that it is language that is the critically determining factor in pupils' capacity to learn.

On the last day of the conference, in a final plenary session which gave expression to the sense of the meeting, it was agreed,

> To redefine our subject in the light of the language needs of all children and their probable needs in a kind of society we cannot predict.

Many teachers might react to this statement of aim by suggesting that it was about time teachers of English looked to their responsibilities, and many others outside the educational system would echo their sentiments. Implicit in this reaction is the familiar idea that '. . . the language needs of all children . . .' can and ought to be met by the work of the English Department. The conference resolution might seem to suggest that a new age was heralded in which pupils would turn up for every class, ready and able to use whatever spoken or written language was required of them by the subject teacher concerned.

If we look at the resolution a little more closely, however, we will find that its implications do not point that way at all. Certainly, the resolution *does* reaffirm the central part to be played by language in the work of English Departments. It does not imply, however, that those who teach 'English' should carry *sole* responsibility for the learner's operational command of language, written or spoken. In order to bring the work of the English Department into line with the sense of the resolution, there would certainly have to be a very sharp focus upon '. . . the language needs of all children . . .'. This means that we need to be much more sharply aware of how they arise, what determines their character, and who would be best able to meet them. It also means that we need to look at a whole range of current class-room practices and ask how they relate to this central question of language need. It would only be possible to answer these questions, however, if we were willing to look at the way in which all teachers and all subjects create language needs particular to themselves. This implies that some redefinition, along the lines of the resolution, will be required for all subjects, if all teachers recognize the part played by language in their own class-rooms.

In particular, an appropriate redefinition of 'English' could not get very far without exploring the basic question of pupils' command of a language, written and spoken. This would lead us to

6

distinguish between the general contribution the teacher of English can make towards this command and the particular contribution that has to come from every teacher in terms of the language needs of his own situation. We would have to look at the ways in which other aspects of the life of the school could affect its pupils' capacity to use language for learning. Such matters as the school's pattern of discipline, its customary view of relationships between teachers and pupils, the relationships it permits between pupils of different age groups or sexes, its attitude towards pupils' everyday speech, all these help to create the climate for language use within each individual class-room. As teachers, we can only show a properly professional approach to '. . . the language needs of all children . . .', therefore, if we are prepared to examine the whole network of relationships between teachers, pupils, subjects and language that go to make up a school. It is the purpose of this book to show how a linguistic approach to the language needs and the language problems of teachers and pupils might enable us to carry out this examination.

2. Terms for discussion

Writing about the field of education presents one particularly acute problem. Almost everyone goes to school; many people go on being involved with schools as parents or as employers; and so talk about education is part of ordinary, everyday life. The result of this is that there are a very large number of words and phrases about education and its processes constantly in use as part of the common language. These words and phrases, moreover, embody our habitual ways of thinking about schools and colleges, teachers and lecturers, pupils and students, and so on. When words and phrases have this sort of function, however, the range of meanings they express can be very wide.

Each person is likely to have his or her own version of what they really mean, and precision is lost through their very accessibility.

If the object of a book is to explore a new approach to established subjects, or new directions in the curriculum, then this can scarcely be done without presenting a challenge to received ideas as to what some of those words and phrases mean, because explorations of this kind will necessarily call into question the habitual ways of thinking that they express. For instance, what needs to be said about language as a function of teaching and learning will very often apply to *all* learning situations, wherever

7

they occur. This is because the things that we have to say are derived from a *general* consideration of the nature and function of language. To couch our argument in terms of the particular divisions and boundaries within the curriculum and the educational process as we know it would merely obscure and distort the value of what a linguistic approach to language in teaching and learning can offer.

The need to cut across boundaries is well illustrated by pairs of words like schools and colleges, teachers and lecturers, pupils and students. In dividing up our world we mark the boundaries we draw by attaching linguistic labels to them. In time we come to think of these boundaries as somehow a part of nature, because we use different words for whatever we place on alternative sides of the boundaries we draw. Moreover, what people normally use to carry on everyday conversation, the common language, very often reinforces this habit of mind, because the common language does not contain words or phrases which readily embrace elements on either side of such boundaries. Consider this group—teacher, pupil, school: and now this—lecturer, student, college. What words and phrases are there to express the common elements which underly both sets of words and yet retain the status of a common language expression? The answer is that there aren't any. If, therefore, we want to point to what schools and colleges, teachers and lecturers, pupils and students have in common, because they are all involved in one process of education, then we shall have to use new terms.

There is a proper scepticism amongst those involved in education, however, about the proliferating terminology of educational studies. Many teachers believe that there is no practical value to be gained by using the new terms these studies introduce. Consider, however, the implications of the following example, taken from the correspondence columns of a leading national daily newspaper, noted for its interest in social questions. One reader wrote to complain about what he regarded as ". . . the terrible jargon the social scientists are at present inflicting upon us". His point was that he had been asked in the street to contribute money for the aid of 'underprivileged children', which he regarded as an 'awful synonym for poor kids'. In reply to his letter, a social scientist pointed out that these terms were by no means synonomous. He said that,

> . . . the term underprivileged assigns responsibility to its rightful owners—the privileged. On the other hand, the term poor . . .

leaves responsibility open, thereby providing people the let out of assigning responsibility for poverty to the poor themselves.

Now the value of this example is that it comes from the market-place. The person who was doing the collecting wanted to express a theory about why poor children are poor, and the term 'under-privileged' does express an underlying body of ideas about why people are poor. The common language phrase, 'poor kids', however, is loosely descriptive and expressive. It is important to see that the use of a term like 'underprivileged' *does* express a point of view, one version of the facts, and it allows us to dispute this version of the facts because the version has been made explicit. The two phrases, 'poor kids' and 'underprivileged children', in fact belong to very different types of discourse, and consequently they give rise to very different styles of discussion. Put bluntly, every man is free to argue his own view of why kids are poor, but disagreement about the underprivileged must make some reference to the facts.

Terms are most needed precisely where their use is likely to cause most irritation, where the subject in question belongs, and has always belonged, in the market-place. Just as the poor are always with us, and therefore have always been a subject for discussion between ordinary members of the community, so have schools and pupils and education. The particular example of the underprivileged is closely paralleled by the familiar educational question of 'ability'. Saying 'dull kids', 'weak pupils', 'the not-so-bright ones', is the equivalent of saying 'poor kids'. These phrases imply many things about our habitual cultural attitudes towards learning, but they do not express a *theory*. Their use does not demand of us a rational and ordered response which takes account of the facts. If we talk about 'the culturally deprived', 'the less able', 'the average pupil', however, we *do* assert a theory and may be properly challenged to state our reasons for taking this view of the facts rather than any of the possible alternative views available to us.

This book, therefore, and those that follow it in this series, ought to use terms that clearly reveal their author's view of the facts. What they say needs to be taken up and challenged, because the explorations that they offer are new. The aim of the series is to provide a basis for discussion, and disagreement, and therefore to stimulate development of the ideas involved.

Let me illustrate this argument by looking at the key phrase in the York conference resolution, 'the language needs of all

9

children'. The use of the word 'children' in this phrase might lead one to think that only those up to the age of nine or ten were being referred to. This book, however, is concerned with all those involved in the educational process from nursery school to college. Its focus is upon the language needs of all *learners*, whatever their situation, age or intellectual ability.

Using *learner* in this way reminds us again of the boundaries built into our thinking by pairs of words like school and college, teacher and lecturer, pupil and student. As teachers, our own situation in the class-room makes us so conscious of the *differences* between learning situations that we lose sight of what they have in common. By using the term *learner* to cover everyone who enters into a learning situation *in order to learn*, whether child, adolescent, or adult, pupil or student, average or able, we are pointing to what they all have in common as learners, *the particular language needs which arise from the learning situation in which they find themselves*. All those, therefore, who enter into the learning situation in order to impart, instruct, lead, organize, guide, or otherwise interact with learners we must call *teachers*.

3. Schools and colleges: institutions or agencies?

The everyday use of language sets up in our minds boundaries between schools and colleges, and between different kinds of school, Nursery and Infant, Infant and Junior, Junior and Secondary. We tend to speak about these different kinds of school as though each one of them accommodates a type of learner *totally distinct in all respects* from any other. By using the term *educational system* we can point to what they all share in common because they are agencies established for the formal transmission of knowledge, intellectual and social and cultural, from one generation to the next.

This use of the word *agency*, rather than institution, is one more example of choosing a term because one particular view of the facts is being advanced rather than another. To talk about schools and colleges as institutions points to their discreteness, their individual autonomy, the fact that they exist as buildings, bricks and mortar, glass and concrete and steel. Institutions are things and they have fixed limits. Where one institution ends, and another begins, is 'obvious'. Consequently it is easy to consider them in terms of their rights and privileges, their spheres of influence and so on. The word institution, therefore, implies a theory

10

about the educational system in which schools and colleges exist independently of anything else and treat with each other as sovereign bodies. But such a view of the educational system will not help us if we need to focus upon the function of language in teaching and learning, wherever teaching and learning occurs.

To talk about schools and colleges as *educational agencies*, on the other hand, implies a very different theory about the educational system. What this view of schools and colleges suggests is the fact that they are not so much buildings, scholastic or administrative units, as collections of people, using certain means to achieve particular educational ends. The word 'agency' points to a theory in which schools and colleges only exist in so far as societies and individuals have need of them. They are so intimately related to the society in which they exist that there is no real sense in which they can be thought of as autonomous. The boundaries of educational agencies are much less easily defined because the essence of their function is to mediate between learners and bodies of knowledge, intellectual and social and cultural. If educational institutions are isolates with impermeable boundaries, then educational agencies are locations for social processes.

All schools and colleges, then, share the task of relaying certain aspects of the culture of their society to those individuals who are in the process of becoming new members of it. 'Culture', in this case, is not to be read as the high culture of the humanist, Arnold's '. . . the best that has been thought and said . . .', but rather what has been so well described by Sir Edward Tyler, the British anthropologist, as,

> . . . that complex whole which includes knowledge, belief, art, morals, law, custom, and any other capabilities and habits acquired by man as a member of society.

If schools and colleges are concerned with the process of mediating between the existing store of '. . . capabilities and habits . . .', and those who are in the process of acquiring them in order to become fully-fledged members of that society, then we are more interested in their mediatory role than in their rights and privileges.

As institutions, schools and colleges appear free to pursue their own ends, and are conscious of the need to maintain their individual identity by a rigorous defence of the boundaries that separate them from each other and from the rest of society; as agencies, however, their focus must be upon the process that relates culture

11

to individual learners, a process that necessarily involves the crossing of many boundaries.

4. The 'needs' of learners

The use of the word 'need' in our key phrase, '. . . the language needs of all children . . .' is a perfect demonstration of the difficulties that arise when we use a familiar word from the common language, and do not set out the particular meaning we intend it to carry. At the present time, as we use it in educational discussion, 'need' is doubly ambiguous, so that we should be particularly careful to distinguish our intended meaning when we do use it.

On the one hand, our use of the word expresses either a concern for the child's personal development as an individual sentient self or a focus upon his parallel development as a social self, a creature made by and through his continuous contact with other human beings. Perhaps we might expect that these two ways of interpreting the word really amount to the same thing, as far as the child's experience of the world is concerned. That this ambiguity has arisen is an indication of the degree to which we feel that this is no longer the case in an advanced industrial society like ours. From the point of view of the educational system, moreover, this ambiguity is reflected in a divergence of emphasis that is vitally important for the language needs of all learners. Those who believe that 'needs' refer primarily to the development of the personal self are likely to emphasize the imaginative and individually creative aspects of language activity, while those who think of 'needs' primarily in terms of the capacity to make relationships with others are likely to stress the public and social aspects of language activity.

On the other hand, we use 'need' to refer either to what society demands of its members, or to what the educational system demands of those who are involved in it as learners. In this case, the ambiguity arises because schools and colleges exist to provide what is *needed* for survival in a particular society, and, at the same time, create their own needs in the process. From the point of view of the language needs of all learners, this ambiguity leads to a blurring of focus as to what kinds of languaging activity ought to be set up in learning situations and for what purposes. There is a divergence between those who think of 'needs' in terms of the kinds of language activity society expects of pupils and students, *because they have been through the formal educational system*; and those

12

who think in terms of the use of language they require of pupils and students, *because they are pupils and students.*

Unfortunately, the way language works encourages us to treat any two somethings, like the two meanings of an ambiguity, as quite separate from each other in every respect, once we have distinguished them. Neither of the pairs of meanings which I have just described ought to be read in this way, however. The distinction between the personal, and the social, needs of the child is clearly a question of the focus. From either point of view, the personal or the social, the focus is upon the developing self of the individual child. The ambiguity only arises because we can view this development, and therefore our assessment of the needs that follow from it, either from a standpoint *inside* the circle of the child's autonomous self, looking out towards the world at large, or from a standpoint *outside* that circle, looking in on it from the direction of the network of demands that the world makes upon him.

The second pair of meanings, the distinction between the needs of society and of the educational system, show a different kind of relationship. In this case, the needs arising from the learner's participation in the educational system are but one example of the needs which arise because he lives in society. We can put this more formally by saying that his needs as a learner are but a sub-set of the whole set of needs that living in a human community gives rise to.

This distinction has a particular significance for the language needs of learners, and leads me to use the terms *language for learning* and *language for living*. *Language for living* will refer to all the ways in which human beings make use of language in the ordinary course of their everyday lives; and *language for learning* will refer to all the ways in which language enters into the process of teaching and learning. A proper understanding of the relationship between *language for living* and *language for learning* is vital to a coherent theory of Language Study. Unless we see clearly the ways in which language for learning relates to, and derives from, language for living, we will never be able to make sense of the language needs of the learners, nor the linguistic problems that face all teachers.

2 Cultural attitudes, language and the learning situation

1. Linguistic perspectives and socialization

We now have so clear a picture of the crucial part played by language in learning that no teacher can really afford to overlook or ignore or leave to others the way in which his own pupils use language to learn. This situation demands an appropriate linguistic perspective towards language which would be available to every teacher for looking at the practical problems of his own situation. Such a perspective would become an essential element in the professional competence of a teacher, in the same way as the teaching of reading is now considered to be an essential element in the professional competence of all first school teachers or a knowledge of the discipline is considered to be an essential element in the professional competence of all subject specialist teachers.

This perspective cannot come from an individual's ordinary everyday acquaintance with language, however, or even from his traditional professional concern with it as a teacher. What is required is a form of Language Study specifically developed to meet the needs of those who are involved in the process of education *as teachers*. Given the nature of the need, and the uniqueness of language as a subject for study, together with the fact that it is the personal possession of everyone who takes up such a study, an appropriate form for it is not going to be easy to find. About the only thing that can be said with absolute certainty is that it will not look anything like the customary pattern of an academic 'subject matter'. Why this should be so is properly the concern of the rest of this book, but perhaps it would be useful at this stage in the argument to outline briefly the sort of consideration which has led to this conclusion. It seems to me that in devising an

14

approach to Language Study there are four matters in particular that no one can properly afford to ignore.

Firstly, there is the fact that questions about language activity in real situations, like homes and shops and factories and class-rooms, do not readily yield to enquiries conducted exclusively within the boundaries of a single discipline. An appropriate form for Language Study is therefore going to have to be interdisciplin-ary. Then there is the fact that the development of a linguistic perspective will make considerable demands upon individual teachers, because it will require them to modify their existing assumptions about language and attitudes towards its use. Modify-ing one's attitudes and assumptions is never an easy matter, and those that we hold in respect of language we hold most tenaciously, because many of them have been acquired as a result of growing up in a particular community, or even indeed as part of the actual process of acquiring language itself. They are therefore a very intimate, if non-explicit, part of our way of viewing the world. We must be able to put forward arguments for a new perspective in such a way that people will not feel their existing attitudes and assumptions are under attack, and therefore need defending, but be encouraged to rethink them in the light of the new understand-ing Language Study has to offer.

A third consideration is more daunting. If this case for Language Study is valid, it is clear that when one says that a linguistic perspective is a vital part of the professional competence of all teachers, then, at present, the vast majority of those whom one wants to involve in Language Study are going to be experienced practising teachers. They do not have the time, nor do most governments have the resources to provide, for a long period of detailed academic study. What is needed is rather a means of developing a way of thinking about particular issues, a way of conducting particular enquiries, than anything that could be pointed to as a recognizable 'body of knowledge'. 'Knowing the facts' is much less important in this context than knowing what questions to ask and what the answers to those questions might conceivably look like.

There is one more consideration to bring in at this stage. I have spoken about '. . . a form of study specifically developed to meet the needs of those who are involved in the process of education *as teachers*'. There are, of course, two participants in that process, for learners also have needs. Language Study must therefore develop a dual focus. In other words, one essential aspect of Language

15

Study is to show how a linguistic perspective can relate to the particular needs of all learners. It must also be ready to show how the learner can develop a new perspective for himself, as his existing attitudes to language may be a key element in preventing his effective use of language for learning. Moreover, Language Study should not stop at the provision of this perspective in relation only to *language for learning*. *Language for living* is an essential part of his ability to use language to learn. If we are going to be serious about attempting to meet '. . . the language needs of all children . . .', we cannot afford to stop at the class-room door.

I must now return to the main line of argument. To say that the development of an appropriate linguistic perspective is necessary for all those involved in the process of education is a very strong claim to make. What I want to do in this chapter is show how that claim arises not merely from the present situation in education, but out of the very way in which, as social beings, we are designed to use language. In order to do this I shall have to take a brief look at the process the sociologist refers to as 'socialization'. What this will show is that the climate affecting the use of language within the school or the college is created as much by the prevailing climate in the home and the community and society as a whole, as it is by the local conditions within the school itself or the educational system to which it belongs. Once I have done this, I will be in a position to go on and consider the way in which current changes in the educational system and in society affect the concept of Language Study.

One of the most necessary tasks for Language Study is to break down the idea that we can deal successfully with the problems of using language for learning by focusing solely upon the framework of the educational process itself. By looking at how a folk-linguistic perspective can shape an individual's view of language and its use, one can show that using language to learn is so bound up with using language to live that it does not make sense to treat them in isolation from one another. It also underlies the fact that every teacher needs to develop an *adequate* linguistic perspective in order to discover the effect of folk-linguistic perspective upon his attitudes to his own, and his pupils' use of language. In so far as we want to make sense of the language activity that goes on in schools and colleges, we must give up our habit of treating them as isolated autonomous institutions. The difference between viewing them as *institutions* and as *agencies* has already been referred to (see Chapter 1, Section 3, page 14). The next step is to relate this

16

distinction to the process of socialization, because it is this process that most intimately connects school and society through the medium of language. Schools and colleges as educational agencies stand in a special relationship to this process, moreover, which is why it is possible to refer to them as 'socializing agencies'. This is important from the point of view of Language Study, because language is one of the primary means by which *educational* agencies perform their function as *socializing* agencies.

To call schools and colleges agencies, then, is to express a particular theory about the part they play in the process by which individual men and women learn how to be effective members of society. Educational agencies play a dominant part in the process by which men acquire the particular '. . . capabilities and habits . . .' they need for survival in our society, as well as the values that bind them together as a society. A contemporary American linguist, whose chief interest is the relationship between language and culture, goes as far as to say that:

. . . language itself is a social institution with the function of value integration.

I would prefer to say 'social agency', but the implications of the remark are clear enough. If we are interested in how men use language to live, we must face the fact that one of their chief uses for it is to give an individual identity to the multiplicity of social groups that go to make up a society, groups such as family, community, office and workshop and school. This identity arises out of shared values and activities which are made available to the newcomer through the process of socialization. Unless we focus on this process, then, we are unlikely to make sense of the ways in which they use language to live, because we will not understand what values those ways are expressing.

Having said as much, it follows that the scope of Language Study must include a consideration of the wider contexts in which the teacher is operating. Certainly, the language activity within the learning situation itself, the pattern of language in use between teachers and pupils in class-rooms, must be at the very centre of its focus. At the same time, wherever the focus is upon the immediate linguistic events involved in a particular pattern of class-room activity, we need to remember that that class-room exists in the social context of the school as a whole; and that that school exists in the context of a particular neighbourhood, in a particular community. Moreover, we must not forget that that school also

17

has a place as an educational agency within the larger context of a particular educational system. In its turn, this educational system exists within the even larger context provided by what we understand as 'society'. Similarly, the neighbourhood and community which provide the immediate social context for the school belong in their turn and in their own way to this same thing we call 'society'. Just to add a final level of complication to the whole picture, it is entirely proper to speak of family, school, neighbourhood and community as each possessing their own culture, and, at the same time partaking of the culture of the larger context to which they belong.

What I have tried to show in this section is that there is no sense in which we are entitled to say that our concern with language in teaching and learning may profitably stop at the boundaries of the class-room or the school. The more we focus upon the problems created in school by the '. . . language needs of all children . . .' the more we are forced to extend our horizons until they embrace the whole range of '. . . capabilities and habits . . .' which go to make up the culture of a society. This we must do, because our concern is with language and the use of language, and language is, as Edward Sapir once said:

> . . . a complex inventory of all the ideas, interests and occupations that take up the attention of the community.

2. Language for living and language for learning

The term language for living introduced in the last chapter may have made some readers uneasy. It might seem to suggest a too heavily emotional attitude towards the part played by language in the lives of men and their society. Nothing of the kind is intended, however. The phrase is offered as a simple descriptive label for the fact that men use language in some way or other throughout the whole spectrum of their activities as individuals and social beings. It *does*, however, imply a particular view of the nature and function of language, a view that regards language as the defining characteristic of man as a species and therefore as a crucial element in his ability to survive, individually and collectively. Professor Max Black, a philosopher whose central interest is the part played by language in our capacity to function as thinking animals, puts it this way,

Man is the only animal that can talk . . . He alone can bridge

18

the gap between one person and another, conveying thoughts, feelings, desires, attitudes, and sharing in the traditions, conventions, the knowledge and the superstition of his culture . . . On this essential skill depends everything that we call civilisation. Without it, imagination, thought—even self-knowledge—are impossible.

What Professor Black says is obviously the case. The trouble is that it is *so obviously* the case that we are constantly being led to overlook its implications, because we live them out in every aspect of our lives, every day that we live. This very obviousness can become a serious liability when we are concerned with the question of the part played by language in education. As I have suggested elsewhere:

> When something enters into every aspect of our lives in the way in which language does, its very familiarity is a barrier to exploration. Existing understanding will always seem sufficient, and exploration merely a process of elaborating an abstruse disguise for what is commonplace and familiar.

One major aim of Language Study is to show that it is precisely the commonplace and the familiar in our use of language, for living which is most in need of exploration, if we are to understand how we use language to learn. We need to be able to create a climate of opinion in which no teacher would be willing to accept that his everyday familiarity with language, as a competent native speaker, was sufficient *in itself* to provide him, as a teacher, with what he needs to know about its nature and function.

If we now consider the second of our terms, language for learning, we can see that the pupil finds himself in a similar situation, because his competence as a native speaker will not *of itself* provide him with what he needs to know about language for learning. In other words, the understanding of the nature and function of language which we derive from our capacity to use it as competent native speakers does not make it easy for us to reflect upon our knowledge of the language, or our knowledge of the use of the language. We learn language in such a way that our knowledge of it, and of its use, are necessarily intuitive. We function successfully as users of language just because we do not need to deploy an explicit body of knowledge in so doing, as we do if we wish to function successfully as users of Physics, or Mathematics, or History, or Social Science. This distinction is a very important one, but its exploration in detail is not material to the argument

19

of this chapter. May I, therefore, refer the interested reader to Chapter Two of *Exploring Language* where I offer an analysis of what we should understand by 'knowledge OF a language'? In particular, I draw a basic distinction between 'knowledge OF a language' and 'knowledge ABOUT a language' in these terms:

> Knowledge OF a language derives solely from the process of learning language, while knowledge ABOUT language embraces the intuitions of folk-linguistic and all kinds of knowledge about that are conscious and explicit.

This distinction between 'knowledge OF a language' and 'knowledge ABOUT a language' is crucial to the idea of language for learning. When we want to focus upon the question of pupils' needs in the context of learning situations, we must be very clear about the kind of 'knowledge' that would be relevant. Pupils are competent speakers of a language because they have acquired a natural language in the process of growing up as ordinary members of a human community. It is this 'knowledge OF the language' which they bring with them into the class-room. It is *operational knowledge* of the language in the sense that it provides each pupil with a capacity to use language for living. This means that he is in a position to produce spoken utterance or written text in so far as he can *read* the situation in which he finds himself. His ability to read a situation and then draw upon his *operational knowledge* in order to meet its demands necessarily depends, therefore, upon his intuitive assessment of how he can use language to live. It follows from this that an individual's knowledge of his language can only become operational for him in so far as he is able to form an intuitive assessment of what using language might look like in a particular situation. Unless we are prepared to show pupils, therefore, what using language for learning really looks like, we must not be surprised if they are unable to deploy their knowledge of the language effectively to meet the linguistic demands of the learning situations in which we meet them.

An individual's knowledge of his language, therefore, becomes *operational* when he adds to his fundamental knowledge of the language a corresponding knowledge of the use of the language. We can speak of these two 'knowledges', then, as different aspects of an individual's *linguistic resource,* and together we can say that they provide him with his capacity. We possess a very strong intuition that this distinction is a real distinction and our sense of it has entered into a whole range of everyday expressions. Consider what we mean by 'words failed me', 'I was lost for words', 'I just didn't know what to say', 'I can't find words to express it', 'I was speechless', 'He hadn't a word to say for himself'. A common element in all these expressions is surely the sense that the 'words' *are* there, but we can't lay our tongues on them at that precise moment in that particular setting. What our intuition points to is the fact that we may indeed be aware that we possess relevant intuitive knowledge of the elements and structure of the language, but be quite unable to deploy them on occasions, because we seem to lack a correspondingly relevant intuitive knowledge of how they might be used.

There is, however, yet another factor to be considered in relation to language for learning; it is the pupils' folk-linguistic intuitions about language and the use of language. These intuitions constitute a third kind of 'knowledge', and influence our capacity to language effectively just as much as either of the other two. They are, however, knowledge ABOUT language rather than knowledge OF language, although, as will be seen, it is knowledge ABOUT of a rather special kind. Consider for a moment popular views about accent or dialect; about the relationship between spoken and written language; about correctness in speech or writing. Consider the fact that many people write and talk about language as though it were made up of 'words' only; that others regard their favoured form of the written language as the correct form, a form of which speech is but an imperfect copy; that others regard usage acquired from another language as necessarily a sign of linguistic decline. Think of the implications of phrases like 'Actions speak louder than words', 'What we want is action, not words', 'Mere talk', 'Don't bandy words with me', 'Don't answer back'. All of these express a particular view of how we use language to live and, even more importantly how some of us think how we all ought to use language to live.

What these views reveal are attitudes and assumptions about the nature and function of language which enter into a person's whole way of regarding the part language plays in his life. He has acquired them by growing up as a member of a particular social group within a particular human community. In that sense they are a product of cultural learning; they are intimately a part of the way in which he looks at the world. This idea can be tested by challenging the expression of such views. The reaction is likely to be very strongly felt. It is also likely to imply that the challenge must be unserious, because the views expressed are so *obvious* to the

21

holder that he can conceive of no other way of looking at the topic to which they refer. These views are intuitive, therefore, in the sense that they do shape a speaker's own use of language, and his response to how others use it, without his being continuously conscious of the fact. At the same time, however, they are knowledge ABOUT language rather than knowledge OF language, and consequently it is possible to create a situation in which people can be made aware of what their own folk-linguistic views might be. It is even possible to create situations in which they can go on to modify their folk-linguistic attitudes in the light of a new perspective on language.

In the final section of this chapter, I want to draw together this discussion of language for living and language for learning by suggesting how the different factors we have looked at come together to create a particular climate for language activity within the environment of school or college. In doing this, I hope I shall be able to show that the need for Language Study arises out of the very nature of language activity itself and its relationship to the environment we create for ourselves as social beings. If I am successful in this, then I will have shown that every teacher needs to be able to reflect upon his own and his pupils' use of language, because there is no teacher who does not contribute to the creation of the climate for language activity within which he and all his colleagues have to work. I will also have shown, moreover, that every teacher's attitudes and assumptions about language not only affect the local climate of opinion in the school, but also contribute powerfully to the attitudes and assumptions current within the larger context of community and society.

3. Language and cultural learning

In the first section of this chapter I spoke about the way in which men use language to create and maintain the individual identity of the human groups which go to make up the total organization of society. I pointed to the process the sociologist calls socialization as the primary means by which these groups are able to perpetuate themselves and suggested that language plays a crucial part in the process. I want to emphasize the fact that this process is concerned with the way in which newcomers to a group learn how to be members of it and that a crucial aspect of the whole business is their induction into the complex web of values, capabilities and habits which go to make up the life of that group. Alternatively,

22

we can say that socialization is the process of cultural learning by means of which a newcomer learns how to function adequately as a member of society. We can think of a child, therefore, as having *to learn his way into* the society to which he belongs by birth or by adoption.

As well as being a member of society, however, he also belongs to a family and a community. Each of these is an example of a *human group* and each socializes the child in two ways. From the point of view of society as a whole, it is through his membership of such *socializing agencies* as these that the child learns what values, capabilities and habits characterize the culture of the society in which he finds himself. Our own experience tells us, however, that some of the things which we learn through being socialized into our own family are not characteristic of families in general, but are unique to that one particular family. This is because a particular social group, whether a family, a school or a community, does have a pattern of values, capabilities and habits uniquely its own, and as we acquire the language of the group so we acquire these values, capabilities and habits which are peculiar to it. Whether we are focusing on the patterns of society as a whole or on those unique to particular social groups the most potent way in which values, capabilities and habits are acquired is through learning the language, because so many elements of the culture are embedded in the patterns of the language itself.

Being a member of a school is like being a member of any other human group in the sense that membership, whether for teacher or for pupil, necessarily involves the individual in a many-levelled process of cultural learning. At one level, schools and colleges act as socializing agencies in that they mediate the values, capabilities and habits characteristic of the culture of the society in which they occur, just like any other social group within that society. At another, they mediate the values, capabilities and habits which combine to give unique identity to a particular school or college. Unlike most other groups, however, schools and colleges also function on a third level as *educational* agencies. Their function is to pass on a quite specific set of values, capabilities and habits, the explicit operational skills like reading and writing, and the organized bodies of knowledge that a society believes it has need of. Moreover, this function is explicitly recognized in society and constitutes the public view of what they exist to do.

We are now in a position to relate the process of cultural learning to the distinction we have made between language for living and language for learning. In so far as the school or college functions as a *socializing agency*, language for living will have to be used *even in the learning situation itself*. How and where, and in what ways, we have been socialized determine how we use language to live. Consequently, the language for living that learners have available for entering into the social life of the school is a language shaped by their background and not by the school. On the other hand, language for learning only arises where the use of language arises out of the need to pass on operational skills and organized knowledge. Language for learning is, therefore, something that the school makes available through its own activities as an educational agency rather than a use of language which learners bring into the school with them from their life outside.

We can now link this to what was said earlier about folk-linguistic attitudes. If we ask the basic question—what *are* folk-linguistic attitudes?—one answer is to say that they represent a society's attitudes and assumptions about language and its use. As this is the case, they are the product of socialization, and as language is one of the major means by which socialization is accomplished, we will find that the process gives rise to attitudes and assumptions about language and its use wherever it operates. When we focus upon language activity within the school, then, we can expect to find a variety of different folk-linguistic attitudes and assumptions occurring side by side.

The school itself will produce perspectives in relation to its function as a social agency and as an educational agency, and there is no reason to suppose that these will be congruent. Teachers and pupils will each have their own perspective, as individuals standing in differing relationships to the cultural values of society as a whole and as members of different social groups, each with its own set of cultural values concerning language and its use. Moreover, these differences in perspective relate to language for learning as much as to language for living.

For this reason above all, I would argue that the point of departure for an effective approach to Language Study must be a consideration of the attitudes of teachers and pupils towards language; what they are, where they come from; what leads to their perpetuation and how they may be modified. I want to end by pointing to one further complicating factor. Language is not only the major means through which we gain possession of the values, capabilities and habits which go to make up our culture, but it is *itself* one of those capabilities, and its use involves the

24

learning of a whole set of linguistic values and habits. Hence, whenever we have to concern ourselves with patterns of language in use, whether for living or for learning, we will find ourselves forced to consider what it means to be socialized into a society, or a culture, or a particular variety of human group, and how the necessary process of cultural learning involves us also in a process of learning how to use language.

3 Language, learners and a changing society

1. Social diversity and its demands upon the individual

Up to this point, the argument for Language Study has been made in terms of the basic needs of teachers and learners. These needs have been shown to arise out of the very nature and function of language itself in its role as the primary medium for cultural learning. The heart of the problem is our need to use explicitly for educational ends within the school and college what we acquire and use intuitively for personal ends within the family and the community.

I want to turn now to the question of change, within the educational system and within society itself. I write from within a complex advanced industrial society, and I am likely to be read by many who live within societies that are very differently organized. I would suggest, however, that it is those elements in the organization of an advanced industrial society which most directly affect the use of language to live and language to learn that are appearing in newly industrialized societies throughout the world.

I want to show that the nature and direction of the changes taking place within society and within the educational system enormously reinforce the need for a linguistic perspective, whether we are considering the use of language for living or language for learning. This is an enormous topic and deserves a whole book to itself. All I can do in this context is to indicate the relevance of Language Study to some of the key problems which are likely to arise in a changing society, especially those problems which are likely to arise in an emergent society when an advanced industrial society is taken as a model for change. Such problems can be seen in terms of patterns of change, their diversity, tempo and cumulative effect upon the life-histories of individual human beings.

26

Perhaps the most obvious difference between the world one's pupils live in and the world their great-grand parents lived in as children is the sheer diversity of function and focus it now contains. The majority of our pupils are urban dwellers. They grow up in the social context of an enormously complex network of relationships, stretching from the intimate circle of the nuclear family, through the circle of the neighbourhood, peer group and the school, to all the contacts that they make with other human beings in the course of using the facilities and services of their community. They may find themselves moving from one community to another in the course of their father's need to follow job opportunities. What they do when they leave school is a matter of choice. In order to find the job they want, or even any job at all, they may have to go on their travels, live a life independent of neighbourhood ties, come into contact with parts of the country quite different from any they have ever met before. In many parts of Europe, this diversity of situation has already come to include other countries and this could easily become the case for those now at school in Britain.

The diversity of focus in our society shows clearly when we observe the large groups within it who develop and maintain their own view of the world. Each group expresses its uniqueness through a particular pattern of values, capabilities and habits. Where we find this diversity we can properly speak of a *plural* society. Looking at these varied patterns it becomes increasingly difficult to talk in terms of a single *unitary* culture, the values of which will be recognized and accepted by all those who happen to speak the same mother tongue. In such a situation, it also becomes increasingly difficult to maintain the fiction that there is, or ought to be, congruence between the values, attitudes and assumptions of any one group dominant in a society and the very different values, attitudes and assumptions to be found in other parts of it. The maintenance of such a fiction, however, is of particular relevance to relationships in schools and colleges, for if the fiction is maintained then there will be the assumption that, they, the schools and colleges, must as educational agencies, mediate the values of this one group. If this happens, then a credibility gap will open between the view of the world which the educational system takes as axiomatic and the view of the world that governs the lives of the majority of the learners it is supposed to serve. This is the situation which we are now faced with in Britain.

27

From what was said in the previous chapter about the role of socialization in integrating our collective activities as human beings, it follows that a key feature of cultural diversity is a corresponding linguistic diversity. The linguistic diversity that matters in the context of a plural society, however, is that which expresses fundamental attitudes and assumptions about the world. For example, we are all familiar with the way in which the sound patterns of a language can show diversity in terms of accent and dialect. This, however, is much more a matter of *locality* than attitude. In these terms, the phonological diversity in the way in which working class pupils from Newcastle or Liverpool or Birmingham form the sounds of the language is far less important than the congruence that exists is their use of language to live, and in their assumptions about using language to learn. Cultural diversity generates linguistic diversity in such a way that teachers and learners are very likely to find themselves repeatedly at cross-purposes, because each assumes that their way of using language is the only way of using language, whether for living or learning. In such a situation, surely we need to be able to stand outside our culture-bound use of the language in order to see how others use it? In the context of the learning situation, it is at least arguable that teachers should take the lead in this activity and this they can only do by developing an appropriate linguistic perspective.

From the learner's point of view, however, an equally important aspect of this diversity is more social than cultural, because it is concerned with interpersonal relations rather than with underlying attitudes and assumptions about the world. It can best be expressed in terms of the multiplicity of roles that the individual now has to assume in the course of his life as an ordinary member of society. There is one pattern of relationships centred on the home, another on work, another on leisure, another involving contact with public agencies, and so on, with very little overlap between them. The following quotation suggests why these relationships are so important from a Language Study point of view:

> Who people are, what they do together, and for what purpose they do it, provides a mesh which yields the picture of a pattern of relationship or a pattern of language, depending on the angle of one's vision.

An individual who has to enter into a very large number of relationships of many different kinds will have a much greater need for a wide variety of ways of speaking than one who lives out his

28

life within the limits of a very small network of relationships. In fact, we can say that the more diverse a man's range of activities, the more diverse the kind and condition of the other people with whom he comes in contact, the greater will be the demand he has to make upon his command of the language in order to survive. We can say, therefore, that survival in such circumstances will depend ultimately upon a man's understanding of the enormous variety of different ways in which people can use language for living within the confines of the society.

If we accept the validity of this position, then we must accept that the development of the necessary operational competence to meet the linguistic demands of an indefinately variable pattern of social relationships is a key '. . . language need' for anyone who has to live in our kind of society. It follows that the development of this competence must be a major objective for our educational system, and therefore properly a feature of every teacher's professional concerns so far as they have responsibility for pupils' use of language. This responsibility, moreover, extends to language for living as well as language for learning, because the life of a school is social as well as educational. In order to meet it teachers need to know what is involved. They need an adequate account of the part played by language in sustaining the fabric of a complex society, social and linguistic, and they need to see how this account could then be related to practical class-room activities designed to bring about the development of the competence that is called for. A Language Study approach ought to take the responsibility for helping the teacher with both these tasks. A first attempt to provide the necessary account of language, relationships and society will be found in chapters five and six of *Exploring Language*, while *Language in Use* offers a concrete example of how this can be worked out in terms of practical class-room activities.

2. The demands of a changing society

If we now turn to consider the *tempo* of change in our society, we find a similarly disturbing situation. This is a feature of our world that is much spoken about and there is little need to detail its characteristics, but perhaps the very familiarity of the idea has blunted our perception of some of the most significant consequences that follow from it. Let me put it in terms of an individual's expectations, his ideas about the sort of world he is going to live in and what he is going to do to make a living for himself and his

29

family. In 1900, a man aged 20 would have believed that the future was going to be very little different from the past. He would do one job for his working life, do it in one town, probably even in one firm. The town was likely to be the town of his birth, the job the same as his fathers. In 1925, a young man of 20 would probably have believed much the same. In 1950, a young man would be much more likely to see himself making moves of one kind or other, changing jobs or changing firms or changing towns. He would still see these moves as major decisions, however, and unlikely to occur more than once or twice in his working life. That he would have been wrong is a measure of the degree to which significant changes in the structure and organization of a society do not always impinge immediately upon the consciousness of those they are going to affect most directly.

If we come now to the present generation in our schools and colleges, the very least that we can say is that the world in which they celebrate their 65th birthday, the world of the 2020ies, will be even more unlike our own world than our own world is unlike the world of 1900. What has happened in this century is that the rate of change has increased out of all proportion to anything men have known in earlier periods. It has reached a point where change grows upon itself, so that we are creating a society in which the *normal* state of that society is one of change. This goes against some of our deepest assumptions, because the way we look at change is a product of our cultural learning and our view of it is expressed through terms which imply the desirability of staying where one is, unless a move is really necessary. Our whole way of speaking about change assumes that what we mean by it is a move from a present position to a future position; each position, the old and the new, is a position of stability and what happens in between is a period of uncertainty which ought properly to be limited in scale and direction. A good example of this is provided by current attitudes to changes in the curriculum. Those who accept change as necessary assume that what curriculum development means is the replacement of the old set of subject contents and received patterns of work by a new set. Once that has been worked out then curriculum change ceases. Hostility occurs where teachers sense that what these present changes point towards is a situation in which there will be no new set to replace the old, only a programme for continuous change.

Their hostility is not surprising when everything in our educational tradition reinforces the idea that change is perhaps necessary, but only as a device for moving from one fixed order to another. For instance, school is still run on the assumption that what you learn there is not only relevant to your needs in adult life immediately on leaving school, but will remain indefinitely relevant throughout adult life because that adult life will remain more or less the same. What I have said about the tempo of change in our society, however, argues a widening credibility between the view of the world our educational system offers and what is actually happening. This situation has produced the tensions which underlie the present call for *relevance* in rethinking the curriculum. The system as it is at present does not begin to meet the needs of learners, now that they face a society in a process of continuous change. One of the best attempts to look at the problem in educational terms is called *Teaching as a subversive activity*. In it Neil Postman and Charles Weingartner sum up the effects of the tempo of change by saying that:

> we have reached the stage where change occurs so rapidly that each of us in the course of our lives has continuously to work out a set of values, beliefs, and patterns of behaviour that are viable, or *seem viable*, to each of us personally. And just when we have identified a workable system, it turns out to be irrelevant because so much has changed while we were doing it.

The cumulative effect upon the individual human being is to place an enormous emphasis upon his powers of adaption. Man is a problem-solving animal and his capacity to survive is bound up with his capacity to deal with the heuristic in his life. Working out what it means to be a problem-solving animal was the central concern of the psychologist George Kelly. His theory of personal constructs is very relevant to the present argument, because it enables me to show how my reference to Postman and Weingartner on the impact of continuous change relates to the current need for a Language Study approach.

Summarizing Kelly's fundamental postulate, Bannister and Fransella suggest that:

> . . . a man checks how much sense he has made of the world by seeing how well his 'sense' enables him to anticipate it.

Kelly stresses that:

> man is in business to make sense out of his world and to test the sense he has made in terms of its predictive capacity.

If the preceding arguments about the diversity and the tempo of change are accepted, then the least we can say is that the task of making sense out of the world, and using the results as a basis for predicting what is going to happen next, will be extremely complicated by the kind of society in which change is continuous. Making sense of things while standing still may be difficult enough in itself, but we have now created a world which everyone is expected to make sense of while standing on a moving stairway. If human beings are in business to produce 'predictive capacity', as Kelly suggests, then a changing society will make his task progressively more taxing. The diversity and tempo of change renders obsolete the sense we make of our world even as we make it.

So we have a situation in which the most important single need for survival becomes the individual's ability to revise continuously the sense he makes of his world because that world is changing continuously, and his effective 'predictive capacity' rests upon the sense that he makes of it. It is reasonable to argue, therefore, that success in developing and operating a 'predictive capacity' will be very closely linked to an individual's success in developing an operational command over spoken and written language. If we remember the part played by language in cultural learning, we can see that, whatever else may be necessary in this situation, human beings must be able to review the part played by language in shaping their view of the world. The ability to 'work out a set of values, beliefs, and patterns of behaviour' is, after all, dependent upon our capacity to language. The linguistic form we give to what we learn through the process of socialization, moreover, is often decisive in determining our view of the world. Altering that view of the world, therefore, will depend upon the degree to which we can draw upon our capacity to language for a range of alternative linguistic forms that will give us alternative ways of looking at the world. It follows then, that another essential aspect of meeting '. . . the language needs of all children' is the creation of a learning environment in which they can come to appreciate how language is used to embody *alternative views of reality*.

3. The effects of change on school and curriculum

In the preceding sections of this chapter, I focused upon the idea of change and the way it now affects the life and organization of society, in order to show that it has created a climate which makes exceptionally heavy demands upon any individual's ability to use language for living. Given the nature of the relationship between

32

society and school a change in the one is certain to bring about parallel changes in the environment for learning provided by the other. This section, therefore, explores the nature of these changes, and looks at the implications for the use of *language for learning*, because change creates new situations, new situations create new patterns of relationship and new relationships demand new ways of speaking for their effective realization. The eventual success or otherwise of these changes in the environment of school and college, therefore, will depend upon the degree to which teachers and learners are willing and able to rethink their use of language for teaching and for learning.

I want to refer once more to the York Conference from which I took my key quotation for Chapter 1. In his own summing up of the work of the conference Professor Wayne Booth of Chicago University set out to place the activities of the conference in the broader context of the current educational scene as a whole. In particular he suggested that the conference represented the efforts of one large group of teachers within the educational system to come to terms with a radically new concept of the child. This he described in the following way:

> the child is an inherently curious, inherently purposive creature, a creature whose thoughts will be passion-ridden and whose feelings are bound with cognitions, a creature made for and by symbol exchange, a creature made in and through the language which by his own irrepressible needs he helps to create.

Although Professor Wayne Booth refers explicitly to *the child*, I want the reader to see that this is really a radically new way of looking at individual human beings, whatever their age. It seems unlikely that so fundamental a form of behaviour would only operate in the earliest years of life. What Professor Wayne Booth says about the child, therefore, can be taken to apply as much to students as to pupils and as much to teachers as to learners.

Professor Wayne Booth is really advancing four propositions about the nature and function of man:

1) '. . . the child is an inherently curious, inherently purposive creature . . .'

To say that he is *inherently* curious and purposive is in accord with Kelly's view of man as a problem-solving animal. This heuristic bias is a product of man's genetic design and therefore must have great survival value for the species. What this suggests is that there is a very powerful drive built into the make up of every human being which compels him to make sense of his world. If he finds that he is unable to do so, however hard he tries, or sees that he is being prevented from doing so, the result will be an enormous sense of frustration.

This proposition can be related to the current educational scene in two quite distinct ways. The pressure towards a more child-centred learning situation, and the idea of the learner as one who should be asked to solve real problems rather than commit to memory other people's solutions, derive from this view of the child as a person who is *designed* to be curious and purposive. On the other hand, it can be suggested that hostility and apathy towards school and college have their origin as much in the frustrating of this basic need to make sense of the world as in anything else. The knowledge we now have about the effects of stress upon the individual indicate that there are two basic responses available, hysteria and apathy. One leads to hostility and ultimately to expressive violence, the other to disinterest and ultimately to withdrawal. From a linguistic point of view, if we try to bring about learning situations that satisfy the needs of learners as problem-solving animals we cannot avoid creating quite new demands upon their use of language for learning. At the same time, hostility and apathy may well arise if pupils are unable to use the language for learning that their teacher demands. It is often the case that no one has tried to make this language for learning available to them, or considered its relevance to their needs in the particular learning situation concerned. In either case, one part of a successful approach to the problem is likely to include a sharp focus upon the patterns of language used in the learning situations, and that focus a linguistic view of language can provide.

2) '. . . a creature whose thoughts will be passion-ridden and whose feelings are bound with cognitions . . .'

If it is true that man is a creature whose 'thoughts will be passion-ridden and whose feelings are bound with cognitions', then a major challenge is presented to the curriculum as we know it. Much of our professional thinking is based upon the implicit assumption that there is a fundamental dichotomy between thought and feeling; that we can happily plan a curriculum which pursues affective and cognitive goals in separation from each other.

I would suggest that the insights contained in this particular proposition underlie a great many of the current efforts at changing

34

the curriculum, such as the development of a new perspective in science teaching, especially the life sciences; in the work towards a new concept of the humanities; and, in this country, in the programmes suggested for those who will now be remaining at school beyond fifteen. I would suggest, also, that it accounts in part for the impetus towards the widespread use of a thematic approach and for the urge to develop effective methods of team teaching.

Once again, there are two distinct ways in which these changes in the curriculum affect the use of language for learning. Firstly, they alter the patterns of relationship within the learning situation, and in the social and cultural life of the school or the college as a whole; and, secondly, they put a premium upon the ability of teachers and learners to find new ways of speaking which will fit these new ways of relating to each other as teachers and learners. In so far as these changes reflect a shift away from the old dichotomy between thought and feeling, however, they create a demand for new varieties of language for learning, because the terms and phrases which provide the patterns for existing *varieties* have this distinction built into them. This is because the technical language we use for the subjects we teach is not only a form of descriptive language, but also a way of recording a particular view of the world. Should that view of the world change in any fundamental way, as it surely must if we accept this new relationship between thought and feeling, then we can only express our sense of the change by modifying the language we have been accustomed to use for the discussion of particular areas of knowledge.

Modifying language habits of this kind usually requires us to modify, in turn, our views of what we want language to do for us in relation to a particular area of operations like the teaching of a curriculum subject. This situation of change, therefore, makes great demands upon our ability to review the whole range of our professional attitudes towards language for learning. Reviewing 'the tools for the trade', however, implies flexibility towards our own choice of language in the learning situation. This is only attainable in so far as we are prepared to develop an adequate linguistic perspective, but even if we are fully prepared to consider the questions involved we cannot do so successfully, without an appropriate form of Language Study to draw upon.

Between the third and fourth propositions we are considering there is a special relationship, in that the most potent system of symbols available to man is the language that he speaks.

3) '. . . a creature made for and by symbol-exchange . . .'

The idea that man is a creature made for and by symbol-exchange is really saying something about the fundamental relationship between the individual and the world he inhabits. It is suggesting that we have to translate our experience of the world into a pattern of symbols before we can be said to 'know' what we have expressed. We are *made for* this process, in the sense that our brains are designed to operate in this way, and we are *made by* it, in so far as we know what we can symbolize, and what we know about the world makes us what we are. As Kelly says 'a particular man *is* the sense he makes of the world'. So far, so good, but unless we can share what we know through an *exchange of symbols*, we have no means of testing the general validity of what we know, and, as Kelly suggests, we are in business to test the validity of our predictions about the world. If we want to see what happens to our knowledge of the world when we cannot test it through an exchange of symbols, we have only to look at the plight of the autistic child or the paranoic.

How then does so abstract an idea relate to the climate of change in the class-room? I suggest that this proposition underlines the importance of our ability to make sense of the world, and of the fact that human beings have a *biological* need to interpret new experience successfully, if they are to maintain their capacity to function as individual sentient selves. The corollary of this is that if they cannot make meaning out of new experiences satisfactory to themselves, they suffer distress which, repeated frequently, leads in the end to a complete breakdown in their ability to relate to the world.

If we have a climate of continuous change in society, then the struggle to make meanings out of a continuous flux of new experience demands an ability to perform rapidly and successfully a whole range of symbol-exchanges. It would be proper to argue that schools and colleges are in business to facilitate symbol-exchange, and that they have a special responsibility in this direction. However, when we remember that the climate of change in society brings about a similar climate in schools and colleges we see that schools and colleges have to cope with the learner's needs both as an individual in a rapidly changing world *and* as a learner in a rapidly changing educational system. After all that has been said so far, it is not surprising that the attitudes of the school, the teacher and the learner, towards language play a decisive part in the success or failure of any attempts to meet this dual need.

36

Indeed, the fourth proposition we have to consider suggests that it could hardly do otherwise.

4) 'A creature made in and through the language which by his own irrepressible needs he helps to create . . .'

This proposition presents one special instance of the operation of symbol-exchange, the human use of language to create meaning out of experience. It underlines the point that language is so intimately a part of us that our view of the world is inseparable from the way we use language to shape it. It also stresses that our own individual identity, and *our knowledge of that identity*, is a product of the activity of using language to live. Finally, it points to the fact that that language which we use for these purposes is not only 'out there', a thing wholly public and external to our functioning as individual human beings, but also 'in here', a thing so intimately ours that we can create unique meanings with its aid.

In one sense, there is little more to say. As language plays so central a part in the autonomy and operational effectiveness of individual human beings, then their capacity for survival is seriously affected, in so far as they find themselves continuously in a situation where their attempts to make sense of new experience is frustrated by their lack of the necessary language for learning or language for living.

Our failure to consider sufficiently carefully *the linguistic demands* that arise from a pattern of change in the curriculum is in the process of creating precisely such a situation in our schools and colleges.

4 Language Study: discipline or process?

1. Relevant considerations

In the last chapter, I suggested that the diversity and tempo of change in our society have brought about a situation in which the individual is increasingly at risk, unless he can respond rapidly and flexibly to continuously varying circumstances, personal, social and cultural. As our ability to make sense of the world and to make relationships with others depends ultimately upon our command of a language, the more demanding and complex the network of relationships we enter into the greater will be the cumulative strain upon our capacity to language. I also suggested that a similar situation has arisen within schools and colleges owing to the special relationship that exists between an educational agency and the society it serves. It is this dual climate of change as it affects the problems and processes of teaching and learning that provides the immediate context for Language Study.

Cumulatively, the three preceding chapters have argued the case for a new approach to the educational study of language in terms of the radical nature of the society men have created in this century and the fundamental nature of their use of language to live and to learn. I must now offer a design for such an approach that could be realized in terms of actual programmes of study in particular schools and colleges.

There are many respects in which this design for Language Study runs counter to the customary ways of thinking about new areas of interest within the educational system or establishing a new subject in the curriculum. I do not think there is any point in talking about Language Study as though it were but one more subject to add to the list for an already overcrowded curriculum, and I would not accept the addition of an element of academic

Linguistic Science to the curriculum of teacher education as an adequate answer to the need for a Language Study approach in that context. The difficulty lies in our need to focus upon patterns of language for living and language for learning, because these are patterns of language *in use* and language in use constitutes a unique focus for enquiry, owing to the way in which we learn how to use language, what we learn along with it, and what we do with it when we have learnt it.

I have focused attention upon the fact that man is a problem-solving animal whose integrity as an individual sentient self depends upon his continuing ability to make sense of his world and to form relationships with other similarly individual sentient selves. His ability to do either of these things is profoundly affected by his capacity to language. Values, capabilities and habits are transmitted through language, moreover, and it is these values, capabilities and habits, which guide him in his interpretation of the world and his relationship with others, because they provide him with his only models for judging what is and is not the case. Language plays a vital part, therefore, in the whole process of cultural learning but it is itself a product of the same process, and therein lies its uniqueness as a focus of enquiry and the heart of the problem for the educational study of language.

The uniqueness of language derives from the fact that it is, at one and the same time, a capability man acquires through growing up as a member of a particular society and the major means by which he can acquire all the other capabilities . . .

that go to make up the personal, social and cultural life of a particular family, community and society. This is to say that, at any one time, a man's capacity to language is the product of a particular way of life, led in a particular community, at a particular time, and has built into it, therefore, one particular set of personal, social and cultural values. They form the basis of his reading of the world, but they have themselves been shaped in his mind by the very language through which he gained access to them.

So we are faced with the inescapable fact that man's major means for making sense of his world has built into its elements and structure a bias towards interpreting experience in terms of a pre-existing set of categories, attitudes and assumptions. Should he live in a world subject to continuous social and cultural change, therefore, this bias must act as a continuous check upon his

39

attempts to make sense of the new, because it will always make it easier for him to language the new in terms of what he found appropriate for languaging the old. There are many who would say that there is nothing we can do about this, because it is simply 'human nature'. 'Human nature', however, is as much a construct as any other concept we use to make sense of the world, and the way we language the concept plays a vital part in our understanding of what we mean by it. Does this not suggest, therefore, that, if we were more adept at seeing how our language shapes the concepts we use, we might find less difficulty in modifying the constructs that go to make them? This implies that the development of a capacity *to reflect upon the part language plays in shaping our view of the world* is a vital part of everyone's equipment for survival in the sort of world we are already living in.

As educators, then, we must say that we cannot afford the comforting pessimism of an unchangeable 'human nature', but are bound to look for ways in which we can help all those we teach to cope with the world in which they have to live. A major priority must be the creation of conditions in which pupils can develop that ability to reflect upon the part language plays in their lives. It is an ability to stand back from the language we use in order to see how and why and in what ways that language mediates between us and our understanding of the world. The development of such an ability rests upon the growth of a *linguistic perspective* and it is for this reason that I would place the idea of linguistic perspective at the very centre of our professional concern with language. The nature and function of a linguistic perspective, where it comes from and how it operates, and what conditions are necessary for encouraging its development in teachers as well as in learners, therefore, provide the central focus for Language Study; whatever we put forward in relation to its design must be judged according to its value in forwarding this aim.

2. Disciplines, perspectives and reflexiveness

Linguistics is still a comparatively unfamiliar discipline, but this is not the place for me to give a detailed account of its structure and objectives. All I need to do is to show how its status as a discipline affects its relationship to Language Study. As I understand it, a discipline is a term for a particular way of looking at the world. If we take the standpoint of the biologist, the psychologist, the geographer or the economist, we view the world through his eyes,

40

which means that we use a particular set of concepts in our inter-pretation of it and use a particular pattern of language when we speak about it. What we are doing is to accept a particular per-spective upon the world, biological, psychological, geographical or economistic. The most characteristic feature of these perspectives is the kind of question they encourage us to ask about the world, and it is commonplace that the questions we ask will determine the kind of evidence we look for, and, consequently, the kind of answers we get.

Let me illustrate this by showing how these four disciplines approach the study of man. Each asks its own questions about man: how does he function as a living organism? how does he function as a thinking being? how is he related to his environment? and how does he organize himself to supply his needs? The intellectual tradition we inherit from the nineteenth century stresses the autonomy of disciplines, the degree to which they exist in order to ask questions the answers to which are of unique interest to the disciplines themselves. Progressively through this century, however, people have become more and more aware of the relevance of the answers one discipline gives to its own ques-tions to the questions which it is necessary to ask in a different field. To give an example which is illustrated by a book in this series: what biologists discover about the structure and function of the brain is highly relevant to what psychologists might have to say about man's cognitive activity. Putting this in terms of *perspective*, we can say that each discipline encourages the develop-ment and use of a particular way of looking at some aspect of the world, but that we are now increasingly aware of the limitations imposed upon our way of looking at things if we adopt the stand-point of a single perspective only. Especially is this the case if the focus of our interest is a complex phenomenon, like man, or his culture, or his society, or his language.

If we now consider the relationship between *linguistic* perspective and Linguistic Science, we will find an ambiguity similar to that which arose in the discussion of the educational use of the word 'need'. There is a proper sense in which we can refer to the particular way of looking at language which derives from the discipline of Linguistics as a 'linguistic perspective'. At the same time, however, it remains a most convenient term to use for man's ability to stand back from his habitual way of looking at language and its use. In the narrow sense, then, linguistic perspective is the linguist's characteristic way of viewing his subject matter: in the

41

broad sense, it is the way in which a 'creature made in and through language . . .' learns to look at what has made him. Using the same term reminds us constantly that we cannot achieve a linguistic perspective on how we use language to live, unless we are prepared to make use of the linguistic perspective the linguist develops in the course of his own particular enquiries. At the same time, it should warn us that that perspective cannot tell us all we want to know, because it derives from one particular area of enquiry into language, and language is so complex a phenomenon in the life of man that no one discipline can ask all the necessary questions, and therefore no one discipline will provide all the answers.

What Language Study is interested in, therefore, is this *broad* sense of linguistic perspective, and the way in which it relates to our folk-linguistic perspective, the product of our habitual way of viewing the nature of function of language, which we operate intuitively, and which provides the basis for our everyday attitudes and assumptions concerning language and its use. What Language Study has to develop, therefore, is a perspective that is properly *reflexive* in the sense in which the social psychologist G. H. Mead used the word. In his theory, this term describes the relationship which arises when,

> . . . the individual's adjustment to the social processes is modified and refined by the awareness or consciousness which he thus has of it. It is by means of *reflexiveness*—the turning back of the experience of the individual upon himself—that the whole social process is thus brought into the experience of the individuals involved in it; it is by such means, which enable the individual to take the attitude of the other towards himself, that the individual is able consciously to adjust himself to that process. . . .

When I referred to the idea of the individual standing back from his habitual way of looking at language, in Mead's terms, I was suggesting that he should acquire the ability to 'turn back' upon himself his cumulative experience of languaging. In so far as the development of a linguistic perspective enables us to see how our capacity to language is primarily a product of a particular place, a particular time and a particular culture, it enables us '. . . to take the attitude of the other . . .', as far as language activity is concerned, because it makes us see that a view of the world is the product of an habitual way of using language, and is, by definition, particular and not universal.

42

3. Linguistics and Language Study

Let me now return to the relation between Linguistics and Language Study. I have laid stress upon the prominent role that we need to give to the identification and modification of attitudes and assumptions towards language, in developing a design for language study. We need to be free, therefore, to make use of the answers the linguist gives to his questions about the nature and function of language, in order to answer our own questions about the educational use of language. I have already given an account of how I see this relationship in Chapter Two, section 4, of *Exploring Language*, where I suggested that:

> Language Study, then, takes the needs of teachers and pupils as its criterion of relevance for selecting particular topics for exploration out of the whole range of Linguistic Studies. It recognises that teachers are interested in two kinds of knowledge about language, what will help them to understand the part played by language in the processes of learning and teaching and what will best show them how this part can be related to language as a feature of living, individual and social.

Language Study, therefore, will only be interested in using the work of academic Linguistic Studies in so far as that work can be related to the particular problems of language in teaching and learning. The primary need to modify the folk-linguistic perspective of teachers and learners, moreover, and encourage the development of a linguistic perspective that is properly reflexive, provides us with powerful criteria for selection and presentation. We cannot afford to make use of the findings of academic Linguistics, just because they are there; nor can we use findings, however relevant to the needs of teachers and learners, unless we can show how they relate to what goes on in actual learning situations.

We need to remember the hard truth we have all experienced in our own class-rooms that a knowledge of the facts does not automatically produce a change of attitude. 'Don't confuse me with facts, I've made up my mind', is a familiar enough saying from the world of public affairs, but it is no less common an occurrence in the world of education. When we are handling something as intimate and value-laden as language, where everyone regards his own view as authoritative, the chance of eliciting this response to an alternative view of the facts is quite extraordinarily high. An individual's feelings towards his own view of language, moreover, are often so strong that he will regard the presentation of an alternative view as a personal attack upon his integrity. Where his own view is expressed through the common language, and appears to be sanctioned by the very fact that the language itself provides familiar words and phrases for it, and where the alternative view must make use of a system of thought and a technical language which are quite unfamiliar, an explosive reaction is very likely, unless this state of affairs has been taken into account at the design stage. It is a common-place that such a reaction, should it occur, merely serves to reinforce a person's original view of the facts, and makes it that much more difficult to win a sympathetic hearing for a new approach. In this situation, encouraging teachers and learners to move towards a linguistic perspective must be a precondition for any extended exploration of language. In so doing, we must remember that the possession of a linguistic perspective on language is not the same thing as knowing what the discipline of Linguistics might have to say about the elements and structure of one's own, or any other, language.

We must now ask what kind of a perspective on language linguists can offer us. They hold differing views about the status of their subject, however, and some of these views are more helpful than others in relation to the concept of Language Study. We start with the common ground that Linguistics is a discipline asking its own questions about an aspect of the world and offering a body of knowledge about it that is rational and ordered. Some would say that a linguistic view is *an*, or even *the*, 'objective' view of the nature and function of language. This is not the place to go into the current debate about whether or not scientific enquiry is 'objective', in the popular sense of the word, but language is so intimate a function of being human that the problems of being a truly 'disinterested observer' are particularly acute, when language is the subject of our explorations. The position has been put most sharply by Professor Michael Polanyi,

> . . . as human beings, we must inevitably see the universe from a centre lying within ourselves and speak about it in terms of a human language shaped by exigencies of human intercourse. *Any attempt rigorously to eliminate our human perspective from our picture of the world must lead to absurdity.* (My italics)

If we need to use the work of a number of disciplines in order to develop a theory of language by means of which individual teachers and learners can develop a *linguistic* perspective, then the

44

last thing we can afford to do is to assume that, whilst teachers and learners have a *human* perspective, of which their view of language is a part, the disciplines themselves do not possess such a perspective, because they are 'objective'.

This point is important, because it is related to a basic division of opinion amongst linguists about what their field of enquiry and mode of operation should be. I shall simplify the position by suggesting that there are two views of the case current at the present time, the narrow and the broad. As in all such distinctions, the two views are here made to seem much more sharply defined than they actually appear in the work of any one linguist, but this simplification will show clearly where the problem lies for the development of a design for Language Study.

What I am calling the narrow view sees Linguistics as a discipline which is concerned exclusively with the organization of the sound patterns of natural languages, and their relationship to the corresponding organization of the internal pattern of those languages, phonological, grammatical and lexical. Those who hold to this point of view tend to believe that the Natural Sciences, especially 'hard data' sciences like Physics and Chemistry, provide the most appropriate models for their enquiries and for the criteria by which the results of those enquiries should be assessed. There is no doubt that this belief has produced most valuable results in certain fields, particularly those concerned with the production and reception of speech, the various branches of Phonetics. It has also produced an enormous body of descriptive information about the grammar and phonology of the world's natural languages. In particular, it has led to the development of a very powerful methodology for recording and analysing the patterns of languages which exists only as spoken languages. In terms of the actual number of different languages involved they constitute a far larger body then those which do make use of a writing system.

The total result has not been altogether happy, however, for two closely related reasons. Linguists have frequently adopted a view of what it is to practise science that does not bear very much relation to how scientists actually work. In particular, they have sought to use what they have understood by 'scientific method', and, in the process, they have set on one side many aspects of language in use, because these were too 'messy' to be accommodated within the terms of the rigorous system of enquiry that they chose to employ. The result has been a certain trivializing of the content of their enquiries in order to preserve the integrity of the methodology they have adopted. In effect, the version of 'science' that informs their thinking would not be readily acceptable to those comtemporary scientists who have tried hardest to understand what it is to practise science. One of the most lucid and articulate is the distinguished British medical scientist, Sir Peter Medawar. Reviewing a recent book on this theme, Dr. Alex Comfort suggested that:

> For Medawar, science is an exercise in critical integrity operating on the fruits of the imagination. Without the imagination, no discovery: without the integrity of self-criticism, stratospheric hokum.

He might have gone on to say that enquiry without imagination, linked to a belief in a methodology that explicitly excludes the observer, leads to monumental irrelevance.

This is so important a question for the design of an approach to Language Study that I want to add to the discussion a key passage from Medawar's own writings. It is taken from the conclusion to his three lectures on *Induction and Intuition in Scientific Thought*:

> The purpose of scientific enquiry is not to compile an inventory of factual information, nor to build up a totalitarian world picture of natural Laws in which every event that is not compulsory is forbidden. We should think of it rather as a logically articulated structure of justifiable beliefs about nature. It begins as a story about a Possible World—a story which we invent and criticise and modify as we go along, so that it ends by being, as nearly as we can make it, a story about real life.

In the terms of my argument, '. . . a logically articulated structure of justifiable beliefs about . . .' language is what I would understand by a linguistic perspective, but ultimately this structure of beliefs has to be 'a story about real life', and a linguistic story that did justice to real life would have to tell the tale in terms of how people use language to live.

The narrow view of Linguistics tends to be accompanied by a strongly institutional view of the domain and function of the discipline and makes much use of dichotomies like 'theoretical' and 'practical', 'pure' and 'applied', 'linguistic' and 'non-linguistic'. In one sense, this is only to be expected in a young discipline, because our educational and academic system puts a premium upon the autonomy of the discipline, and is only prepared to tolerate a newcomer so long as it can show exclusive right to a field of enquiry. The controversy in this country over the

46

'right' of sociology to exist as an autonomous field of enquiry is only the most recent of many examples. Some readers may remember the similar controversy that surrounded the attempt to establish 'English' as a discipline, a controversy that can still erupt in the form of a challenge to the English Department to show what its 'content' is, what it actually 'teaches'. Unfortunately, an institutional view of linguistics is very hostile to the idea of 'using' linguistics in the ways which are necessary for a Language Study approach.

4. Language Study as a human science

Turning now to the broad view of Linguistic Science, I would suggest that it sees Linguistics as a *human* or *social* rather than a *natural* science. It is concerned with language as human behaviour, with language as 'the nervous system of our society', and as the medium through which we maintain a 'network of bonds and obligations'. These phrases are taken from *The Tongues of Men* by the late Professor Firth, a key figure for the idea of Linguistics as a human science. Elsewhere he has provided the most succinct definition of the broad view of linguistics that I have ever come across. When asked to define Linguistics, he said that 'the object of linguistic analysis is to make statements of meaning so that we can see how we use language to live'. This proposition implies that we should see linguistics associated with those disciplines which exist to pursue 'the proper study of man', especially Psychology and Sociology, the study of individual and social man respectively. As man makes himself a self in and through the language he speaks, and as he creates a society by using language to form a network of relationships with others, it is reasonable to suggest that the study of man as an individuating animal, and the study of man as a social animal, should be joined by the study of man as a talking animal, to form a triumvirate at the centre of our endeavour to understand ourselves.

What this view implies is the idea of a discipline as an *agency* rather than an institution. From this point of view, a discipline in the field of human science would be expected to show an openness towards other fields of enquiry interested in the same phenomena, a readiness to see the results of its enquiries used in the exploration of those complex problems which defy the resources of any one discipline. Conceived of as an agency for the mediation of knowledge, a discipline would reveal a willingness to forego the luxury

47

of treating enquiries as necessarily self-sufficient. It would reveal a willingness to tolerate indeterminate boundaries between what is 'pure' and what 'applied', and to make use of a range of different approaches chosen according to the nature of the particular problem at hand. Above all, it would show a willingness to tolerate the messiness of real events, because the story that needs to be told is a 'story about real life', and real life has a habit of slipping out of the door when human science focuses too closely upon the elegance, simplicity and rigour of research design.

I have said that I see Language Study as a process. In this sense, it goes one stage beyond the broad view of a discipline as an agency, because it exists in order to mediate between the disciplines which have something to say about language and the people who need to understand the true story about language as it is used for teaching and learning. In this sense, and unlike a discipline, Language Study does not ask questions unique to itself, nor does it have techniques of enquiry peculiar to itself. Its 'content' is not a content which the syllabus maker could ever draw a line around and say that these things and these alone constitute 'the foundations of the subject'. What it does do is provide a meeting point between the questions concerning language and the use of language, which arise in the context of teaching and learning, and the disciplines which might well be able to offer some contribution towards their answers. 'Might be able' is not a polite circumlocution. It points to the fact that one of the most important tasks for Language Study is to show that some key questions do not have answers as yet. For example, we do not yet know how human beings go on extending their command of a language after its initial acquisition. Putting together what we do know about such a question, however, can be very useful. It enables us to suggest what a definitive answer might look like and this can carry us well beyond the limits of our habitual assumptions about the problem.

Language Study also has to show that some of the questions about language which teachers most often ask are so formed that they can never have answers. Two examples must suffice. Those who look to linguistics for a justification of their belief in an absolute form of the language, against which all usage can be properly measured, with the faulty found wanting, will be disappointed, because they will find that natural language does not work like that. Those who hope to find a justification for their views about fluent and slovenly speech, good and bad accent, rich and impoverished dialects, by taking a linguistic view of language,

48

will be equally disappointed, because they will find that their questions about speech, accent and dialect are complex questions involving social and cultural, as well as linguistic, patterns rather than simple questions about the elements and structure of a particular language.

My last point is to link what has been said in this chapter about the design for Language Study to the climate created by a changing society. As society is subject to a process of continuous and rapid change, and the educational system reflects this process, the questions that teachers and learners ask will necessarily change also. Even if the questions themselves were to remain the same it is very unlikely that the relevant answers would remain the same. This situation implies the need for a very great flexibility in the process of relating the questions from the educational context to the disciplines which might be able to provide the answers. It suggests a willingness to discard what has been learnt, to review the relevance of what has *seemed* useful, and to realign in new configurations and relationships the components of old and tried answers. It also requires a willingness to assert the urgency of the new question over the institutional convenience of the received answer. In a changing world, it is better to know that you are asking the relevant question than comfort yourself that you have an impeccable answer to a problem that no longer exists.

5. 'God's truth' and 'hocus-pocus'

I want to end this chapter by looking at some of the problems which confront us when we set out to develop a design for Language Study, problems which arise from the nature of curriculum development rather than from the contingencies of class-room practice. The first of these is the great diversity we find in teacher education. In this country alone, it is so great that there sometimes seems to be as many different approaches to the education of teachers as there are institutions and agencies to provide that education. When we consider the practice of other countries in addition, the diversity becomes quite daunting. In these circumstances, it is necessary to focus upon the *design* for a particular approach rather than the details of particular courses and syllabuses. What is needed is a clear statement of the components which make up the approach and the principles which have led to their selection. With both of these available to them, those who wished to develop a Language Study approach would be in a position to

49

work out for themselves how best the components could be realized in terms of the actual courses and syllabuses that would meet the particular needs of their own learning situations.

To speak of a principled basis for selecting the components which will go to make up the framework of a particular approach raises the question of what we mean by the phrase 'developing an approach to'. One very common response to 'developing an approach to' is to see it as a matter of fitting together various items from different sources in order to produce a programme for class-room use. The emphasis is upon the list of different bits and pieces in the kit rather than the models that can be made with them, and there is no scope for asking whether these bits and pieces are the most suitable for building those models or why we should want to build these models rather than any others. This is to say that a course put together in this way lacks 'necessity'. There is no way of relating any part of it to an underlying theory or set of postu-lates which could provide a rational classification for putting the course together in one way rather than another.

To many people, a lack of necessity for what they put into their courses and syllabuses does not seem to matter. Perhaps they would even regard it as irrelevant so long as their choice of content or approach 'worked in the class-room'. Leaving aside for the moment the very difficult question as to how we know that some-thing 'works', I would want to argue that the climate of change in the educational system has created a new situation in which it is much more important than ever to know what we are actually doing in a learning situation, and why we are doing it. This is because we need to see how a particular pattern of work matches up to the actual needs of learners, and those needs are no longer a fixed quantity, because they reflect the pattern of continuous cultural change.

In this situation, we need to be able to ask three basic questions about any pattern of work set up within the educational system: why were these features selected rather than any others? what was the total range of alternatives from which these features were selected? what objectives are to be served by the features selected? To answer these questions successfully involves course and syllabus having a principled basis, an explicit formulation of the theory which underlies their content and their organization. This would enable us to formulate answers to our three basic questions that did have 'necessity' and avoid some of the commonest answers which we offer at present: that the course has always had these things in

50

it; that the students like it; that that is how students/examiners/ Board of Studies/University/society/God/wants it to be; that that is all we can teach; that that is the only way we know how to teach; that anything else would be contrary to the Laws of Nature. All or any of which may be good and sufficient reasons for doing what we are doing, but they do not really help to justify the existing elements and structure of course or syllabus, unless they are derived from *an explicit set of principles* which relate content and organization to an underlying explanatory theory.

The question of why teachers and learners do what they do is not a theoretical question that concerns only the professional curriculum developer, but a severely practical matter that involves everyone who has to create patterns of activity for learning situations. Let me demonstrate this point by referring to the aim of this book. It sets out to show that a Language Study approach is relevant to the needs of teachers and learners. In effect, its argument invites the reader to assess for himself how far he needs a Language Study approach to make sense of his work as a teacher, and how far he considers such an approach relevant to the language needs of all learners. The book puts the reader in a position to do this by making explicit the theoretical basis for what it advocates. The reader will reach his decision on the relevance of what is offered, therefore, according to his assessment of the validity of the theory that guides the selection of the components and the objectives which are presented to him as the constituents of a Language Study approach. In this sense, what looks like an abstract question for the professional curriculum developer ends up by being a highly relevant practical question for the individual teacher, because it is the presence of an explicit principled basis for Language Study which allows him to judge for himself, on rational grounds, whether or not he wants to have anything to do with it.

The first three chapters of this book explored certain major aspects of man as a languaging animal, and as a social and cultural animal, in order to show that a connection can be made between the way men use language to live and the language needs of all teachers and learners. The implication was that there are certain conclusions about the part played by language in teaching and learning which can be seen to follow *necessarily* from the nature and function of language in the life and society of man. These conclusions constitute a theory of language which provides us with the principled basis for the Language Study approach that this book advocates. What follows in Chapter 5, therefore, is an explicit working out of this basis so that the reader can test the validity of that basis for himself. Only then does it make sense for him to go on and consider what this approach could offer him in terms of his own situation.

In setting out this basis, I make use of twelve postulates which can guide us in our selection of a number of relevant areas of enquiry for Language Study. This is a useful way of formulating a principled basis, because it enables the reader to see the whole foundation of the argument set out in a relatively short space so that the relationship between its different elements stands out clearly. There is a danger in doing it this way, however, because it is always easy to overlook the fact that a set of postulates of this kind is only one out of the number of possible sets which could have been offered. If I stress the fact that what I offer is only one out of a number of possibilities, however, I lay myself open to the charge that what I offer is of no value, because it is not *the* answer to the problem.

There is an old debate in Linguistics as to whether the linguist is trying to reveal God's truth about a language through his description of it, or merely using his own hocus-pocus of a linguistic theory to set out one possible version of the facts as far as that language is concerned. I think it will be obvious to all readers that I would be the last person to claim God's truth for anything I was putting forward. What I am offering is one possible version of the facts as far as the development of an approach to Language Study is concerned. I hold very strongly to the view that all theories are *arbitrary* in the sense that all we can ever hope to do in our explorations of some aspect of reality, linguistic or social or cultural, is to offer one version out of the several alternative versions the facts make possible. We put this version together according to our own reading of the facts, and in doing so, we necessarily adopt only one out of a number of possible alternative ways of viewing the aspect of reality with which we are concerned. We put forward this version, and invite others to question its validity. The only constraint we have to accept in taking up this invitation is that that there is no point in trying to assess the validity of one version by using the theoretical postulates of another. We won't get very far if we insist on judging one man's hocus-pocus according to the dictates of our own belief in God's truth.

Let me end by trying to relate this argument to the quotation from Professor Medawar on page 50. He says that we start an enquiry by postulating '. . . a logically articulated structure of justifiable beliefs about nature'. In our case, this 'articulated structure' is the principled basis for a Language Study approach. Medawar insists, however, that this structure is only a story about a *Possible* World. In other words we are implying that if these and these facts are indeed true, then this is what one aspect of the world, or reality, really looks like. As he says, 'it is a story, which we *invent*', but he also says that it is a story which we 'criticise and modify *as we go along*', so that 'it ends by being . . . a story about *real life*' (My italics). This is the argument for putting forward at this stage in time an account of Language Study in terms of its principled basis and the components which can be derived from that basis, because we must begin by inventing our Possible World of Language Study, and then proceed to criticize and modify it as we try to make it approximate more and more closely to what would be, in terms of the language needs of teachers and learners, 'a story about real life'. This we can only do if we can see what principles shape the plot, the characters and the action of the story, because it is to these *principles* that the modifying criticism of others must be directed, if they have alternative stories to tell, and not to the detail of the courses that could be derived from them.

5 A Design for Language Study

1. The principled basis

The last chapter set out the framework of the design for Language Study which this book advocates. In order to provide the necessary support and guidance for the development of particular courses and syllabuses, there are four aspects of this framework which have to be set out in detail:

1) A *theory of language* which will provide the principled basis for the particular approach to Language Study which I am advocating.
2) A set of *components* which will provide an *operational focus* for Language Study.
3) A set of *areas of concern* which will define an *operational domain* for Language Study.
4) A set of *objectives* by which the activities in learning situations that Language Study gives rise to may be guided, and their effectiveness assessed.

The distinction I am proposing here between an *operational focus* and an *operational domain* is a distinction between the way in which we show interest in a particular aspect of reality and the human activities which give rise to that interest. The *components* of Language Study, which make up its *operational focus*, provide the framework within which we can formulate the kinds of questions about the nature and function of language that we want to ask, because we are interested in the use of language in the context of teaching and learning. On the other hand, the *areas of concern*, which arise out of this interest, reveal the source of those questions in terms of actual personal, cultural, social and educational con-

54

texts and thus provide us with an *operational domain* for Language Study. It is the possibility of setting up such a domain which provides the justification for the claim of Language Study to be considering questions that are not explored elsewhere.

Our point of departure, then, must be the statement of a theory of language which is derived from disciplines which have something to say about man the speaking animal. In *Exploring Language*, I have suggested that a theory of *language* is not the same thing as a theory of *linguistic description*. It is a:

> ... rational and explicit attempt to answer questions which ask *why language is as it is*, rather than *what one particular language contains or how its parts fit together*.

A theory of language must try to explain the patterns of natural languages in terms of the use that their speakers make of them. I have implied throughout this book that this is the only theory of language which can provide the basis for an exploration of the needs of teachers and learners as users of language, because it focuses attention upon language as the medium through which men make themselves and their society.

An outline for a theory of this kind appears in *Exploring Language*, Chapter Seven. A linguistic basis for it can be found in the volume of papers by Professor M. A. K. Halliday, in this series; a biological basis for it is offered in the forthcoming volume in the series by Roger Gurney; and the social and cultural basis will be explored further in another volume in the series by my wife and myself. All I need do in this context, therefore, is to present the fundamental postulates about the nature and function of language upon which the theory rests. While there are many different ways of formulating these postulates, and while each is open to a range of widely differing interpretations in terms of an operational theory of linguistic description, the substance of what they say about man as a languaging animal would be needed by any theory capable of justifying a Language Study approach.

Beginning with language itself, we can say:

1) That a language is a very complex autonomous organization, involving a finite number of elements, which can be combined in different ways, according to a statable set of rules, in order to yield a finite number of types of structure.

2) That, however, this self-consistent and finite organization is a symbolic system capable of producing an unlimited

number of utterances differing in meaning from each other.

3) That there is a set of rules, moreover, which governs the relationship between structures and meanings of such a kind that utterances are *predictable*, in the sense that speakers of the same language are able to derive meaning from them, and at the same time *original*, in the sense that the meanings expressed by these utterances may be unique to them.

4) That using this symbolic system to make utterances involves ' ... a simultaneous selection from among a large number of interrelated options (which) represent the "meaning potential" of language'.

M. A. K. Halliday

The activity of languaging, therefore, consists in the use of a self-consistent symbol system to convert 'meaning potential' into meaningful utterance and to derive meaningfulness from the 'meaning potential' encoded in the utterances of others. The essential thing to grasp about language is that it is composed of a large store of many different types of 'elements and structure', invariable in their nature and function, which can be put together, by the act of languaging, to meet the needs of innumerable unique situations. This act of languaging is guided by rules which determine what choices of 'elements and structure' are available to the speaker in making any particular utterance: 'inventiveness' enters into the situation in so far as the speaker *has to* exercise a process of choice in order to fashion any utterance. The 'elements and structure' may be given, but their deployment in actual utterances is open to limitless individual variations along many dimensions of difference.

If we now focus on the idea of man as a languaging animal, we can add the following postulates about language as a form of behaviour unique to human beings. We can say:

5) That language has survival value for the species; consequently there is a biological basis for the capacity to language which will be found in the genetic design of human beings.

6) That a *particular* language is learnt, however, by individual human beings in the course of continuous interaction with other human beings, who already possess an operational command of that language.

That is, an individual speaker's capacity to language is the product of a genetically-programmed potential for learning a natural

56

language exercised in a particular and local human environment, personal, social and cultural.

If we now consider the individual user of a language, we can suggest,

7) That an individual uses language to discriminate between one experience and the next; he calls upon the categories of his language for classifying and recording what he experiences; and he makes use of the resources of the symbolic system in his possession to understand what it is that he has experienced.

8) That an individual's capacity *to know himself as an individual*, his ability to develop a sense of *self*, a personal identity that is uniquely his, because it differentiates him from all other individuals, is a function of his capacity to language.

These two postulates reinforce the central importance of the fact that learning a language and learning how to use a language are intimately bound up with who we are, and where, and when, and in what manner, we grow up, because we *are* our language.

Man is a cultural animal, however, and language is the primary means available to him for the transmission of the values, capabilities and habits which go to make up a culture. It has been said already that acquiring a capacity to language is the same thing as acquiring a capacity to make meanings. Therefore we can say:

9) That, as the meanings we acquire are necessarily those that have currency amongst the individuals with whom we interact in the process of learning our language, learning a language is necessarily a form of cultural learning.

10) That the acquisition and use of language is a function of communities; that the use of language required by the exercise of capabilities and habits is the active life of communities; and that the part played by language in mediating the values is the continuity of communities.

This is to say that communities provide the immediate environment for man as a cultural animal; and that language is the essential cohesive element in the formation and perpetuation of individual communities.

Man is also a social animal, and consequently we must consider how '. . . language functions as a link in concerted human activity . . .' (Malinowski): that is, how language enables men to sustain patterns of behaviour that are social and interactional. We can say:

11) That men use language in order to initiate and maintain relationships with each other; to exercise control over each others' actions and thoughts; to create social groups which are able to maintain their coherence and identity over extended periods of time; and to articulate the larger structures required by collective social action.

12) That, as relationships are patterns of social action which occur in particular social settings, and as we learn how to language by our activity in particular social settings, the settings we have known will play a large part in shaping the way in which we use language to relate to others, and to exercise control over them.

This is to suggest that language functions for us successfully in so far as it is public rather than private. Its value to us in terms of survival derives from its capability as a symbolic system which can convert 'meaning potential' into *meanings potentially accessible to any other speaker of the language,* solely by virtue of their being speakers of the language. There is a final paradox in this, however. While language is a symbolic system for making public meanings upon which the whole fabric of human life depends, it is also each individual human being's most intimate and private possession, the system he uses to symbolize a unique view of the world. In our approach to Language Study we must never lose sight of either view.

2. The components of Language Study

These twelve postulates provide us, then, with the principled basis which supports this particular framework for an approach to Language Study. We cannot move easily from a set of theoretical statements at this level of abstraction, however, to the detailed provision of courses and syllabuses. In order to do so, we need to set up a middle ground which will relate our principles to what we decide to put into our actual programmes of work, so that they will not lack necessity. This middle ground comprises a set of *components* for Language Study, which derive from our principled basis, and a number of *areas of concern,* from which we derive the questions about language in teaching and learning that we wish to explore.

58

Let us look now at these components. As I have suggested, they are not 'subjects', or even subject contents, but a set of specific points of focus upon the nature and function of language. They can be formulated in the following terms:

I. Language as a function of its own internal organization as a self-consistent symbolic system, and the way in which that system is related to 'meaning potential' on the one hand, and modes of expression on the other.

II. Language as a generalized capacity, genetically-programmed and specific to man as a species. (A focus upon the degree to which language exists, because there is survival value in being a talking animal.)

III. Language in the creation and projection of the self. (A focus upon the degree to which we are dependent upon language for our capacity to make sense of the world and transmit our understanding of it to others.)

IV. Language as the medium for invention, mediation and modification of the values, capabilities and habits that make up a culture.

V. Language as the means of initiating, maintaining and controlling relationships with others. (A focus upon the basis of our ability to create social groups and articulate social structures.)

In developing a framework for our approach to Language Study, we can then ask a sequence of three basic questions in respect of each of these five components:

1) What is there to say about this aspect of the nature and function of language in so far as we are focused upon the general question of man's use of language to live?

2) How can we relate what we learn about this aspect of language to the particular questions we want to ask about the language needs of all learners?

3) What are the implications of this enquiry for the organization of activities in learning situations and the structure of their environment in schools and colleges?

Alternatively, we could phrase these questions so that we ask of each component:

1) What is the case, if we want to know how men use language *for living*?

2) What follows, therefore, if we want to know how men use *language for learning*?

3) What follows from this, if our aim is to develop a linguistic perspective on language for teachers and learners relevant to the needs of formal learning situations?

What I want to do next is to take each of the five components in turn and suggest how we might formulate more specific questions under the general heading of the first of our three basic questions, 'What is the case, if we want to know how men use *language for living*?

I—*Language as a self-consistent symbolic system*

1) What can formal linguistic descriptions tell us about the way in which 'meaning potential' is realized in terms of particular configurations of 'elements and structure'?

2) What would such a description have to say about the range of options open to the speaker at a particular point of utterance?

3) How do the elements and structure of this system relate to the sounds we make in the air and the marks we make on the page; and what is the relationship between these two modes of expression?

II—*Language as a phenomenon specific to the species*

1) What is the relationship between brain process and language production?

2) What is the relationship between the maturation of the organism and the development of a capacity to language?

3) What are the biological bases for the malfunction or breakdown in this capacity to language?

III—*Language as the medium for individuation*

1) How does the individual make use of language to categorize, order and interpret his experience of the world?

2) How does he use language to develop, maintain, project and modify a sense of self; and what part does language play in enabling us to perceive of ourselves as being *the same person*, irrespective of a multiplicity of local changes in time, space and situation?

3) How does he use language to create Possible Worlds; and how does he use language to express a unique view of the world?

IV—*Language and culture*
1) What part does language play in the process of transmitting culture from one generation to the next?
2) What do we mean by cultural learning and how closely is it initially bound up with our learning of a language?
3) What problems arise out of the way in which we use language to mediate values when a society no longer possesses a unitary culture?

V—*Language and social action*
1) What is the role of language in interaction; how do we use it to relate ourselves to others and what constraints does this place upon our freedom of action as individual selves?
2) What is the relationship between verbal and non-verbal channels in the context of face-to-face interaction?
3) To what extent are patterns of social action patterns of language in use; and how do we create these patterns of language in use in order to serve our needs as members of social groups and organizations?

What I have tried to do in presenting these questions is to indicate the kind of enquiry into the nature and function of language which is relevant to the particular context of Language Study. Exploring the answers to any one of them should be carried out bearing in mind the basic aim for Language Study, the development of a linguistic perspective. The aim is not to find out the facts for their own sake, but to discover what is relevant to a better understanding of the language needs of learning and teaching.

Each one of the questions I have enumerated would constitute a major theme in itself. The next stage is to break down each question into a large number of much more specific questions that would point to local and concrete enquiries into particular topics. A reader who would like to see how this can be done should take a look at *Language in Use*, the approach to Language Study which I and my colleagues developed for the Schools Council in this country. It is a resource for the teacher, which suggests how he can initiate Language Study for the pupil or student by working from their own existing intuitions about, and understanding of, language. For those who might already know the volume, and for those who might be interested enough to consult it, I would point out that four of the five components I have discussed in this

61

section relate directly to the structure of *Language in Use* in the following way:

Language in Use	*Language Study Component*
Part I. Language, its nature and function.	I. Language as a self-consistent symbolic system.
Part II. Language and the Individual.	III. Language as the medium for individuation.
Part III. Language and Social Man.	IV. Language as the medium for cultural action.
	V. Language as the medium for social action.

3. Areas of concern

So far in this chapter, I have been looking at the framework for a Language Study approach from the direction of the theory of language that provides it with a principled basis from which we can derive its components. I want now to look at this framework from the opposite direction, the *areas of concern* which give us the questions we want to ask about language in teaching and learning.

Let me now suggest six of these areas of concern. I think I have made it clear already that a list of this kind is not an exhaustive account of what might concern Language Study, but a *minimum* set of possibilities, those areas of concern which no approach to Language Study could properly afford to overlook.   They are:

1) The nature and function of language as a medium for teaching and learning.
2) The activities of teachers and learners as users of language for learning.
3) The character of the contexts in which language is used for teaching and learning.
4) The question of extending the learner's command over language for living and language for learning.
5) The question of developing pupils' awareness of how they use language to live and language to learn.
6) The question of developing a reflexive linguistic perspective for teachers.

Each of these primary areas of concern can be made to yield a number of much more specific topics which would form the basis for particular explorations. Let me show what this might look

62

like by taking (2), the language activity of teachers and pupils as participants in learning situations.

If we take the teacher first, we need to consider the way in which he creates a climate for learning through his decisions about what is to be learnt, and how it is to be learnt. We have to focus upon the linguistic implications of the fact that:

1) He determines the local content of what his pupils and students are expected to learn.
2) His own use of language, and the materials he provides, determine the character of the language through which his pupils or students gain access to that content.
3) It is his own attitudes towards the language for learning he expects his pupils or students to use, whether he reveals them implicitly or explicitly, that determine the character of the language for learning they will believe it possible to use.
4) The attitudes and assumptions he reveals, implicitly or explicitly, about language for living, set the limits within which his pupils or students feel free to draw upon their knowledge of the language as competent native speakers in order to participate in the learning situation.

If we now look at the learner, we can suggest that, as a participant in a learning situation, he is expected to:

1) Master a content, which he does not normally provide himself.
2) Make sense of this content through the use of a language for learning, which he does not himself select.
3) Render an account of the success of his learning, spoken or written, using this same language for learning.

At the same time, we can say that he will certainly bring into the learning situation:

4) His own folk-linguistic intuitions about the kind of language he expects to have to use for learning, and about the kind of language which he believes to be acceptable in the context of a learning situation.
5) His own attitudes and assumptions about the way in which people use language to live.

It seems to me that we could formulate two basic objectives which a Language Study approach might derive from this

63

breakdown of one aspect of a key *area of concern*. As far as the teacher is concerned, the objective is to put him in a position to answer for himself, in relation to his own learning situation, the following question:

> How can I create a situation in my own class-room that will give my pupils the incentive and the opportunity to develop the operational command of the language for learning that they need; and how can I best draw upon their existing command of language for living in the process?

As far as the learner is concerned, there is a dual objective:

1) To create a situation in which he can develop an appropriate command of the language for learning which he needs and an accompanying awareness of how he uses language to learn.
2) To use the learning situation to develop his overall command of language for living by developing his awareness of how he uses language to live.

4. Objectives

At the end of the preceding section, we were in a position to see how the examination of one particular area of concern and its breakdown into a number of specific topics or questions led us to formulate two particular objectives for a Language Study approach. I do not have the space to provide a detailed breakdown for the other areas of concern, but I can suggest two particular objectives for each of them. Taken together, the twelve objectives will then provide us with an overall picture of the specific contributions Language Study would hope to make to a better understanding of the part played by language in teaching and learning.

In order to fulfil the claims that we make for it, let us say then that Language Study would have to show how we could reach the following local and particular objectives.

In relation to the first of our areas of concern, the nature and function of language as a medium for teaching and learning, we can suggest these two objectives:

1) To show what characterizes the varieties of language, ways
64

of speaking as well as ways of writing, that arise specifically in the context of school or college.

2) To show how these varieties of a language relate to the ways in which it is used for living in the context of family, community and society.

The second of our areas, the activities of teachers and learners as users of language for learning, has already been dealt with at the end of the preceding section. Our third area, however, yields us these two possible objectives:

3) To show what personal, cultural, social and linguistic factors brought into the learning situation by teacher and learner do most to determine the climate for language activity.

4) To show what the school or college as a social organization contributes to this climate.

The question of extending command over language for living and language for learning is the fourth of our areas of concern. From this, we can derive these two objectives:

5) To make available a theory of competence which would provide a principled basis for developing activities and procedures designed to encourage growth of competence.

6) To enable the teacher to use such a theory in order to assess the effectiveness of the language activity in his own situation, judged from the point of view of its contribution to the growth of competence.

The fifth is closely related to the fourth, the question of developing pupils' awareness of how they use language to live and to learn. This would give us the following objectives:

7) To demonstrate the degree to which the success of language activity in learning situations depends upon the attitudes of teachers and learners towards language for learning.

8) To show how the development of awareness in the use of language for learning is related to a prior development of awareness in the use of language for living, and how growth of competence is also related to this dual development.

Our sixth and last area of concern specifically involves teachers. In a sense, the question of a reflexive linguistic perspective for teachers is the logical outcome of the other five. Given that we accept the validity of the objectives so far enumerated, then it is hard to avoid the conclusion that they require of the teacher a particularly developed awareness of the nature and function of language. Let us, therefore, suggest these two objectives for our final area of concern:

9) To show what knowledge about the nature and function of language is most relevant to the context of language in teaching and learning, and where that knowledge may be obtained.

10) To show how teachers might be able to develop a linguistic perspective and what difference it would make to their class-room practice were they to do so.

I would stress the fact that these ten objectives represent only one way of formulating the questions involved. At the same time, I do not think an approach to Language Study which ignored the substance of these ten would provide a very satisfactory mediator between the language problems of teachers and learners and the sources which might be able to produce answers for them. I would also say that we could take each of these objectives and break it down further, either in terms of what Language Study ought to provide or what teachers and learners could be expected to achieve by working towards that objective.

While I do not have the space to deal with each one of these objectives in such detail, I would like to take one of them, (7), and suggest what the pursuit of this objective might make available to the teacher:

1) It would put him in a position to see that pupils and students can only meet the demands made by language for learning if they are free to bring into the learning situation, and make use of it, their native speakers' command of language for living.

2) It would demonstrate to him that this is only possible where there is congruence between their understanding of how they use language to live and their understanding of what it means to use language to learn.

3) It would make him aware of his own fundamental contribution to the language of the learning situation in terms of:
   i) His folk-linguistic attitudes towards language and the use of language.

ii) His customary professional view of the use of language for living.

iii) His awareness of the linguistic attitudes and assumptions which his pupils or students bring into the learning situation and their probable divergence from his own.

4) It would make him aware of his own use of language in terms of:

i) What he says, formally through instruction, informally through consultation and advice, and in his exercise of social control.

ii) What written text he makes available or recommends.

iii) What demands he makes upon his pupils' and students' capacity to language, spoken or written.

I want to end this section by formulating a *global aim* for this approach to Language Study, an aim which would define its particular contribution to the professional competence of all teachers. The objectives I have described in this section can only be realized in so far as teachers are able to modify their customary ways of regarding language, whether for living or for learning. Collectively, therefore, they suggest that Language Study must be concerned with the development of a linguistic perspective. This gives a global aim and we can set it out in the following terms:

1) A teacher needs to understand the part played by language in the work of every area of the curriculum, whatever his own particular responsibilities.

2) He must be able to assess his individual contribution to the language climate of school or college in terms of:

i) His own individual language activity, inside and outside the learning situation.

ii) The activity he demands and expects from all the pupils and students with whom he comes into contact.

3) He needs to understand the part language plays in every aspect of our lives as human beings, personal, cultural and social.

4) He must be aware of the intimate relationship between the two aspects of language in use, language for living and language for learning.

What follows in section five is an outline of the evidence the work of the Schools Council *Language in Use* Project provides for suggesting how we can begin to work towards such an aim.

5. The evidence from the *Language in Use* project

This project set out to develop a Language Study approach to work in English at pupil level. Some of its effects upon teachers who used it are, however, relevant to the present context. Through their actual work in the class-room, based upon pupil's own existing experience of using language and employing a thorough-going exploratory approach, they came to review their whole attitude to language in the class-room context and beyond.

In their comments and reports, six points consistently recurred:

1) Language Study was accepted as relevant to their pupils' problems, and their own, in connection with the use of language for learning and teaching.

2) Their own folk linguistic attitudes had come to be considerably modified. Three factors seemed particularly important in making this possible:
   i) Continuous use of *Language in Use* teaches about language as it teaches: in other words, teachers learn as much as pupils by the same process of involvement in the exploration of their own experience as users of language.
   ii) Starting with pupils' own experience of using language to live powerfully modifies the idea that they do not know how to use language properly until they are taught to do so at school.
   iii) Looking at language as a human activity reveals the degree to which many common class-room problems are basically *linguistic* problmes.

3) Using the units of *Language in Use* involves teachers in using the theory of language implicit in their design. As they grow more familiar with the theory, they come to see its relevance to their work and want to know more, initially, about the principles underlying the units, but ultimately about the nature and function of language itself.

4) Teachers find that this familiarity with the theory also comes to provide them with a conceptual framework that they can use to shape the questions about language which they want to ask and into which they can fit the answers they discover.

5) In effect, they find that this framework gives them the rudiments of a principled approach to the linguistic aspects of their work and thus provides:
   i) A means of assessing the potential of any activity in terms of its ability to generate in pupils the command of language for learning necessary for its effective pursuit.
   ii) A means of planning an approach to his own and his pupils' use of language that is consonant with what we know to be true about its nature and function.
   iii) A basis for assessing the relative contributions of all subjects to the pupils' linguistic competence and the particular nature of the contribution properly to be expected from the English Department.

6) Using the units provides a first-hand experience of using an approach that is ordered and coherent, yet does not impose rigid structure and direction upon the pattern of work that derives from it.

Given that this is what happened when the units were used in the ordinary course of day-to-day teaching, we can necessarily ask why it happened. These results were possible because of certain features in the basic design. For our present purposes they can be summarized as:

1) A formal framework for 'content' that offered:
   i) Flexibility within a rational ordering of options so that a multiplicity of individual 'courses' can be built up from the units.
   ii) A principled basis for selecting options.
   iii) A rationale for any work undertaken.

2) A notion of 'content' that broke away from the idea that the study of language in the class-room must *necessarily* show the same kind of explicitness of analytical statement common in other subject areas.

3) A pattern of class-room activity that enables both teacher and pupils to learn new ways of operating together in the process of following out a clearly defined objective. The focus is upon the enquiry and the 'new ways' seem to arise naturally out of the work to be done.

4) Objectives for the units that combine growth of awareness of the nature and function of language with growth of competence in the use of spoken and written English.

5) An overall strategy where the aim was to create patterns of work that would modify attitudes. You cannot *tell* people what to think about language, because it is too intimate and familiar a possession; therefore you have to let them work towards a situation in which they come to see for themselves the limits of their existing views. The key process, here, is the 'working towards', the process of the enquiry itself.

Part II
A Guide to Reading in Language Study

by
Geoffrey Thornton

Introduction

The suggestions made in this second part of the book do not claim to constitute either an exhaustive or a definitive list of books concerned with various aspects of Language Study. They represent a selection of those books available at the time of writing (April 1972) which the authors have found particularly helpful, not only in their own reading in the subject but also in the course of their work with teachers. The books and articles referred to are grouped in sections to correspond with the schema described in chapter 5, section II. In each case a book will be identified by the author's name and title (e.g. HALLIDAY: EXPLORATIONS IN THE FUNCTIONS OF LANGUAGE), with full bibliographical details given in an appendix.

1. Language as a self-consistent symbolic system

Two essays in SAPIR: CULTURE, LANGUAGE AND PERSONALITY make a good starting point—the first, called simply 'Language', and the third, 'The Status of Linguistics as a Science'. The first chapter, 'Introductory: Language Defined' of SAPIR: LANGUAGE, which is subtitled 'An Introduction to the Study of Speech' also makes good introductory reading.

Commonly held, if frequently fallacious, views of language are sometimes called 'folk-linguistic notions of language'. (See DOUGHTY, PEARCE, THORNTON: EXPLORING LANGUAGE, chapters 1 and 2.) The contrast between the folk-linguistic view and the view of language held by the linguist is pointed out in chapters 2 and 3 of CRYSTAL: LINGUISTICS. Chapter 3 is followed by 'Interlude: An Example', a most readable attempt to illustrate concretely some of the 'hallmarks of a scientifically responsible approach to language study'. In the first two chapters of PALMER: GRAMMAR will also be found some comparison between 'traditional' notions about language and those now held by the linguists. For further reading see the introduction to (Ed.) LYONS: NEW HORIZONS IN LINGUISTICS, where the editor discusses some of the 'key concepts of modern linguistics'.

For a brief introduction to phonetics and phonology see CRYSTAL: LINGUISTICS, pp. 167–86. This may be followed by the introductory chapter, and chapters 2 and 3, of CHAO: LANGUAGE AND SYMBOLIC SYSTEMS, and chapter 3 of LYONS: INTRODUCTION TO THEORETICAL LINGUISTICS. ABERCROMBIE: ELEMENTS OF GENERAL PHONETICS gives a good, comprehensive account. For a description of the way in which intonation functions as part of the grammar of spoken English, see HALLIDAY: INTONATION AND GRAMMAR IN BRITISH ENGLISH.

A short introductory course of reading in syntax might begin with CRYSTAL: LINGUISTICS, pp. 187–230; CHAO, chapter 4; LYONS: INTRODUCTION TO THEORETICAL LINGUISTICS, chapters 4 and 5; and PALMER: GRAMMAR, already referred to.

For a short introduction to the concept of 'meaning potential' (p. 60) see 'The problem of meaning', a chapter in FIRTH: THE TONGUES OF MEN & SPEECH, and THORNTON, BIRK AND HUDSON: LANGUAGE AT WORK. The papers which comprise HALLIDAY: EXPLORATIONS IN THE FUNCTIONS OF LANGUAGE (in this series) bring together a number of related treatments of the idea. See also HALLIDAY: 'LANGUAGE STRUCTURE AND LANGUAGE FUNCTION' in (Ed.) LYONS: NEW HORIZONS IN LINGUISTICS, and HALLIDAY: 'LEARNING HOW TO MEAN'.

For a discussion of the relationship between "the sounds we make in the air and the marks we make on the page" see CHAO, chapter 8. For a description of the writing system of English see ALBROW: THE ENGLISH WRITING SYSTEM. Related to this, but with specific reference to the teaching of reading and writing is the Teachers' Manual to MACKAY, THOMPSON AND SCHAUB: BREAK-THROUGH TO LITERACY.

2. Language as a phenomenon specific to the species

Introductory reading—GURNEY: LANGUAGE, BRAIN AND INTER-ACTIVE PROCESSES (in this series).

The work of E. H. Lenneberg is perhaps the best known in this area. See LENNEBERG: 'A BIOLOGICAL PERSPECTIVE OF

LANGUAGE' in (Ed.) OLDFIELD and MARSHALL: LANGUAGE, and his book LENNEBERG: THE BIOLOGICAL FOUNDATIONS OF LANGUAGE.

For reading in the biological background, see NATHAN: THE NERVOUS SYSTEM, and WOOLDRIDGE: THE MACHINERY OF THE BRAIN. Also GREGORY: THE INTELLIGENT EYE (especially chapter 8).

For a series of readings on the impact of biological factors on the individual's potential for language acquisition see Part Two (Biological Factors) of (Ed.) HUDSON: THE ECOLOGY OF HUMAN INTELLIGENCE, and the section called 'From Biology' in (Ed.) RICHARDSON AND SPEARS: RACE, CULTURE AND INTELLIGENCE.

A survey of what is currently known about the mechanism of speech production and reception might begin with EXPLORING LANGUAGE, chapter 8, part i, followed by FRY: 'SPEECH RECEPTION AND PERCEPTION' and LAVER: 'THE PRODUCTION OF SPEECH', both in (Ed.) LYONS: NEW HORIZONS IN LINGUISTICS. GOLDMAN EISLER: PSYCHOLINGUISTICS gives an account of her research into the significance of hesitation pausing in fluent speech. On this, see also BOOMER: 'HESITATION PAUSING AND GRAMMATICAL ENCODING' in (Ed.) OLDFIELD AND MARSHALL: LANGUAGE.

For an introduction to the literature of language disorders, see LENNEBERG: 'SPEECH AS A MOTOR SKILL WITH SPECIAL REFERENCE TO NON-APHASIC DISORDERS' in (Ed.) PRIBRAM: ADAPTATION and TALLAND: DISORDERS OF MEMORY AND LEARNING.

WILKINSON: THE FOUNDATIONS OF LANGUAGE brings together a great deal of information on many related topics. See particularly, in this area, chapters 6 and 7.

3. Language as a medium for individuation

Introduction—EXPLORING LANGUAGE, chapters 3 and 4, and THORNTON: THE INDIVIDUAL'S DEVELOPMENT OF A LANGUAGE, in THORNTON, BIRK AND HUDSON: LANGUAGE AT WORK.

For discussion of the way in which the individual sets up categories in order to make sense of experience see ABERCROMBIE: THE ANATOMY OF JUDGMENT, chapters 2 and 3; LEACH: 'ANIMAL CATEGORIES AND VERBAL ABUSE' in (Ed.) LENNEBERG: NEW DIRECTIONS IN THE STUDY OF LANGUAGE, and BROWN: 'HOW SHALL A THING BE CALLED?' in (Ed.) OLDFIELD AND MARSHALL: LANGUAGE.

On problems attendant upon creating and maintaining a sense of self see GOFFMAN: STIGMA and GOFFMAN: THE PRESENTATION OF SELF IN EVERYDAY LIFE. See also BANNISTER AND FRANSELLA: INQUIRING MAN and BRITTON: LANGUAGE AND LEARNING, chapter 1.

FIRTH: 'PERSONALITY AND LANGUAGE IN SOCIETY' in his PAPERS IN LINGUISTICS, 1934-51 would form a good introduction to WHORF: LANGUAGE, THOUGHT AND REALITY, a collection of essays that has had an important influence on the arguments of the last ten years.

In BERGER AND LUCKMANN: THE SOCIAL CONSTRUCTION OF REALITY the authors explore the social foundations of what the individual comes to accept as reality.

Various influences contributing to the individual's construction of reality are examined in some of the readings in (Ed.) WISE-MAN: INTELLIGENCE AND ABILITY (see especially HEBB: 'THE GROWTH AND DECLINE OF INTELLIGENCE' and J. MCV. HUNT: 'INTELLIGENCE AND EXPERIENCE') and in (Ed.) HUDSON: THE ECOLOGY OF HUMAN INTELLIGENCE. See especially extracts number 12-16. HUDSON: FRAMES OF MIND follows HUDSON: CONTRARY IMAGINATIONS in looking at some of the factors predisposing the individual to one view of reality rather than another. Some recent points of controversy in this area are discussed in contributions to (Ed.) RICHARDSON AND SPEARS: RACE, CULTURE AND INTELLIGENCE.

4. Language as a medium for cultural action

SPROTT: HUMAN GROUPS provides a good introductory read to this section. It might be followed by SAPIR: LANGUAGE, chapter 10 and by a number of essays in SAPIR: CULTURE, LANGUAGE AND PERSONALITY.

HALL: THE SILENT LANGUAGE is a book which the author says 'is written for the layman . . . in such a way as to lead the reader gradually from the known to the unknown' and make him aware of the infinitely subtle ways in which culture is transmitted from generation to generation.

DOUGLAS: PURITY AND DANGER and DOUGLAS: NATURAL SYMBOLS discuss the symbolic significance in the life of society of such things as rules of hygiene.

The first part of (Ed.) HUDSON: THE ECOLOGY OF HUMAN IN-TELLIGENCE is called 'The Cultural Context'. See, especially, the first extract, D'ANDRADE: 'SEX DIFFERENCES AND CULTURAL INSTITUTIONS'.

In FRANKENBERG: COMMUNITIES IN BRITAIN the author brings together a number of studies of various kinds of community in Britain. See chapters 5 and 7. Chapter 9 contains very useful definitions of the sociologist's concepts of 'role' and 'network'. (See EXPLORING LANGUAGE, chapters 5 and 6). SHARP: ENGLISH IN A BI-LINGUAL COMMUNITY (in this series) explores the implications for those living in communities which have two languages of the relationship between those languages.

5. Language as the medium for social action

BERGER : INVITATION TO SOCIOLOGY makes a good introduction to the reading suggested in this section.

For discussion of recent work in socio-linguistics see PRIDE: THE SOCIAL MEANING OF LANGUAGE, chapters 1–7. The editorial introduction to GIGLIOLI: LANGUAGE AND SOCIAL CONTEXT reminds us that questions to be asked about the part played by language in social interaction may be summarized as, 'Who speaks to whom in what language and on what occasion?' The excerpts in Part Two of that volume, headed 'Speech and Situated Action', form a useful anthology.

The eighth excerpt is BERNSTEIN: 'SOCIAL CLASS, LANGUAGE AND SOCIALIZATION', which is also reprinted in BERNSTEIN: CLASS, CODES AND CONTROL, Vol. 1. This is a collection of Bernstein's writings over the last twelve years, prefaced by an introduction in which the author traces the development of his ideas during this period. BERNSTEIN: CLASS, CODES AND CONTROL, Vol. 2 will be a collection of papers by various authors on aspects of the relationship between social class and educability. See particularly HASAN: CODE, REGISTER AND SOCIAL DIALECT. See also LAWTON: SOCIAL CLASS, LANGUAGE AND EDUCATION for a discussion of the issues and a summary of relevant research up to the time of publication.

The relationship between society and its educational agencies (see p. 14) may be approached through some of the contributions in COSIN et al: SCHOOL AND SOCIETY, particularly sections I and II. The introduction to (Ed.) YOUNG: KNOWLEDGE AND CONTROL, followed by the first three pieces in the volume, will enable the exploration to be taken further. These are YOUNG'S own 'AN APPROACH TO THE STUDY OF CURRICULA AS SOCIALLY ORGANISED KNOWLEDGE', BERNSTEIN: 'ON THE CLASSIFICATION AND FRAMING OF KNOWLEDGE' and ESLAND: 'TEACHING AND LEARNING AS THE ORGANISATION OF KNOWLEDGE.'

(Ed.) HOOPER: THE CURRICULUM is a collection concerned with the context, design and development of the curriculum, including such topics as 'Education and social change in modern England' and 'Freedom and learning: the need for choice'.

Section III of SCHOOL AND SOCIETY, entitled 'Learning and its organisation in school', contains half a dozen pieces which look at some of the ways in which the organization of schools affects those who go to them. This is also considered in HANNAM, SMYTH AND STEPHENSON: YOUNG TEACHERS AND RELUCTANT LEARNERS, and in some of the contributions to (Ed.) RUBINSTEIN AND STONEMAN: EDUCATION FOR DEMOCRACY. LETTER TO A TEACHER describes convincingly the way in which attitudes in school can discriminate against some categories of pupil.

There is a growing literature concerned with the school as an environment for language development. See, for example, BARNES AND BRITTON: LANGUAGE, THE LEARNER AND THE SCHOOL, BARNES: CLASSROOM CONTEXTS FOR LANGUAGE AND LEARNING and KEDDIE: 'CLASSROOM KNOWLEDGE' in (Ed.) YOUNG: KNOWLEDGE AND CONTROL. CREBER: LOST FOR WORDS provides a well-argued consideration of the connection between educational failure and the climate provided in the school for language use. See also POSTMAN AND WEINGARTNER: TEACHING AS A SUBVERSIVE ACTIVITY, especially chapter 7, 'Languaging', and, in this series, THORNTON: LANGUAGE, EXPERIENCE AND SCHOOL.

For a more specific consideration of language in discussion as a context for language development, see EXPLORING LANGUAGE, chapter 8, part ii; ABERCROMBIE: THE ANATOMY OF JUDGMENT, chapters 5 onwards; the relevant parts of BARNES AND BRITTON; and HANNAM, SMYTH AND STEPHENSON, chapter 6.

It might be useful at this stage to look at problems arising from folk-linguistic notions of dialect, accent and correctness. On accent and dialect see EXPLORING LANGUAGE, chapter 10; and—in ABERCROMBIE : STUDIES IN PHONETICS AND LINGUISTICS—the chapter entitled 'RP and Local Accent'.

On 'correctness' see MITTINS: WHAT IS CORRECTNESS? and MITTINS et al: ATTITUDES TO ENGLISH USAGE.

The relationship between language for living and language for learning will be discussed in more detail in DOUGHTY AND DOUGHTY: LANGUAGE AND COMMUNITY (in this series). The question of the place of language in the work of the English department, and the role of the English department in the curriculum, is considered in DOUGHTY: LANGUAGE, 'ENGLISH', AND THE CURRICULUM.

Two other books in this series consider specific areas of language work in school—ASHWORTH: LANGUAGE IN THE JUNIOR SCHOOL and HARRISON: ENGLISH AS A SECOND AND FOREIGN LANGUAGE. The latter has much to say about the teaching of immigrants.

For lecturers in Colleges of Education (Ed.) DENNIS: LANGUAGE STUDY IN TEACHER EDUCATION offers a number of suggestions as to the way in which courses of Language Study might be set up and fitted into college curricula.

Appendix

Language in Use, Exploring Language **and Language Study**

In this section we link together, in a selection of examples, units from *Language in Use*, chapters from *Exploring Language* and some of the literature to which they might lead. These examples are offered in order to illustrate ways in which components of a course in Language Study might be built up, beginning at points within the language and experience of the student and gradually leading on to explorations in the literature.

1. Language

Language in Use Units D1, D2, D3 and D4.

These units are concerned with, respectively, 'the internal organization of language, sounds, words and meanings, and how they inter-relate'; 'the . . . fact that language works because much of what we say is predictable'; 'what limits there are upon . . . (our) . . . freedom' to say what we want to say; and the way in which 'language is composed of many inter-related patterns'.

Exploring Language, chapter Nine—Spoken and Written.

This chapter looks at the nature of spoken language, and its relationship to written language.

FIRTH: 'The Problem of Meaning' in TONGUES OF MEN & SPEECH.

See, for example, p. 177 and the notion of 'pivotal points' of language, and their relationship to meaning.

FRY: 'SPEECH RECEPTION AND PERCEPTION'.

The early pages discuss 'the vast store of information' about language that has to be carried in the brain of any language user, the way in which this information has to be systematized and the

81

way in which one has to be able to predict what other people are going to say if one is to understand them.

For an introduction to the way in which linguists describe the 'elements and structures' of language see references on p. 78.

Language in Use Units C6 and C7.

These units serve as an introduction to intonation, and (C7) the possibilities open to a language user of implying rather than making explicit what he means.

Exploring Language, chapter Nine.

HALLIDAY : INTONATION AND GRAMMAR IN BRITISH ENGLISH for a description of the intonation system in British English.

C7 ('Implications') might serve as an introduction to meaning in spoken language, language as code (see HASAN: 'REGISTER, CODE AND SOCIAL DIALECT'), the concept of 'meaning potential' and Halliday's use of the term 'socio-semantic' (see 'LANGUAGE IN A SOCIAL PERSPECTIVE' in HALLIDAY: EXPLORATIONS IN THE FUNCTIONS OF LANGUAGE).

2. Language and the individual

Language in Use, Unit C3.

This unit is concerned with the 'physical features which go to make up the uniqueness of a particular voice', called indexical features.

See ABERCROMBIE: ELEMENTS OF GENERAL PHONETICS for a phonetician's description.

Language in Use, Units F1, D7, D8.

These units are concerned with categories as language makes them available to the individual.

Exploring Language, chapter Four.

This chapter is concerned with the way in which experience is categorized by the language and the language-learner.

ABERCROMBIE : THE ANATOMY OF JUDGMENT, in which the author discusses the process of categorization.

DOUGLAS: PURITY AND DANGER.

Some categories, like those of cleanliness and dirtiness, are deeply significant for the life of the individual and for the life of society. Chapters 7 ('External Boundaries)', 8 '(Internal Lines') and 9 ('The System at War with Itself') consider the importance of boundaries between categories, and how they are maintained.

In his Introduction to CLASS, CODES AND CONTROL, Bernstein

records how Professor Douglas helped to focus his work 'upon the idea of the variable strength of boundaries and their relationship to the structuring and realizing of experience'. For an application of this to the educational world see BERNSTEIN: 'ON THE CLASSIFI-CATION AND FRAMING OF EDUCATIONAL KNOWLEDGE' in both CLASS, CODES and CONTROL and (Ed.) YOUNG: KNOWLEDGE AND CONTROL.

Language in Use, Units H3, H5, H6.
These units are concerned with various aspects of self.
Exploring Language, chapter Five.
This chapter, Language and Relationships, takes the argument further, and points towards BERGER: INVITATION TO SOCIOLOGY, and other works referenced at the end of the chapter.
GOFFMAN: STIGMA and THE PRESENTATION OF SELF IN EVERYDAY LIFE might well come in here, to be followed by a consideration of the theory of 'personal constructs'. See BANNISTER AND FRANSELLA: INQUIRING MAN and BRITTON: LANGUAGE AND LEARNING.

3. Language and culture

Language in Use, Unit F2.
The starting point of this unit is 'the fact that certain tasks are traditionally thought to be the prerogative of one sex or the other' and explores the way in which this is reflected in the language.
Exploring Language, chapter Three and THORNTON: THE INDIVI-DUAL'S DEVELOPMENT OF HIS LANGUAGE look a little more deeply at culturally determined differences between male and female in society.
HUDSON: FRAMES OF MIND, chapter 3, 'Masculine and Feminine', points to some educational implications of this differentiation.
D'ANDRADE: 'SEX DIFFERENCES AND CULTURAL INSTITUTIONS' in (Ed.) HUDSON: THE ECOLOGY OF HUMAN INTELLIGENCE considers 'some of the very complex mechanisms that play a part in the development of sex differences in all human societies'.

Language in Use, Units H1 and H2, 'Family Names' and 'Personal Names', look at the part that names play in relation-ships.
Exploring Language, chapter Five, examines relationships more closely.
BERGER AND LUCKMANN: THE SOCIAL CONSTRUCTION OF REALITY argue, as their title implies, that what the individual comes to

accept as reality is socially constructed, and they 'analyse the process in which this occurs'. In the chapter entitled 'Society as Subjective Reality' they say, of names that we are given, 'Every name implies a nomenclature, which in turn implies a designated social location'. This particular 'pathway' through the reading could usefully be linked with that suggested under the heading of 'self' in the previous section, and with the same authors' treatment of 'role' in THE SOCIAL CONSTRUCTION OF REALITY.

4. Language and society

Language in Use, Units J4 and J5.
Both units are concerned with the way in which language is used to establish and maintain contact with other people.
Exploring Language, chapters Five, Six and Eight.
Five and Six discuss, among other points, relationships in society. Chapter 8, part ii, begins to look at relationships in the class-room, and how such relationships constrain language. To take this further, see
BARNES: CLASSROOM CONTEXTS FOR LANGUAGE AND LEARNING and, on relationships in school, HANNAM, SMYTH AND STEPHENSON: YOUNG TEACHERS AND RELUCTANT LEARNERS.

Language in Use, Units C4 and F10.
One notion which may act as a constraint on the use of language is that of accent. These units may be used to begin a linguistic consideration of accent, and may be followed by *Exploring Language*, chapter Ten, 'Accent and Dialect'.
ABERCROMBIE : 'RP AND LOCAL ACCENT' in STUDIES IN PHONETICS AND LINGUISTICS is also very useful.

Language in Use, Units D6 and F9.
Allied to 'folk-linguistic' notions of accent and dialect may be notions of correctness. F9 explores the linguistic basis of 'popular notions of "corrections" ', and D6 looks at the kind of corrections made on pupils' written work. Grammatical notions of 'correctness' are examined in PALMER: GRAMMAR, section 1.3 'Correct and incorrect'. See also MITTINS: 'WHAT IS CORRECTNESS?' and MITTINS et al: ATTITUDES TO ENGLISH USAGE.

Language in Use, Units K1 and K2, 'Schools and colleges' and 'School traditions'.
These units may be used to begin a detailed look at school organization and structure.

84

Many of the excerpts in COSIN et al: SCHOOL AND SOCIETY will be helpful. See the Introduction, and the section introductions—especially that to section III, 'Learning and its organisation in school'.

Various aspects of school organization are touched upon in CREBER: LOST FOR WORDS. (How certain types of school organization help to educate for failure.)

LETTER TO TEACHER. (How some pupils start at a disadvantage and become more and more disadvantaged until they drop out altogether.)

HANNAM, SMYTH AND STEPHENSON: YOUNG TEACHERS AND RELUCTANT LEARNERS, chapter 4. (How young teachers have to fit into the authority structure of a school.)

Language in Use, Units E7 and G9.

E7, 'Write me an essay', tries to show how words used to describe tasks in school are 'a function of the social context provided by the school', while G9, 'The language of school subjects', 'considers the crucial part played by key terms in the understanding of new concepts'—especially as those concepts appear in school subjects.

Exploring Language, Chapter Seven, Command of a Language, 'is concerned with the way in which a speaker extends his command over spoken and written language'—particularly in the context of demands upon him in school.

DOUGHTY: LANGUAGE, 'English' and the curriculum takes the exploration further.

The study of the language of school subjects might now form the starting point for a look at the status of subjects within the curriculum. Especially helpful are various contributions to (Ed.) YOUNG: KNOWLEDGE AND CONTROL. (See references on p. 81.)

See also various contributions to (Ed.) HOOPER: THE CURRICULUM.

Bibliography

Abercrombie, D. *Studies in Phonetics and Linguistics* (O.U.P. 1965)
— *Elements of General Phonetics* (Edinburgh, 1967)
Abercrombie, M. L. J. *The Anatomy of Judgment* (Penguin, 1969)
Albrow, K. H. *The English Writing System* (Papers in Linguistics and English Teaching, Series 11, Longman, 1972)
Ashworth, E. *Language in the Junior School* (Edward Arnold, in this series, forthcoming)
Bannister, D. and Fransella, F. *Inquiring Man: The Theory of Personal Constructs* (Penguin, 1971)
Barnes, D. 'Classroom Contexts for Language and Learning' in *The Context of Language* (Educational Review, Birmingham University, 1971)
Barnes, D. and Britton, J. N. *Language, the learner and the school* (Penguin, 1969)
Berger, P. L. *Invitation to Sociology* (Penguin, 1966)
Berger, P. L. and Luckmann, T. *The Social Construction of Reality* (Penguin University Books, 1971)
Bernstein, B. *Class, Codes and Control, Vol. I* (Routledge and Kegan Paul, 1971)
(Ed.) Bernstein, B. *Class, Codes and Control, Vol. II* (Routledge and Kegan Paul, forthcoming)
Boomer, D. S. 'Hesitation Pausing and Grammatical Encoding' in (Ed.) Oldfield R. C. and Marshall J. C. *Language*
Britton, J. N. *Language and Learning* (Penguin 1972)
Chao, Y. R. *Language and Symbolic Systems* (C.U.P. 1968)
Cosin, B., Dale, I. R., Esland, G. M., Swift, D. F. *School and Society* (Routledge and Kegan Paul, 1971)
Creber, J. W. P. *Lost for Words* (Penguin, 1972)
Crystal, D. *Linguistics* (Penguin, 1971)
(Ed.) Dennis, G. W. *Language Study in Teacher Education* (Edward Arnold, in this series, forthcoming)

Doughty, P. S. *Language, 'English' and the curriculum*. (Papers in Linguistics and English Teaching, Series 11, Longman, 1972)

Doughty, P. S. and E. A. *Language and Community* (Edward Arnold, in this series, forthcoming)

Doughty, P. S., Pearce, J. J. and Thornton, G. M. *Language in Use* (Edward Arnold, 1971)

— — — *Exploring Language* (Edward Arnold, 1972)

Doughty, P. S. and Thornton, G. M. *Command of a language: towards a theory of competence in teaching and learning* (Papers in Linguistics and English Teaching, Series 11, Longman, 1972)

Douglas, M. *Purity and Danger* (Penguin, 1970)

— *Natural Symbols* (Cresset Press, 1970)

Firth, J. R. *Papers in Linguistics, 1934–51* (O.U.P. 1957)

— *The Tongues of Men & Speech* (O.U.P. 1964)

Frankenberg, R. *Communities in Britain* (Penguin, 1966)

Fry, D. B. 'Speech Reception and Perception' in (Ed.) Oldfield R. C. and Marshall, J. C. *Language* (Penguin)

(Ed.) Giglioli, P. P. *Language and Social Context* (Penguin, 1972)

Goffman, E. *Stigma* (Penguin, 1967)

— *The Presentation of Self in Everyday Life* (Penguin, 1969)

Goldman Eisler, F. *Psycholinguistics* (Academic Press, N.Y., 1968)

Gregory, R. L. *The Intelligent Eye* (Weidenfeld and Nicholson, 1970)

Gurney, R. *Language, Brain and Interactive Processes* (Edward Arnold, in this series, forthcoming)

Hall, E. T. *The Silent Language* (Doubleday, 1959)

Halliday, M. A. K. *Intonation and Grammar in British English* (Mouton, 1967)

— *Explorations in the Functions of Language* (Edward Arnold, in this series)

— 'Language Structure and Language Function' in (Ed.) Lyons J. *New Horizons in Linguistics* (Penguin)

— 'Learning how to mean' in (Ed.) Lenneberg, E. H. *Foundations of Language: A Multidisciplinary Approach* (UNESCO and IBRO forthcoming)

Hannam, C., Smyth, P. and Stephenson, N. *Young teachers and reluctant learners* (Penguin, 1971)

Harrison, J. B. *English as a Second and Foreign Language* (Edward Arnold, in this series)

Hasan, R. 'Register, Code and Social Dialect' in (Ed.) Bernstein, B. *Class, Codes and Control, Vol. II*

(Ed.) Hooper, R. *The Curriculum* (Oliver and Boyd, 1971)

Hudson, L. *Contrary Imaginations* (Penguin, 1967)

— *Frames of Mind* (Penguin, 1970)

(Ed.) Hudson, L. *The Ecology of Human Intelligence* (Penguin, 1970)

Laver, J. 'The Production of Speech' in (Ed.) Lyons, J. *New Horizons in Linguistics*

87

Lawton, D. *Social Class, Language and Education* (Routledge and Kegan Paul, 1968)

Lenneberg, E. H. *The Biological Foundations of Language* (Wiley, 1957)

— 'Speech as a motor skill with special reference to non-aphasic disorders' in (Ed.) Pribram, K. H. *Adaptations* (Penguin)

(Ed.) Lenneberg E. H. *New Directions in the Study of Language* (M.I.T. 1966)

Letter to a Teacher by the School of Barbiana (Penguin, 1970)

Lyons, J. *Introduction to Theoretical Linguistics* (C.U.P. 1968)

(Ed.) Lyons, J. *New Horizons in Linguistics* (Penguin, 1970)

Mackay, D., Thompson, B., Schaub, P. *Breakthrough to Literacy, Teachers' Manual* (Longman, 1970)

Medawar, P. B. *Induction and Intuition in Scientific Thought* (Methuen, 1969)

Mittins, W. H. 'What is correctness?' in *The State of Language* (Educational Review, University of Birmingham, Nov. 1969)

Mittins, W. H. et al. *Attitudes to English Usage* (O.U.P. 1970)

Nathan, P. *The Nervous System* (Penguin, 1969)

(Ed.) Oldfield, R. C. and Marshall, J. C. *Language* (Penguin, 1968)

Palmer, F. *Grammar* (Penguin, 1971)

Postman, N. and Weingartner, C. *Teaching as a Subversive Activity* (Penguin, 1971)

(Ed.) Pribram, K. H. *Adaptation* (Brain and Behaviour 4, Penguin Modern Psychology, 1969)

Pride, J. B. *The Social Meaning of Language* (O.U.P. 1971)

(Ed.) Richardson, K. and Spears, D. *Race, Culture and Intelligence* (Penguin, 1972)

(Ed.) Rubinstein, D. and Stoneman, C. *Education for Democracy* (Penguin, 1970)

Sapir, E. *Language* (Harcourt Brace & World Inc., 1921)

— *Culture, Language and Personality* (Univ. of California, 1949)

Sharp, D. *Language in Bi-lingual Communities* (Edward Arnold, in this series, forthcoming)

Sprott, W. J. H. *Human Groups* (Penguin, 1958)

Talland, G. A. *Disorders of Memory and Learning* (Penguin, 1968)

Thornton, G. M. *Language, Experience and School* (Edward Arnold, in this series, forthcoming)

— 'The Individual's Development of Language' in Thornton, G. M., Birk, D. and Hudson, R. A. *Language at Work* (Papers in Linguistics and English Teaching, Series 11, Longman, 1972)

Whorf, B. L. *Language, Thought and Reality* (Wiley, 1956)

Wilkinson, A. *The Foundations of Language* (O.U.P. 1971)

(Ed.) Wiseman, S. *Intelligence and Ability* (Penguin, 1967)

Wooldridge, D. *The Machinery of the Brain*, (McGraw Hill, 1960)

(Ed.) Young M. *Knowledge and Control* (Collier-MacMillan, 1971)

LANGUAGE, EXPERIENCE AND SCHOOL

Geoffrey Thornton

Acknowledgements

I am grateful to those who have helped, in various ways, with the writing of the book, especially Eric Ashworth and Peter Doughty, Stephen Lushington and Frank Skitt. The responsibility for where the argument leads is mine.

Geoffrey Thornton

Introduction

Most teachers would agree that a fair proportion of the discussion in educational circles at the present time is concerned with the idea of 'the pupil's needs', and these 'needs' are usually discussed in terms of how the curriculum, and the teaching which implements it, can best meet them. Now this is a very important change of focus, a change which asks every teacher to ensure that what he teaches, and how he teaches it, always relates to the pupil who has to do the learning rather than the subject which has to be taught. There is a very important aspect of 'the pupil's needs', however, which has been somewhat overlooked—the pupil 'needs' teachers who are aware of *all* the factors which can influence the effectiveness of his learning. He needs teachers who are as aware of the part played by the life of the school as they are of the part played by the syllabus of a subject, or the dictates of an examination, in shaping how and what can be learnt. He needs teachers who are as conscious of the *process* of learning, and its critical medium, language, as they are of the *content* of what they teach and its potential relevance to the lives of their pupils.

If such needs as these on the part of the pupil are to be satisfied, however, teachers in their turn will have new needs. It is not enough to 'know your subject', or even, how best to 'put it over'. There is no sadder sight at the present time than the prospect of a well-informed and professionally very capable teacher slowly turning from enthusiasm to dismay, and then to disillusion, because all his best efforts have come to nothing, defeated, not by his choice of what to teach, or by his inability to teach it, but by his unawareness. He has not seen that there are features of the school community in which he works, the boundaries it sets up, or its 'message systems', or its attitudes to learning, or to language for learning, which have come between him and his pupils. Geoffrey

91

Thornton has taken this situation as his basic theme for *Language, Experience and School*. He sets out to show every teacher that the way the life of a school is organised, the way it has come to function as an autonomous community, setting its own goals, writing its own laws, and inventing its own patterns of social behaviour, is decisive in determining how successfully teaching and learning can take place within it.

A reader may wonder at this point why such a book should appear in a series called *Explorations in Language Study*. The answer is simple. Just as language is the crucial means by which we create human communities, so language is the decisive factor in creating the life of the school community. For this reason, Geoffrey Thornton begins by looking at the way we learn language before he goes on to describe how language functions in the context of the school. He wants the reader to have before him at each stage the clear sense that every pupil already knows how to use language as a member of a human community before ever he enters school. As he says, however, 'Schools are *communities* which exist to promote learning'. The school does in little what is done by the larger community outside. It uses language to promote, maintain and regulate relationships. It uses language to create and transmit values. It uses language as a major means for conveying information of all kinds. For the majority of teachers, however, 'language' in school is only what is used for conveying that particular form of information they call 'knowledge' backwards and forwards between teacher and pupil.

Throughout this book, Geoffrey Thornton asks the teacher to focus upon all those other ways of using language that go on in school, and to consider how they form a single pattern of interrelated 'message systems', the function of which is to give the school its own social and cultural identity. He points out that some of the most important of these 'message systems', like rules about dress or social behaviour, reveal an intimate interrelationship between verbal and non-verbal ways of conveying meanings. Perhaps as a result of their continuous preoccupation with the language of intellectual processes, teachers are often inclined to overlook the importance of message systems that are not wholly verbal, but it is just these systems which create the collective social and cultural life of the school community. For this reason, Geoffrey Thornton argues that a teacher should always be aware of three major aspects of the language activity of his school community: (1) how language is used as a 'pure' medium in

92

relation to intellectual processes; (2) how language is used as a 'mixed' medium to give the school its social and cultural identity; (3) what effect the school's 'mixed' message systems may have upon the use of language for learning in the context of his own classroom.

These three aspects, taken together, vitally affect the success or failure of the school's central function, the promotion of learning. There is yet another factor, however, which has just as vital an effect upon this success or failure. Geoffrey Thornton points out that the pupil comes to school already possessing a highly developed experience of language, an experience intimately bound up with his knowledge of the message systems of his own community. Given the present nature of our society, the school's view of its function, and the teacher's view of his role, what this means in so many cases is a head-on clash between the pupil's experience of language for living and the school's attitude to language for learning.

In Chapter 5, he shows how the clash between the language habits of the home community and the school community's attitudes towards language can have so disastrous an effect upon the climate for language activity in the class room. In Chapter 6, he goes on to take a close look at what is demanded of pupils in terms of language for learning. In particular, he examines five examples of what the school regards as appropriate language for learning and shows how they present the ordinary pupil with the equivalent of a complex and difficult 'language game' for which he has not been given the rules. Finally, in Chapter 8, he gives a most thought-provoking analysis of one effort one particular student made to bridge the gap between the language she could use so successfully as a member of her home community and the language demanded of her by the context for learning she had been placed in. What this example demonstrates so admirably is the need for every teacher to ask himself how far his own school community promotes a language climate favourable to learning and how far it inhibits, or actively discourages, the pupil from using in school the only language he has, the language of his home community. The aim of this book is to help the teacher to do this successfully.

PETER DOUGHTY

1   Language in school

There is a haunting remark in a paper by Bernstein, called 'Social Class, language and socialisation', where he says,

'. . . differently-focused experience may be disvalued and humiliated within schools, or seen, at best, to be irrelevant to the educational endeavour.'[1]

There is a passage in Halliday's *Language and Social Man* which contains more than an echo of this:

'. . . but as things are, certain ways of organising experience through language, and of participating and interacting with people and things, are necessary to success in school. The child who is not disposed to this type of verbal exploration in this type of experiential and interpersonal context 'is not at home in the educational world', as Bernstein puts it. Whether he is so predisposed or not turns out not to be any innate property of the child as an individual, an inherent limitation on his mental powers, as used to be generally thought; it is merely the result of a mismatch between his own symbolic orders of meaning and those of the school. . . .'[2]

And in a paper called, 'Code, Register and Social Dialect', Ruqaiya Hasan makes this point:

'educational failure may not be as much a result of the pupil's inability to master the concepts as that of the educational system which fails to establish any relevance between these concepts and the pupil's living of life, especially where the life in the school is not a simple extension of life outside.'[3]

These quotations express a common concern with problems of educational success and failure, while the writers share a conviction that explanations of success and failure are to be sought, ultimately, in the inability of the school system always to enable

95

the pupil to make the best use of his basic resource for learning, his language. They suggest, in other words, that 'as things are', some pupils enter school predisposed to success while some enter it predisposed to failure.

It is the intention of this book to explore the basis of this contention; and to ask how it comes about that schools can be charged with discounting as 'irrelevant to the educational endeavour' the experience of language and life (the only experience that they could have had!) that some pupils bring into school with them. This entails looking for the factors which make for educational success or failure in the relationship that is set up between school and pupil, and asking why it is that some kinds of relationship point the pupil towards failure and some towards success.

This will involve setting up an opposition between the pupil, an individual human being with a capacity for using language, and the school, an institution which, by its very nature, exists to make constant, quite special, demands on the languaging capacity of its pupils.

The focus of the exploration will be language, language conceived as something that was evolved for *use* in the furtherance of the daily communion with other people of which life consists. We learn language through growing up in a human community. We go on using language throughout the rest of our lives in the process of establishing and maintaining relationships in community with other people. We learn language through contact with other people, we use language in contact with other people, and we make a mistake if we regard language as something that can be divorced from the situation in which it is used, and the purpose for which it is used in that situation.

Language is social. Within a social context, language has purpose and point; it is functional. And its function is to enable human beings to exchange meanings with each other. Language is for meaning.

As human beings, most of us learn that this is so during the early years of life, when we acquire an ability to put into language a range of meanings adequate to our needs. Most children enter school with an already well-developed potential for language, yet—as pupils in school—many of them quickly find that they are unable to meet the language demands that school makes upon them in a way that the school regards as adequate.

This book is not intended to be another contribution to the

discussion about the relationship between language, social class and educability. Nor is it intended as a formulation of another 'deprivation theory', whether social or linguistic. The effect of all explanations of educational failure based upon a notion of the pupil's deprivation, of whatever kind it is thought to be, is to place the onus of failure, ultimately, on the shortcomings of the pupil himself, and therefore to absolve the school from its responsibility.

It is the school which constructs the context in which the pupil succeeds or fails, which creates the conditions under which the pupil will, or will not be able, to exploit the potential that he comes into school endowed with—his language and experience, and his own amalgam of knowledge, interests and abilities. It is the school which has the responsibility of matching the contribution brought to the learning situation by the pupil, of—in the old phrase—'starting where the pupil is'. In fact, you can't start anywhere else.

If this is to mean anything at all, it means starting where the pupil is in terms of his own language, and, for this to be done, there must be, on the part of the teacher, a real understanding of what language is, and how it works, so that he may recognise the pupil's linguistic potential for what it really is, and know how to tap it.

This means understanding that language is social and functional, and recognising that the school is a community in which the pupil is also a person. The demands which the school makes on him as a pupil are also made upon him as a person. The way in which he can respond to those demands is determined not only by the nature of the demands themselves but also by the position he is put in to respond to them. The position, that is, that the school has put him in. A school is not merely a collection of individual pupils responding to the demands of learning situations. It is a community in which people, teachers and pupils, live part of their lives, and life inside the school is as real as life outside, not least because the relationships within the school are real. And it is the nature of the relationships that determines the way in which people within the school, teachers and pupils alike, can behave, and perform, succeed and fail.

This means that any search for explanations of why pupils succeed or fail must look at the relationships set up between pupil and teacher, and at what each brings to the relationship.

Chapter 2 will start by looking at the language which a pupil brings. It will discuss initial language acquisition as a process

97

whereby what is acquired is the ability to make meanings in language. The question to be asked is, 'What has the child learnt to do with language by the time he arrives in school?'

In order to begin to answer the question, 'What can he do with his language in school?' Chapters 3 and 4 will look at the nature of the school as a community, and the place of the pupil within it, while Chapter 5 will examine attitudes to language prevalent in school. Chapter 6 will look at the kind of demand typically made upon pupils' language in school, and Chapter 7 will ask what opportunities pupils are normally given to develop the ability to meet them.

The final chapter, asking 'What is to be done?', argues the need for all teaching to be informed by an adequate and relevant knowledge of the nature and function of language as a first step towards achieving a situation in which some pupils need no longer enter school already heading for failure.

2　Language and meaning

'Looking at the early stages of language development from a functional viewpoint, we can follow the process whereby the child gradually "learns how to mean", for that is what first-language learning is. If there is anything which the child can be said to be "acquiring", it is a range of potential, which we could refer to as his "meaning potential".'

Language and Social Man—M. A. K. Halliday

The process of language learning: 'learning how to mean'

Human beings are, with few exceptions, born into the world with a brain that has the potential to learn language. Individual human beings are born into a community where spoken language is in constant use between the people who make up that community. The language that each individual acquires will be the language of that community, which he learns for himself as he experiences language while growing up.

The individual has, in other words, a potential for learning language physically located in his brain, and this potential is realised by the language which he hears in use around him. The process is one whereby an *individual*'s potential is realised by a *communal* act or, rather, an unending succession of communal acts, as language enters into the transactions of daily life around him.[4]

Man evolved language in order to convey meaning. To make meaning with language, the sounds and words of which it is composed have to be combined in ways that other people can understand. We can say, with J. R. Firth, that the 'elements' of which language is composed have to be put together into 'structures'. Another way of viewing the process is to regard language

99

as having three levels, levels of sounds, of words, and of meanings. Sounds are organised into words, and words put together in order to make meanings.

This, however, is only a rough outline of what happens. At the level of sounds, there is much more involved than the sounds themselves. There are all the features of spoken language, features such as intonation, stress, and the kind of pause which makes 'I scream' mean something different from 'ice-cream'. When the level of sounds is referred to, in linguistics, as the level of *phonology*, it is taken to include all these features of spoken language which may be used to make the meaning of one utterance different from another.

At the level of words, it is necessary to remind ourselves that words have to be organised and combined into larger stretches of language if they are to carry meaning. How words are put together in a language constitutes the grammar of the language. Thus, the level of words is more properly the level of words and grammar, or the lexico-grammatical level. The phonological and lexico-grammatical levels exist in order that we can make meaning with language. That is, they exist for the sake of the third level, the level of meaning.

In a well-known paper, 'Relevant Models of Language', M. A. K. Halliday suggested that an individual learns for himself, in infancy, that the function of language is to make meanings by encountering, and experiencing for himself, language used for at least seven different purposes. These he called the Instrumental ('I want') purpose, the Regulatory ('do as I tell you'), the Heuristic ('tell me why'), the Imaginative ('let's pretend'), the Interactional ('me and you'), the Personal ('here I am'), and the Informative ('I've got something to tell you').

Using these as the basis of his observation, Halliday subsequently observed, and described as a process whereby what is learnt is how to make meanings, the language development of a child in the first years of its life. He shows how, in the case of the infant under observation, 'early vocal sounds, although still pre-linguistic in the sense that they were not modelled on the English language, were used effectively for just these purposes—to obtain goods and services that he required (instrumental), to influence the behaviour of those closest to him (regulatory), to maintain his emotional ties with them (interactional) and so on. The meanings that he can express at this stage—the number of things that he can ask for, for example—are naturally very

100

restricted, but he has internalised the fact that language serves these purposes.'[2]

The child learns very early in life what language is for. Indeed, Halliday notes that, by the age of 18 months, the child 'could use language effectively in the instrumental, regulatory, interactional and personal functions, and was beginning to use it for pretend-play (the imaginative function) and also heuristically, for the purpose of exploring the environment', that is, for six out of seven functions. The informative function is the last to be mastered, for reasons which will be discussed later.

Looked at from this 'functional viewpoint', that is from the viewpoint of seeing language as something that is used for practical purposes, Halliday can claim that, 'By the age of two and a half or even earlier', the child has laid the foundations for his subsequent mastery of language. 'The framework is all there.'

Because it sees language learning as being essentially a process of learning how to make meanings in language, this is a strikingly different account of the first stages of language learning from that which is commonly held. Popular beliefs about early language learning, beliefs of the kind described in *Exploring Language*[5] as 'folk-linguistic notions of language', centre around the tendency to equate language with words. The utterance of a child's first word is normally hailed as the first step along the road of linguistic development. But by the time the child utters his first recognisably word-like combination of sounds, he has already travelled some distance along the road. He has already taught himself how to structure sounds and intonations into ways of making meanings.

He has not only grasped, intuitively, the fact that language is for making meanings with but is able to exploit the phonological level for this purpose before he develops the ability to exploit the lexico-grammatical level as well. It is worth noting, because the point will have to be considered later, that this intuitive grasp of the nature and function of language that a child displays early in life normally becomes overlaid, later on, with culturally taught 'folk-linguistic notions' of language. There persist in our culture deep-rooted misconceptions about language, which are transmitted from generation to generation, despite the penetrating insights into language made available by linguists in the last thirty years and despite the obvious fact that the way in which language is used in the course of our daily lives is completely at variance with the way in which most adults seem to think it is used.

By the age of about three, any normal child will have mastered the sounds of the language in use around him, and will already be able to put together basic lexico-grammatical structures. Thus early in life, he will have laid the foundations of his langage.

He will also be learning that language is not the only method by which human beings communicate, that is share meanings, with each other, although it so happens that language is the most complex and subtle system so far evolved for the purpose. Communication between people, at least in face-to-face situations, takes place in ways which involve exploiting bodily features in systematic ways. Facial expressions, bodily postures and gestures all play their part in the process of exchanging meanings. Although it is convenient, as in a book like this, to distinguish between verbal and nonverbal communication, it is important to remember that when two human beings are communicating in a face-to-face situation they are using verbal and nonverbal means interdependently. The expression which accompanies 'Are you coming?' will help to determine whether what has been said means a question, a command, or a threat. The length of the silence before an answering 'No' may convey as much meaning as the 'No' itself.

'When we study communication as the process by means of which people relate to each other, we must look at the context in which it occurs—the human relationship. And when we examine a human relationship, such as a simple conversation between two people, we almost immediately discover that there are multiple modalities or channels operating in addition to language. We discover that the modalities, verbal and nonverbal, are learned as patterns of the culture (as language is learned) and that they are systematic (as language has grammar, for example). Furthermore we discover that they all fit together: they are systematically interrelated.'
Nonverbal Communication and the Education of Children—Paul and
Happie Byers[6]

The context of language learning

Language is learnt by the child from those around him as they use it in the course of their daily lives, but it is not learnt simply by a process of imitation. Such is the capacity of a human brain, that it can, during those early years of life, pick out the elements of language from the noise around it and teach itself how to put the elements together in structures that can convey meaning to others. It can take meaning from utterances that it has never heard before, and can put together structures that no one else has put together before.

Every child whose brain is thus developing the capacity to use language is a unique human being, at the centre of a unique network of relationships with other human beings. A number of factors will operate to ensure that this is so, factors such as sex, number in the family group, age of siblings already born, and so on. The son born as the eldest child will have a different relationship with his parents from his sister born a year or two later, while a boy born as the tenth child to a family already consisting of five girls and four boys will establish a pattern of relationships different from that already established by his brothers and sisters. And it is essentially in the course of establishing and maintaining those relationships that language is used in the life of day to day, as it is encountered by the child growing up. The relationships are the matrices within which language functions interdependently with the other means of communication mentioned in the last section. Who we are, and how we relate to the other person, determine what we want to mean, as a typical example of language in action will illustrate.

I go into a pub at lunch-time, and say to John behind the bar, 'Half of lager, please, and a cheese and onion jacket.' He takes a glass, puts it under the tap, turns the tap, and waits while the glass fills up. While he waits, we might exchange remarks about the weather, about the number of people in the bar, about the fact that I am alone when I am often with colleagues. If it is summer, and the television in the other bar is showing the Test Match, I might ask what the score is. I might, on the other hand, say nothing. It would not be considered odd if I did say nothing. In fact, John might, while he waited for the glass to fill, be carrying on a conversation with someone else.

When the glass is full, he puts it on the bar in front of me, and turns to the telephone at the end of the bar. He picks it up, and says, 'One cheese and onion jacket. Number six.' He puts the phone down, picks up a small plastic disc with the number 6 on it, and puts it on the bar in front of me, saying, 'Nineteen, please.' I offer him two tenpenny pieces, which he takes. He turns to the cash register, operates it, and turns back to me with a penny, which he hands to me. I put it in my pocket, pick up the plastic disc in one hand, the lager in the other, and turn to find a seat.

103

About five minutes later, the landlady comes in with a plate, on which is a potato that has been baked in its jacket, and cheese and onion added before it has been browned under the grill. It is a 'cheese and onion jacket'. She calls out, 'Number six.' I raise my hand, or call out something like, 'Over here.' She brings it across, puts it on the table, picks up the plastic disc, and says something. Invariably, she says something—about the weather, the number of people in the bar, the imminence of Race Day, something—before she goes to collect the order for 'Number seven'. Silence is, for her, not an option.

So a bit of language like 'cheese and onion jacket', not perhaps at first sight a lexico-grammatical structure likely to be meaningful, becomes meaningful in the social sequence in which it occurs, a social sequence in which people, and language, and actions, and things, interrelate. When I say, 'and a cheese and onion jacket', I know that the barman knows what I mean. When he says, 'Nineteen, please', he knows that, at that point in the sequence, I will understand him to mean that he is asking me for nineteen pence, the price of the lager and the cheese and onion jacket. It is a familiar routine, in which the interweaving of language with things and actions is taken for granted, just as the relationships of the participants in the scene are taken for granted.

Uses of language like this, asking for what we want, giving orders, fulfilling requests, maintaining friendly contact with people at work, are aspects of everyday living. What we say, and how we say it, in order to mean, is shaped by who we are talking to, the nature of our relationship with them, and when and why we are talking to them.

We begin the development of our own language by gradually becoming part of the everyday interchanges of life in a particular environment, the one into which we are born, where people have been habitually using language for a long time. The infant begins, tentatively, to encode meanings in sounds, and thus become part of new interchanges. He experiences which of the meanings get a response, and in what form, and builds such experiences into subsequent attempts to make meanings. At first, he encodes meanings in sounds, that is, only at the phonological level. In time, although it is, as we have seen, a comparatively short time, he develops the ability to use the lexico-grammatical level as well, and is ready to begin a career as an adult language user.

104

Differing contexts of language learning

Halliday's 'Relevant Models' can be regarded as a description of the functional contexts within which language learning can take place. These functional contexts provide for the child the opportunity to learn (*a*) that language can be used for such and such a purpose, e.g. for getting what he wants, like a biscuit, and (*b*) the linguistic means of achieving his objective, e.g. 'bikky', 'bikky, please', or 'Can I have a biscuit?'

This way of looking at the language learning process provides us with a valuable way of comparing the differences which may exist, linguistically speaking, between environments in which children grow up.

Let us set side by side two extreme examples, which may be no more than ten geographical miles apart but which may be separated by a very wide social gulf. The first family consists of a teacher and his wife, herself a teacher before she married, and their three-year-old only son. The second family consists of a husband and wife, neither of whom can read and write, and three children under five, two boys and a girl. Both husband and wife work—he as a labourer, she as a cleaner.

We can, I think, fairly safely make a number of predictions about the amount and kind of language to which the teacher's son is exposed, compared with that which the youngest son of the labourer experiences. As the teacher's son begins to ask questions, it is probable that he will have them answered, not necessarily all the time, but frequently enough for him to grasp the notion that language is for asking questions and getting answers. (Halliday's heuristic model). Alone with his mother most of the day, he has no difficulty in realising that language is for talking to adults with. Doubtless his father will reinforce this realisation when he comes home, and, during the holidays, the way in which the boy is allowed, and encouraged, to talk to and with relatives and visitors, will also be a factor (Interactional). The way in which he is encouraged to play, by himself and with others, will influence his development of language for Imaginative purposes. By contrast, it is likely that the labourer's youngest son will be left in the company of his brother and sister for long periods. He will thus have less opportunity of talking to adults. He may, indeed, be positively discouraged from so doing, either because the parents are too busy, can't be bothered, or are simply not there. Questions may habitually go unanswered, so that the child cannot come to appreciate the potential of language as a means of asking questions and getting answers. He cannot, therefore, develop his own potential. This doesn't mean that he can't, linguistically, construct a question ('Why . . .?'/'where . . .?'/ 'when . . .?'/'can't we . . .?'/'did he . . .?') but rather that he doesn't come to appreciate the possibilities of question and answer, because there is so little occasion in his life to experience the possibilities. We can take this contrast much deeper by looking closely at two more of the 'Relevant Models', the Personal and the Informative.

Who we are, and what the world is likely to have in store for us, is something that we learn, as we learn our language itself, from those around us. In fact, we learn these things largely in and through language itself. What it means to be a boy, or a girl, in a particular culture, or sub-culture, we learn by observing how men and women around us behave towards each other, and towards our brothers and sisters. We see what roles seem to be allocated to one sex or the other, what differences of dress and appearance distinguish one sex from the other, what is considered appropriate behaviour for each, how members of each sex talk about each other and about members of the opposite sex, and so on. The child comes eventually to see himself as a boy, or herself as a girl, and, on that foundation, to see his or her place in the world.

Dan Fader, the author of *Hooked on Books*,[7] once remarked that the only people who could afford to talk about the future were those who thought that they had a future. The future he meant was the kind predicated in statements like, 'I'm going to be a doctor', or 'I want to be an architect'. It is much more likely that the son of the teacher who is the subject of the comparison will, one day, make such a remark than will the girl who is the middle daughter of the illiterate labourer and his wife, and this for a number of reasons. An important one, of course, is that one is a boy, the other a girl—it is still much easier for a boy to become a doctor or an architect than for a girl. Another reason centres on the expectations of the parents: it is more than likely that the teacher and his wife will think in terms of a 'professional' career for their son. Another may have to do with the fact that the teacher's son is an only child, while the labourer's daughter is a second child. The son will inevitably spend more time in adult company, talking to and being talked to by adults. His exposure to adult concerns, and the language of adult concerns, is therefore

106

greater than that of a second (or third, or fourth) child, who will naturally spend time in the sole company of an elder brother or sister.

But the main point here is that, if there is, in the family, an anticipation that a child may be able to take a path towards a particular career, then it will be talked about—in all its aspects. And if it is talked about, the consequences for the child will be profound. He will come to realise that it is possible, indeed natural, to talk about such matters. He will have the opportunity of learning appropriate resources for talking about them, to hear and practice for himself language in which to discuss, probe, evaluate, and qualify. Language is thus playing its part in 'the process whereby the child becomes aware of himself', the process through which the child creates a self-image.

Another way of looking at what was going on when parents and child were discussing the future is to regard it as a process of exchanging information about the world. Halliday defined his Informative Model of language as the one which refers to 'the processes, persons, objects, abstractions, qualities, states and relations of the real world'.

It is the last of the seven 'Relevant Models' that the child learns how to function with, and this for a very significant reason. It makes more use of purely linguistic resources. It is language less bound to the context in which it occurs, language used to fashion abstractions and generalisations, language used in longer-than-usual stretches so that more sophisticated use has to be made of these linguistic devices which bind language together. (See p. 68.)

It is language use which needs experience and practice; language used to enable us to tell each other about what interests us, or is important to us, about what we think, or feel, or believe, about our understanding of the way the world is, and of the people in it. It is language used to discuss truth and beauty, right and wrong, the functioning of the international money market, or whatever, if we can language our meaning in such a way as to enable someone else to share it in a context which has made it possible.

Consider the following headline:

OUR MIRAGE SHOULD FOIL IRISH GAMBLE

An essential clue to the meaning conveyed by the language is that the paper in which it appeared was a local sporting paper, published on Race Day. *Our Mirage* was the name of a horse, apparently fancied by the writer against an Irish entry regarded as something of a gamble. Those with sufficient knowledge of racing knew what he meant. They had access to the meaning which was being put into language, an access given by their experience of what is often called, aptly, the 'racing world', and its language.

A selection of the headlines appearing during the course of one week above the racing column in a national daily will emphasise the point.

CARSON GIVES HINT FOR GOLD COAST
PUNTERS PLUNGE AGAIN ON CAVO DORO
NEGUS HAS FINE CHANCE OF BIG DOUBLE
SNOWFIELD TO IMPROVE ON FIRST EFFORT
REALIST NAPPED TO RECOVER EBOR LOSSES

It is not simply a matter of knowing the names of jockeys (Carson), or horses (*Cavo Doro*), or understanding technical terms (napped, big double), or knowing that a horse called *Realist* had not run well in a race called the Ebor Handicap. It is a matter of knowing all this, and much more—of understanding the significance of the fact that Carson, the Champion Jockey, had chosen to ride a horse called *Gold Coast* when he could have chosen to ride another, of knowing what *Snowfield*'s 'first effort' had been, so that the significance of the opinion that it might be improved on might be properly estimated, and so on. When you know all this, you know what the language stands for, you know what it means.

Many people who go to France with the linguistic resource bequeathed by the French they learnt in school discover that they are able, more or less, to ask for a room, to order a meal, to buy petrol, ask the way, and engage in similar linguistic exchanges firmly wedded to a context, of reasonably short duration, and of fairly predictable outcome. They may even be able to hold a short conversation about the weather. But they are quite unable to sustain a discussion about the Common Market, the Channel Tunnel, or the Tour de France. They haven't the language, or the experience of language, necessary to encode their own meaning, or to gain access to somebody else's.

There are children who grow up without the opportunity to have abundant experience of language, especially the kind of language which constitutes the Informative Model. Whether

108

this is so or not will depend, essentially, on the number of adults in the family, and the use habitually made of language in the furtherance of the various relationships in the family.

There may be only one parent in the home, because of death, separation, or, temporarily, demands of a job which take the father away. Shift work, or handing over children to an *au pair* girl whose English is itself not very good, may lead to under-exposure to adult language, and thus a minimising of chances to experience and use it. Large numbers in a family may make for dilution of adult-generated and directed talk. And, over and above this, there must be taken into account habitual ways of using, or not using, language. 'Bugger off out of it', while meaning-ful, neither enhances the status of language as a form of com-munication nor affords opportunity to gain rich experience of language in the course of linguistic exchanges with other people.

There are children, on the other hand, who experience, as they grow up, language used by their parents, and perhaps other adults, for a variety of purposes. They hear all sorts of things being dis-cussed, and they themselves may be encouraged to participate. They thus learn that adults can be talked to and with about a multiplicity of things; they gain access to, and experience of using, the kinds of language in which things various can be talked about. Above all, they come to appreciate the possibilities of communicating in language, to see the power of language in enabling one to transcend the immediate context, to understand the potential of language for making meanings.

In this way, children acquire through experience their potential for making meaning in language, their 'meaning potential'. The process begins because the human brain can respond to the language heard in the environment, and the meaning potential initially acquired is intimately related to the environment in which it is acquired.

The process might, in fact, be described as one of acquiring a repertoire of meanings useful in the environment in which the child has grown up, intimately bound up with that environment, born out of the day-to-day exchange of meanings with those who people that environment, and the relationships he has with them. These meanings will be languaged in the habitual language of the environment—its phonology, its lexico-grammatical patterns—as the child makes it his own.

Each child might, then, be said to have his own, individual linguistic history, which will have endowed him with a linguistic

109

resource, a capacity for making meanings in language. This comprises not only his ability to put together the elements and structures of language at a given time, in response to a given situation, but also his knowledge about language—his intuitive knowledge of what language is for, of how and when to use it, and for what purpose.

But this resource is also a potential, for out of it he will draw what he can do with language in the future. Language learning, in the sense of being able to go on making more and more meanings in language, is a process that can go on throughout life. To what extent we can go on learning depends partly on the opportunities we get, and partly what we can make of them if we get them.

The child of five has learnt, with the opportunities that he has had, what he can do with language. Now he will have to learn what the school wants him to do with language. For some this will be easier than for others. Some will encounter obstacles that do not seem to appear in the way of others.

To begin to identify these obstacles it is necessary to look first at some aspects of the way in which the school functions as a community.

3   Schools as communities

'Only the Sixth Form may use the grass, the centre path and the path leading to the front door. The First Forms will use the path round the back, the Second Forms will use the path by the wall. Running on the paths is not allowed.'

Extract from School Rules

Schools are communities which exist to promote learning. It follows that, since language lies at the heart of nearly all learning, schools are communities which should allow, promote and encourage the use of language by the pupils for whose sake the schools exist.

Language is for use between people in social situations. For an individual wanting to use language (i.e. to make meaning) in a social situation, who and what he is, are, we have already insisted, factors which act upon his ability to draw upon his linguistic resource to make meaning. The small boy in the playground talking with two or three of his friends is in a very different situation from the small boy in the Head's study trying to explain why he threw glue at a small girl.

Life in school is an unending succession of situations calling for the use of language by people, both teachers and pupils, very conscious of their identity, of who and what they are, within the community. Schools are, in fact, very closely-knit communities which exert a fierce pressure on those who make up the community. Very conscious of its identity as this or that school, the school has a great capacity for making its members conscious of their own identities within it. This self-awareness is bound to be a powerful influence on opportunities for languaging meaning within the school.

Boundaries

The establishing and maintaining of boundaries is a universal human need. We construct identities for ourselves, which we seek to protect. Against threats to identity we react vigorously. This leads us to mark out that bit of territory which we think of as ours, and defend it when we think it is being attacked. This is true at the individual level, when we think our jobs or our possessions or our beliefs are under attack, and it is true at the institutional level, when we defend the institutions in which we work against what we take to be a threat not only against their existence but also against what we see as making for order within the institution. Schools, and those who work in them, are no different, in this respect, from other institutions.

Schools which display a notice like PARENTS SHOULD NOT PROCEED BEYOND THIS POINT are, in effect, drawing a boundary across which they do not wish the parents of their pupils to penetrate. The Headmistress who wrote to a parent, 'We don't really encourage parents', was perhaps making the same point. The notice ALL VISITORS MUST REPORT TO THE OFFICE is defining a category—VISITORS—which is alien to the institution, and must, in case they should constitute a threat, be identified.

Within any institution there are people who are deeply concerned to see that its boundaries are maintained, since their own identities are heavily mortgaged in the institutions of which they are part.

The Head of a school sees himself as Head of that school. He has a conception of what being the Head of a school means, and has known this since he first realised that he wanted to be a Head and believed that he could do the job as he conceived it to be. He is thus bound up with his school, of whatever kind it happens to be: Infant, Junior, Primary; Secondary Modern, Comprehensive, Grammar, Bi-lateral; Middle, Upper, High, Sixth Form College; Boys, Girls or Mixed; Direct Grant or Independent; Aided or Controlled, whether Church of England, Roman Catholic or Jewish.

However, the Head is not the only one whose identity is bound up with the school. The whole staff is concerned, by virtue of their roles within the school. Most school staffs are arranged in hier-

112

archies; the bigger the school the more elaborate the hierarchy. In small Primary Schools there will be a Deputy Head, with very little of a formal hierarchy beyond that created by age and experience, while in large Comprehensive Schools there will be a pyramid, with the Head at the top and, in rank order, various categories of staff—Deputy Heads, Senior Masters or Mistresses, Heads of Department, or Faculties, or Houses, or Years, various other posts of responsibility, and, at the bottom, young teachers and probationers.

Sooner, or later, any one of them will be concerned to maintain what he regards as a proper boundary between what he sees as his role in the school and that of any of his colleagues who may be thought to be trespassing.

Some such boundaries may be demarcated physically within the school rooms set aside for the Head, the Deputy Head, the Reception Class, the Library, the Science Department, and so on. These areas become territories to be defended, so much so that the Science Department in one school was known, to both staff and pupils, as 'The Kremlin', because no members of staff other than members of the Science Department went in.

But boundaries may be erected in much more subtle ways than this. There is the claim to performance of certain duties ('that's my job'), possession of things ('that's my peg/chair/mug'), wearing of special clothing, such as gowns, track-suits or lab coats. At one school, there used to be two 'tea-clubs' within one department, one for graduates and one for non-graduates, while in another students on teaching practice were relegated to a stock cupboard to take their morning break. By such strategies as these, strategies which are regrettably absorbed into the routine of living, boundaries are set up and maintained, and there will inevitably come times in the life of every member of staff when they find themselves vigorously defending what they regard as their boundaries against what they conceive to be a threat.

New members of staff, especially those who join a school at junior level, have to learn to recognise boundaries, and to adjust their behaviour accordingly. They will soon, however, quickly learn not only to recognise boundaries but how to define their own. They will thus join the small army of boundary-maintainers of whom the school is composed. This is an inevitable process. A sense of stability is essential to life, and the existence of boundaries is an ingredient of stability.

Nevertheless, the way in which boundaries are set up and maintained within schools, the way in which members of staff regard certain boundaries as vital to their own sense of identity and react to defend them, will have a profound influence on the way in which the school behaves as a community. This, in turn, will act upon the way in which individuals in the school can behave as members of the community, and this, of course, includes linguistic behaviour—what we have the opportunity of meaning, and how, to whom and when. A probationer will soon learn, if he doesn't already know, the unwisdom of stopping the Head in the corridor, and saying 'By the way, I've been thinking about the way you do Assembly.' But in a Staff Meeting, where the subject of School Assembly has been put on the agenda, he (or she) is entitled to contribute to the discussion.

Schools as message systems

The point was made in the last chapter that when two people communicate with each other, in a face-to-face situation, they make use of various ways, both verbal and nonverbal, of conveying meaning. Likewise, schools, as institutions, make use of a variety of ways of communication. These methods range from explicit, official, verbal messages to ways that are nonverbal, subtle, and unofficial, in the sense that they do not have behind them the full weight of the school's authority.

The school is, in effect, making use, all the time, of a multiplicity of message systems to convey meanings to pupils, meanings connected with daily routine, meanings connected with recurrent events in the school year, meanings which have to do with the existence and purpose of the school, and the behaviour of those in it. In one sense, the output of messages is random, in that they originate from many sources, from the Head downwards, in no particularly co-ordinated fashion. However, the effect of all this activity may be far from random, since its total impact may be such as to be clearly and unambiguously understood by pupils, although this impact may, in fact, be unappreciated by those in authority responsible for sending the messages, since they are not in a position to evaluate the relative effects of various kinds of message as their pupils are, and so measure the total impact. The emphasis placed on this message, or on that; the

114

sanctions invoked to obtain compliance with this, or that rule; the public recognition given to this achievement, or that; the status afforded to this area of activity rather than that. All these add up, until, as might be said, the pupils *get the message*.

Perhaps the most explicit nonverbal system for conveying meaning is the bell, used to signal the beginning and end of school, or the whistle used to signal the beginning of school and the end of break or the lunch-hour. Schools vary in the forms of behaviour which they want linked to the sound of bell or whistle, and which they make verbally explicit, in lists of times posted in strategic places and/or in School Rules.

Pupils arriving after the First Bell will be registered as late.
Pupils must not be on the premises after the Last Bell unless engaged in an authorised activity.

School Rules appear to be the most explicit verbal statement of the school's meaning, but they tend to have an implicit meaning according to the seriousness with which they are taken, and the way in which they are enforced. Newcomers to a school have to learn not so much the rules themselves, but about the rules— which are thought important, and how they are enforced.

This can be illustrated with regard to school uniform. A Primary School sends out a notice to parents.

UNIFORM

Boys   Grey shorts, grey shirt, School tie, grey pullover, black blazer, School cap.
Girls   Grey skirt, white blouse, School tie, grey pullover. Cotton frocks are worn in summer.
      Messrs. Freemantle, in the High Street, are the sole suppliers of School ties, badges, caps and berets.

The key question is, how is the wearing of school uniform encouraged? Is it compulsory, and if so how is the compulsion enforced? Would the school go to the lengths of asking a representative of Social Services to call on parents who said they couldn't afford school uniform and explain that a grant was available? If it is not compulsory, what strategies are used to suggest that the school regards the wearing of uniform as desirable? Is it only pupils who wear uniform who are given jobs of responsibility, or asked to show visitors around, or in any other way given public recognition? It is not necessary to have an explicit system of rewards and punishments to convey the school's approval or disapproval of certain forms of behaviour and certain kinds of achievement. It can be done in a number of subtle ways, although the full subtlety may not always be appreciated.

A boys' Grammar School, which reckoned to get 150 out of the 180 in any one entry up to O Level standard in four years, was faced with the problem of what to do with the remaining thirty. They couldn't go into the Sixth Form with their contemporaries, since they hadn't got the requisite number of O Levels, and therefore they couldn't wear Sixth Form uniform. The solution was to allow them what the school saw as the privilege of wearing Sixth Form blazers, but with bone instead of silver buttons. What the school didn't appreciate was that, since there were only thirty boys in the school wearing that particular uniform, and since what they had in common was their *failure* to achieve sufficient O Levels in four years to enter the Sixth Form, they were being distinguished, by their dress, as failures within the school.

Such distinctions between what the school regards as success and what it regards as failure can be made in other ways.

School magazines usually record achievements—sporting achievements, examination successes, distinctions won by former pupils. The way in which they are recorded is significant. The middle-page spread in a magazine from another Grammar School began with a list of scholarships and exhibitions to Oxford and Cambridge, continued with a note of those who had gained entrance to Oxford or Cambridge Colleges, and went on to those who had gained entrance (whether by scholarship or not) to other Universities. Then came a list of those who had gained places in other institutions of Higher Education, such as Poly-technics, Colleges of Advanced Technology and, at the end of the list, Colleges of Education. The school thus publicly stated a higher regard for the gaining of a place at Oxford or Cambridge than the winning of an entrance scholarship to another University.

The message is not lost on pupils, especially when it is reinforced by similar messages carried by other systems. Girls who have gone from Grammar School to Colleges of Education have testified to being made to feel second-rate within the school because they were not judged capable of aiming at University. Perhaps they were not in the top set, or doing subjects with the highest status, or in an Upper Sixth which had special privileges of accommodation, or were not considered first choices for positions of responsibility, or had to listen while enthusiasm was shown in Assembly for the success of those who had gained University places. In the end, the cumulative effect of such messages was clear: girls who were able

116

enough to go on to Colleges of Education and become teachers themselves were made to feel second-rate within the community of their own school. There is little doubt that many of their teachers would be surprised and distressed to learn that the meaning of the school had been communicated so unambiguously to the pupils.

Every school sees itself as having a certain function to perform, and makes routine, regular and public declarations of its aims. Speech Days, Open Days, Open Evenings, Parents' Evenings, all such occasions afford opportunities to the school to explain what it thinks it is doing for its pupils, and why—small one-form-entry Primary Schools no less than twelve-form-entry Comprehensive Schools. But the way in which the school seeks to realise these aims in practice leads to the establishment of what is sometimes called 'the hidden curriculum', the strategies by which schools, like all institutions, as Berger and Luckmann put it in *The Social Construction of Reality*, 'by the very fact of their existence, control human conduct by setting up predefined patterns of conduct, which channel it in one direction as against the many other directions that would theoretically be possible.'[8]

This 'hidden curriculum' has the effect of enforcing a disposition towards certain forms of behaviour, and puts a premium on certain forms of achievement. Its specification remains implicit in the life of the community, its existence conveyed by an assortment of methods whose cumulative effect may be to press very hardly on those who have difficulty in decoding the messages, or who cannot meet its demands. There are those who pass the examination in the 'hidden curriculum', just as there are those who pass exams based upon more explicit criteria, and those who do not.

Those who do pass the test set by the 'hidden curriculum' are usually those whose cultural background is sufficiently close to that of the school to enable them to understand. Such pupils start their school life with an advantage that others do not have; they begin with a potential for success denied to others. And within the school context, it is success—success by the school's own criteria —that counts, success that is acclaimed.

One of the main arguments of this book is that, in any situation involving two or more human beings, who we are, and what we are, in that situation, has crucial consequences for what we can do in that situation, and that includes what we can mean. The status of pupils acclaimed as successful, as against those condemned

117

as failures, is an important factor bearing upon the ability to perform in a given situation.

Among the messages most clearly received by pupils are those which tell them of their status within the community.

4   The making of a pupil

7) Pupils

         a) Dress and appearance
         b) Movement
         c) Pride in school

         Extract from agenda for Staff Meeting

Children enter the world of school for the first time, usually, at least in our society, at the age of five, to become pupils. They bring with them their own world, and a concept of themselves in that world. They bring with them, in other words, their own versions of reality, a version which they have constructed for themselves out of their experiences in the environment in which they grew up.

They enter the world of school, and meet people who have their own versions of reality, centred around their roles as teachers. And deeply embedded in these versions of reality are notions of normality and appropriacy regarding the behaviour of pupils, as pupils.

These notions may be no more than a loose congerie of expectations as to what are appropriate levels of performance. Such expectations are sometimes, especially in moments of stress, given expression in the admonition, 'You're not in the —— now', with the slot being filled by items like, 'Infants', 'Juniors', 'First Form', 'Fifth Form', and so on. The criteria on which the admonition is based are rarely made explicit. The teacher seemingly expects the pupil to know what is expected of him, appropriate to the point on the chronological-developmental scale he has reached. Pupils (presumably those who have been unable to discover the 'hidden curriculum') have been known to remark that, since they are never told what is expected of them as Juniors, or First Formers, or whatever, they feel that they can 'never win'.

The existence of these expectations is also implied in the perennial complaints that are heard—by Junior School teachers about what is not being done in the Infant Schools, by Secondary School Teachers about what is not being taught in Primary Schools, and by Lecturers in Universities and other institutions of Higher Education about what the schools are not doing. So successful does this kind of pressure become, that education tends to become a process whereby the pupil is merely prepared for the next stage. Educationalists are apt to talk about such things as 'The Needs of the Primary Child'. It would be more appropriate, perhaps, to talk about, 'What is needed to turn a child entering school into a Bottom Infant, then into a Middle Infant, a Top Infant, a Bottom Junior, and so on.'

Pupils and knowledge

'. . . the form master must be firm and ensure that posters and pictures are always in the best taste and suitable for an academic atmosphere, i.e. not soccer heroes, lingerie advertisements, etc.'

Extract from School Rules

There is bound to be an initial gap, or mismatch, between John Smith, child, as he is when he enters school for the first time, and John Smith, pupil, as the school expects him to be.

Each child is an individual, who will come into school endowed with that mixture of abilities, interests and knowledge which growing up in a particular environment has allowed him to develop from his genetic potential. As Roger Gurney says in *Language, Brain and Interactive Processes*, 'The development of any organism provides ample evidence of the importance of interactive processes in producing the mature adult. In biological shorthand, we speak of the genotype (the individual genetic make-up) interacting with the environment to give the phenotype (the individual's personal characteristics). In short, $G \times E = P$, where G is Genotype, E is Environment and P is Phenotype. The phenotype may be expressed in terms of height, hair colour, temperament, intelligence and so on, while the genotype consists of the genes controlling the development of these characteristics. Environment refers to any, or all, of the influences which bear upon the structure in question.'[9]

The gap will be partly that between what the school expects him to have in the way of knowledge when he comes in, and what knowledge he in fact possesses. The school may, on the one hand,

120

expect him to have certain knowledge which in fact he does not have, and, on the other hand, may not regard as legitimate, legitimate to the school context, knowledge which he does possess.

What *is* regarded as knowledge legitimate to the school context will depend partly on the teacher's own knowledge, and therefore his ability to appreciate, understand and share in the child's knowledge, and partly on what is traditionally regarded as educationally respectable.

At all levels, complaints can be heard.

'They don't know what —— is.'
'But he/she/they ought to know ——'

Perhaps, by certain criteria, they ought. But everybody's experience is limited, everybody's knowledge is partial. We all know something that somebody else doesn't; we are all ignorant of something that somebody else knows. We all, however, tend to think that what we know everybody else should know. This seems to be especially true in schools, however arbitrary the bit of knowledge is. But, if pupils don't know when it is thought they should, and if conditions are not provided in which they can come to know, then many will fail, ever, to close the gap between where they are, in terms of their own knowledge, and where their teachers think they ought to be.

This means, in fact, that, unless the school tries to close the gap by accepting the child for what he is, and for what he knows, and by providing him with an environment which will enable him to capitalise on the resources he brings with him into school, then as a pupil he starts his school career at a severe disadvantage. And if the school should start not merely by refusing to accept his knowledge for what it is but by devaluing what he brings into school, they will succeed only in devaluing him, thus virtually ensuring that the gap will never close.

The child whose background has endowed him with interests and knowledge that overlap with the concerns of the school has an obvious advantage over the child whose interests and knowledge are somewhat removed. Having access to the meaning of what is being discussed, the former is able to participate, and thus to capitalise on his language. The latter, unable to reach the language of the classroom, remains dumb. He is in an impossible position. What contribution he could make is likely to be, in Bernstein's word, 'disvalued', yet he is unable readily to share in the contributions made, with approval, by others. The seeds of his failure have thus been sown by a system unable to make use of, or, more precisely, to allow him to make use of, what he possessed when he came into school. And the onus of failure is then normally thrown on the pupil, or on his background: social deprivation, or linguistic deprivation, or both, are invoked to explain the system's inability to provide for some the means to success that it provides for others.

Initial slowness in coming to terms with the concerns, the language, the meanings of the school may lead remorselessly to greater and greater failure, a process which seems to feed on itself, and which is clearly signalled to the pupil at every stage.

Pupils and abilities

Of all the abilities that the child/pupil possesses, the most highly valued in school is what is called intellectual ability. Most of the labels hung on pupils reflect this: Able, Less Able, Very Able; High I.Q., Low I.Q., 'only an I.Q. of 110', and so on. It is not being argued that to place high value on intellectual ability is improper. For one thing, the development of people to their full intellectual capacity is not merely desirable in an advanced industrial society; it is a condition of survival. What is being argued is that when the regard for intellectual ability is enforced in such a way as to prevent the full realisation of the potential of those who do not appear to possess intellectual ability, this, apart from anything else, represents a gross under-use of talent.

Pupils in school operate, as pupils, within the framework provided by the school as a community. Exclusive regard for intellectual achievement has a damaging effect on the status within the school of those who appear to be incapable of such achievement, and we have already seen how message systems operate effectively to convey key meanings within the school. Yet the criteria used to estimate intellectual ability are often grossly inadequate.

Judgment is based, roughly speaking, on the way in which pupils respond to the demands made upon them in school, how quickly and, in the eyes of the teacher, how successfully. From achievements, judgments are made about the capacity which is presumed to underlie those achievements. And to reinforce 'subjective' judgments, so-called 'objective' tests are called upon. We shall see in the next chapter how misconceptions about pupils' language can issue in mistaken judgments about their intellectual potential, but it is worth noting here that tests designed

122

to measure intelligence are themselves not free from the same sort of confusion, since they are, in the main, still based upon inadequate ideas of the way in which language actually works.

For one thing, they ignore what we know about the effect of the context itself upon ability to use language in that context. Tests are often administered under conditions calculated to induce anxiety, especially in pupils who have already been convinced of their inadequacy, so that results obtained cannot be other than misleading. Indeed, the procedure is seemingly designed to discover not how much language pupils have but how little! And even those which seek to measure 'non-verbal' abilities contain implicit demands for language. The front page of an N.F.E.R. Non-verbal Test (Test BD—formerly Non-verbal Test) contains the following instructions:

DO NOT OPEN THIS BOOKLET UNTIL YOU ARE TOLD
TO DO SO

FILL IN THE FOLLOWING PARTICULARS:
YOUR FULL NAME   Surname....................................

                                               Block Capitals
                    Other Name (s)
NAME OF YOUR SCHOOL
CLASS YOU ARE IN
BOY OR GIRL
YOUR AGE..................YEARS...................MONTHS
DATE OF BIRTH DAY...............MONTH...............YEAR
              (write the month as a word)
TODAY'S DATE............................19......

READ THE FOLLOWING CAREFULLY:
1. Do not open this booklet until you are told to do so.
2. The test is in sections. You will be told how much time is allowed for each section.
3. When you come to the end of a page, FOLLOW THE INSTRUCTIONS given at the bottom.
4. Each time you are told to stop, STOP WORKING AT ONCE.
5. Work as quickly and as carefully as you can.
6. If when you try a question you find you cannot do it, DO NOT WASTE TIME BUT GO ON TO THE NEXT.
7. Make any alterations in your answers CLEARLY.
8. ASK NO QUESTIONS AT ALL DURING THE TEST.
9. If you should require another pencil, put up your hand.

A certain degree of literacy is here assumed before the pupil can embark upon what is called a 'non-verbal' test, while during the test the pupil will have to make use of language, inside himself, in order to solve the problems posed by the test. The degree of literacy possessed by the pupil at the time of the examination may, or may not, be related to his intellectual capacity. The relationship between capacity to language and intellectual ability is a very complex one, and is not yet sufficiently understood to allow more than tentative assessments to be made in individual cases. Yet the results of such tests, encoded as I.Q., are the basis of labels which categorise pupils throughout their school careers. These labels need contain no explicit reference to I.Q., but their effect is insidious and pervasive, as we see when we consider ways in which pupils are grouped, and regarded, in school.

The basic method of grouping pupils in school is by age, although experiments in grouping children of various ages in teaching groups are being made in some sectors of the educational world. That this procedure is known as 'vertical grouping' emphasises the fact that it is a departure from the norm. The traditional way is to pass children who come into Primary School through the stages of Bottom Infants, Middle Infants, and Top Infants, Bottom Juniors, Middle Juniors and Top Juniors. Likewise, in Secondary Schools pupils proceed from the First to the Fifth Forms, with some going beyond to the Sixth.

When a pupil is judged by his teacher (or teachers) as being unable to keep up with his contemporaries, he will be designated a Slow Learner, and will soon begin to attract one or more of the numerous labels in common use, publicly or privately. This process begins early. There are 'slow tables' in Infant School, and it is not unknown for titles like 'The Problem of the Slow Learner in the Infant School' to be the subject of books, conferences, and papers.

The following extract from 'Notes for Visitors to the School' shows clearly how a Secondary School with, as demonstrated in the first paragraph, a high regard for children as individual, social beings, inevitably sorts them out as pupils, grading them from 'least able' upwards, by means of devices such as 'coarse setting'.

'All forms are non-streamed, the children being allocated on intake from the primary schools in such a way as to secure a spread of academic ability through all first year forms. We make certain exceptions to this random spread: we place children with the same first year form teacher as their brothers and sisters, and we keep together or separate children if advised to do so by the primary school. Since none of the forms is streamed, children can be easily transferred for social reasons, if for example they fail to develop satisfactory relationships with either their peers or their form teacher.

In the first three years, the least able children are withdrawn in small groups for regular tuition in English and/or Mathematics by specialist remedial teachers.

Setting is used to varying degrees in Mathematics, Science and French. In the first year, the six forms are opened out into 8 sets in Mathematics (in each half of the year, one top set, two parallel second sets and a small fourth set), and in Science (one top set, one second set and two parallel third sets). Provision is made for coarse setting late in the year in French, the six forms being timetabled in 2 groups of 3 from which graded sets can be created.'

Into the category of public labels for 'slow learners', that is, labels that are built into the school curriculum, come Less Able, G (for General, as opposed to Academic) and Remedial, or such recent euphemisms as Progress and Opportunity, as in Progress Department and Opportunity Department.

Among private labels, apart from adjectives like 'thick', 'dim' and 'dull', which are in the common language, we find such terms as 'dimbos', 'peasants', 'thugs', 'tail-enders', 'noddies' and 'grots' in frequent use, and the description of particular classes, or groups, as 'the Tip', 'the Sink', 'the Drain', 'a sink-band', or even 'second-band scum'.

There may be an impression that the use of such terms is unknown to the pupils. If so, it is an illusion. You do not need the institutional formality of division by streaming, or setting, or banding, to bring it home to certain categories of pupil that their status within the school is lower than that of certain other categories. There are, as we have already seen, many message systems at work to make the institution's meaning clear to pupils. One very powerful one is the way in which they are referred to by their teachers, in contexts where the categorisation is totally irrelevant.

'He's one of our Remedials. You'd never guess it, would you?' As it happened, no. The boy in question was giving a very promising performance as Puck in a rehearsal of *A Midsummer Night's Dream*.

125

HEADMASTER (*to visitor*): This is our Remedial Department.
PUPIL (*to teacher, when they had gone*): Sir, what does Remedial mean?

So John Smith, who, outside the school, is a son, a brother, a nephew, a cousin, is, within the school, 'one of our Remedials'. When put into a category which has low status within the school, his chances of ever gaining higher status are slim.

Whether or not his inability, at a particular point in time, to meet the demands of school has been mistaken for an innate incapacity to meet them, the fact remains that he can only be led to a more adequate performance in school by teaching methods which make proper use of what resources he has. This is particularly the case with regard to his language, which lies at the centre of his learning potential. The teacher who described his class, more or less in their hearing, as 'not very bright' was not being over-helpful in giving them an exercise which involved drawing a map and discussing 'The Location of Industry in the British Isles'. In fact, in a very real sense, he was making sure that they couldn't do it, so confirming his judgment and fulfilling his predictions of their ability. A more carefully chosen starting point, within reach of the language and experience of the pupils, might have given them some chance of at least narrowing the gap between what they could bring to the learning situation and what was being demanded of them within it.

5 Attitudes to language in school

'I ain't got none, Miss.'
'No, it's not that. It's "I haven't any".'

'There is no reason to believe that any non-standard vernacular is in itself an obstacle to learning. The chief problem is ignorance of language on the part of all concerned.'
The Logic of Nonstandard English[10]—W. Labov

A child takes with him into school, a language, and a way of speaking it, that is peculiarly his, his own idiolect, a product, as we saw in chapter 2, of his individual linguistic history. This language is, for the child, the chief means by which he represents his reality to himself; it is also the chief means by which he conducts his relationships with other people; and it constitutes his potential for learning.

He will, in his first school, and thereafter throughout his school career, and indeed throughout life, come into contact with people, teachers and others, who have ideas about language in general and about his in particular. Regrettably, it must be said, many of these ideas still derive from those popular misconceptions of language already referred to as 'folk-linguistic notions of language'. They bear little relationship to any kind of truth about what language is and how it works, but derive from mistaken ideas on such matters as how it is 'proper' or 'correct' to speak.

Since early language learning depends, as we have seen, on the child's ability to grasp intuitively what language is for, and how it works, it is curious that, almost inevitably, the soundly based intuitions about the nature and function language that we display very early in life should become overlaid with culturally

127

transmitted notions about language that are quite at variance with the facts of language.

Language and speech

The most noticeable feature of a person's language is his way of speaking it, what is sometimes called his accent, or his dialect. Certainly, accent is the most frequent, though not the only, target of the remarks, judgments or criticisms that most people allow themselves to make from time to time about the speech of their fellows.

This person's accent is 'pleasant', or 'musical', or 'country', it has a burr, or a brogue. That person's, on the other hand, is 'ugly', or 'harsh', 'rough' or 'uncouth'. Sometimes the remarks are dressed up as pseudo-linguistic judgments. Speech may be said to be 'slovenly', with 'dropped consonants' or 'dropped aitches', containing 'glottal stops' or 'impure vowels'. It may even be said to have 'no grammar', despite the fact that any language must, by definition, have a grammar. What such remarks really mean is that we don't like a person, or where he comes from, or what he represents, and therefore we don't like his language, and seek to justify the dislike in pseudo-linguistic terms.

It is perhaps significant that the accents which attract the most censure as being 'ugly' or 'uncouth' are those spoken in large conurbations like East London, Birmingham, Liverpool or Tyneside. The fact is that, for a child who grows up with what is regarded as a Birmingham, or Liverpool accent, the accent is not 'harsh', or 'ugly', or 'uncouth'; it is natural. And all those features which his accent is said to have, like 'dropped consonants', 'glottal stops', or whatever it might be, can be shown linguistically to be features of anybody's language. A linguistic perspective gives a very different view of the matter than that enshrined in the folk-linguistic.

We all, as individuals, possess language, and a way of speaking it. In England, there is a form of language known as standard English, and there are various ways of speaking it. That it should be called standard English must not be taken, in any way, to suggest that it is a standard to which all should aspire, or which one does not reach at one's peril. It merely records the fact that it is the form of English most widely and generally spoken, although spoken in different ways, as a journey northwards from Potters Bar will demonstrate. There are also spoken in England

128

various forms of non-standard English, often called dialects, although, as John Pearce points out in *Exploring Language*, chapter 10, not always consistently. The existence of various speech-forms of standard English, and of a number of kinds of non-standard English, constitutes what Abercrombie, in 'RP and Local Accent', the second of his *Studies in Phonetics and Linguistics*,[11] calls 'a rather unfortunate state of affairs—a kind of situation from which many other countries (perhaps all of them) are free.'

The state of affairs is unfortunate largely because of the attitudes towards forms of non-standard English that pervade our society. We have already seen how these attitudes find expression in pseudo-linguistic judgments, and when such attitudes and judgments are directed at pupils in school the effect may be educationally highly damaging.

The short exchange recorded at the head of this chapter took place in the Reception Class of an Infant School, in East London, where the form, 'I ain't got none', is a feature of the local speech. In order to place the exchange in a proper linguistic perspective, it might be useful here to make again, and add to, a number of points about language that were made in Chapter 2.

Language has three levels, phonological, lexico-grammatical and semantic, the level of meaning. 'I ain't got none', like any bit of natural language, operates at all three levels, and operates efficiently. The sounds (which the teacher understood) were organised into a grammatical combination of words, into a combination as grammatical as the alternative offered by the teacher. It is a characteristic of the non-standard forms of English that they contain grammatical constructions which differ from the grammar of standard English. But such constructions are, linguistically, as efficient, and, indeed, as structurally complex, as those found in standard English. They are different, but as bits of language they work equally well. There is no sense in which they are debased. There is no question of the grammar being 'bad' or 'incorrect'. There is moreover no question of the meaning of what the little boy said being in doubt. It was quite unambiguous.

Nevertheless, the teacher thought it right to correct what the child had said. 'No, it's not that.' As far as the child was concerned, it was *that*, and had been for as long as he could, linguistically speaking, remember. 'I ain't got none' was the form that he had grown up with, and had learnt how to use when the occasion

129

demanded. To say to him, 'It's not that. It's "I haven't any"',
was to say something that, to him, was utterly without meaning.
By what possible criteria could the child interpret the remark, 'It's
not that'? How could he possibly have access to its meaning? If
the teacher wished him to learn the alternative form, and so add
to his linguistic resource in so far as he would then have the possibility of using it when he judged it appropriate (as when, for
example, a teacher thought he ought to use it), then she could
hardly be said to have set up a productive learning situation.
However, it is much more likely that she regarded 'I ain't got
none', as, in some way, the hallmark of a substandard rather than
a non-standard language.

It is sometimes claimed that attitudes towards the accents and
dialects of non-standard English have, in the past ten years or so,
become more tolerant, although one can still be asked such
questions as, 'How can we root out their Birmingham accents'?
It may be that some of the cruder forms of intolerance have been
softened, but disapproval of certain non-standard Englishes is
still widespread. Any attitude towards a pupil's language based
upon such disapproval is bound to have a damaging effect upon
his educational chances.

Devaluing a person's language, which is what you do when you
accuse it of being inferior, is to devalue him. To do this within the
society of the school is to weight the scales against his chances of
success. A barrier has been erected which he has to overcome, even
if it exists only in the teacher's mind, a barrier which is not there
for someone whose language is accepted for what it is. A process of
inevitable failure may then be put in train. Pupils' language is
thought, because of what it sounds like, to be substandard. He
doesn't have much success in school. Therefore others who sound
like him aren't likely to have much success either, because their
teachers come, unconsciously, to think that there are bound to be
limits to what they can achieve. They are thus predisposed to
failure, literally, as soon as they open their mouths.

But the important thing about a pupil's language is not what it
sounds like; it is what he can use it for. It is the meaning potential
that his language gives him, and here again he is likely to run up
against misconceptions about the nature and function of language
that will, in practice, set limits to the enlargement of his range of
meaning potential.

Functions of language

When describing his seven 'Relevant Models of Language', Halliday remarked of the seventh, the Informative Model, 'This is the only model of language that many adults have.' He meant by this that many adults, including, notably, teachers, seem to think that language is used only for expressing ideas and exchanging information, as indeed it often is in the classroom, despite the range of uses to which they, and those with whom they mix, put language during the course of their daily lives.

Human beings living and working together in the close proximity enforced by an institution like a school have to get on with each other. To do this they need to use language frequently to make what is sometimes called social talk. The starting point of such talk may be the weather, last night's television, gardening, cars, sport, holidays, clothes, domestic problems of various sorts—anything, in fact, about which two or more people can exchange meanings in language for periods ranging from a passing snatch of conversation in the corridor to the lunch-hour. Such talk goes on all the time. But the curious thing is that equivalent talk between pupils is frequently dismissed as 'idle chatter', 'idle gossip' or 'playground talk'. One assumption behind this dismissive judgment seems to be that talk within the school setting that is not inspired, licensed or directed by the teacher is 'idle', and therefore, presumably, profitless. Another assumption seems to be that linguistic exchanges between adults are always, and exclusively, in Halliday's sense, 'informative', that is, concerned with 'processes, persons, objects, abstractions, qualities, states and relations of the real world . . .' A moment's reflection should serve to show how far removed from linguistic reality that is, even at High Table in the Senior Common Room.

It is fatally easy to move from the belief that language used by pupils outside the classroom is of little value, because it does not serve what the teacher regards as an educational purpose, to the belief that they have no worthwhile language at all. This belief is given expression in at least two ways.

'They have no language when they come to me' is a remark that can be heard from teachers at various levels, put in different ways, from Reception Class Teachers in Infant Schools to Lecturers in Colleges and Universities. In fact, it is not very long since a Lecturer in a College of Education was reported as saying, at an Educational Conference in the North of England, 'Many of my own students have to learn their own language at the age of 18 or 19.' A walk through the playground of any Infant School at break or during the lunch-hour, when the place is usually alive with language, is enough to show how far from linguistic truth such an opinion is, whether aimed at five-, eleven- or eighteen-year-olds. Yet, quite recently, a teacher said at a Conference, of pupils who had already been in Secondary School four years, 'They don't even speak English—they just grunt.'

A more subtle, and therefore somewhat more insidious form of this belief about pupils' language is given expression as, 'They have two languages—one that they use in school, and the other that they use outside.' A Junior School Headmaster added, 'I was surprised the other day to find how precise their language is', and thereby revealed what he really thought about 'their' language.

Out of their linguistic resource people have to try to meet the demands of situations in which they find themselves. This entails, among other things, matching the language to the situation, knowing, for example, that talking to the Headmaster requires a different choice of language from that appropriate to a discussion with a peer in the playground. All language users are involved, constantly, in such choices. As a result, all language users may be said to have not two but many languages—even language users of five.

As Eric Ashworth says in *Language in the Junior School*,

'By the time that the children arrive in the Primary School, they will all have learned to perform their language with a high degree of skill. Even the most backward child there will know how to operate complex systems of words and how to select from among grammatical systems in order to make a range of meanings that is enormously wide. So great will be the ability of the children that it would not be stretching the imagination to call them experts.'

It is these 'experts' who are then said, in school, to 'have no language'. As it was put in an Infant School scheme of work, 'Where language is entirely lacking a cautious approach brings best results.' Pupils are then written off as 'inarticulate', or 'unable to express themselves', or 'unable to communicate'.

We live our lives in a succession of contexts which are socially constructed (and this includes the context of the classroom) and which appear to us as situations in which we can mean something, or we can't. We can mean something when the language used puts meaning within our reach, and when our role in the situation makes it possible for us to contribute meaning.

132

The function of education is to increase, for the pupil, the possibility of making meaning. This can be done only by enabling him to draw upon his linguistic resource, which in turn can happen only if the teacher accepts that resource for what it is, and assists the pupil to exploit and expand it.

When the pupil's language is disvalued because of what it sounds like, or its potential underestimated because of misconceptions about the way in which language functions, then indeed 'educational endeavour' can become very difficult.

6 Demands on pupils' language

'First formers do ask such stupid questions.'

A pupil in school is constantly faced with demands upon his linguistic resource. In one sense, he is, in this respect, in no different situation from most other human beings most of the time. As human beings we live by and through language. But pupils not only live by language, they learn through language— simultaneously. And the business of learning entails responding to demands for language related, in highly specialised ways, to specific contexts which are sometimes quite remote from the kind of context in which the language of every day functions.

We have already seen that the way in which we are regarded as human beings within the community of the institution will have its effect on our ability to use language successfully within the institution. By this is meant, in the terms in which language is conceived in this book, the ability of the individual pupil to draw upon his linguistic resource in order to meet the demands for making meanings in language. And before he can begin to meet the demands, he must, of course, be able to understand them, that is, he must be able to reach the meaning carried by the language used to formulate the demand.

In this chapter, we shall look closely at the nature of typical demands made upon the language of pupils in school, and in the next we shall ask what opportunities are provided for pupils to develop the abilities to meet these demands.

Such an examination could be made, in principle, at any stage of the educational career. The predicament is fundamentally the same, whether we are considering first entry to school at 5, transfer to Junior School at 7, to Middle School at 8 or 9, Secondary School

134

at 11 or 13, Sixth Form College or College of Further Education at 16 plus, or any of the institutions of Higher Education thereafter. Demands will always be made upon a pupil's capacity to put meaning into language, and judgments will constantly be made, on criteria operated by the teacher, upon his apparent ability to meet those demands adequately and, usually, quickly. The point of reference for the analysis in this chapter will, however, be transfer to Secondary School at 11.

There are a number of reasons for choosing this point. Eric Ashworth, in *Language in the Junior School*, in this series, has taken a critical look at the language experience that pupils can expect to have in school between 5 and 11. Despite the development, in some areas, of Middle Schools, it remains true that most pupils in England transfer to some form of secondary education at 11, and it is also true that this transfer brings with it inevitable difficulties for the pupil, not least in the area of language.

Any transfer from one school to another involves the pupil in the task of finding his way through what we have called the 'hidden curriculum' of the new institution, but transfer to some form of secondary education brings with it particular difficulties which derive from the fact that secondary education is still, to a large extent, subject-oriented. This means, in effect, that he will be taught by teachers for whom the language of a particular subject, or subject area (like Humanities, or Social Studies, or Creative Arts) has, through long experience and use, become very familiar.

It is very easy for a subject specialist, immersed in it as he is, to believe that the language of his own subject is part of what he imagines to be a 'common language', the kind of language that everyone has, or should have, in common. Such an assumption is, of course, yet another of the misconceptions about language use discussed in the last chapter. It is at one with the demand for 'good plain English' that is so frequently heard.

'Why can't he put it in good plain English?'

'It' may be anything, or rather any *meaning*, according to who 'he' is, where 'he' is, and the meaning that he is trying to language. The assumption clearly is that there is an available language into which any meaning can be encoded, irrespective of what that meaning is, or of the audience for whom it is intended, and of how much meaning and language they already share with the speaker (or writer). OUR MIRAGE SHOULD FOIL IRISH GAMBLE is 'good plain English' to those who have access to its meaning.

To those who don't, it may seem like gibberish. But, given the context, with all that that implies about the nature of his audience and the knowledge he shares with them, the writer of the headline was being plainly meaningful. Language use must always take account of the audience for whom it is intended, and the situation in which it is being used.

A first-former in a Secondary School will arrive, on a typical school day, at the appointed time, join up with some of his peers, and make his way to the place within the school where, for him, Registration takes place. He will probably take part in some form of Assembly, at the end of which it will not be unknown for him to have to listen to a succession of notices taking twenty minutes to read out. Thereafter, he (or she) will move about the school as a member of a group, or as a member of different groups brought together for different purposes, according to the organisation of the school. As he does so, he will be responding to language with language, meaning with meaning, or trying to. It may be the language of his friends, outside the class-room situation or the language of the teacher inside the class-room situation; in the main, language as speech. If he is particularly unlucky, his efforts to participate in the sharing of meaning will be rewarded with the kind of remark quoted at the head of the chapter.

Spoken and written

In the classroom situation there will come, sooner or later, demands for language as writing. There is speech, and there is writing. Being literate is having the ability to move from spoken to written language, and back again, freely and at will. In the linguistic history of each individual, just as in the history of the evolution of human language, speech comes before writing. Learning to be literate requires the pupil, at some stage, to invest in mastering the writing system that knowledge of language, and how it works, that he acquired in its spoken form by living and growing up with it.

The relationship of written language to the spoken language to which it corresponds is a complex one, more complex than is often acknowledged, and than is apparently assumed in, for example, phonic approaches to the teaching of reading, or traditional attitudes to spelling. Spoken language consists of sounds made

136

with the mouth, written language of marks made with the hand. Spoken language occurs normally in face-to-face situations in which language and other channels can be used together to convey the meaning which it is intended to convey. Moreover, as we speak in such a situation, we can register the effect of what we are meaning on other people present, and can modify what we say as we go along.

Written language exists not in time but in space. It lacks the immediacy of context provided by the face-to-face situation, and cannot make use of such characteristics of speech as intonation, pausing and stress. At the same time it has features, like punctuation marks and capital letters, that have no equivalent in speech. It is usually required in longer, perhaps more complex, structures than spoken language, which consists typically of what have been described as 'structured chunks of syntax and meaning' rather than complete sentences. This tends to require more sophisticated demands on the resources of language itself. It normally requires a more formal style, in the sense in which Martin Joos used the term in his book, *The Five Clocks*,[12] than is the case with spoken language. It, also, as far as school is concerned, tends to be 'informational' type language.

Written language, moreover, is normally a written form of the standard language. Written forms of non-standard languages, or dialects, are usually confined to characters in novels or pieces in local papers by writers trying to preserve local dialects. Such forms are not functional, in the sense that they are not forms of language in everyday use in the life of the community.

The speaker of non-standard language has, if he is to meet the demands made upon him in school (demands which are also non-functional, although in a different way, in that they are not related to life outside the school), to acquire an ability to handle the written form of the standard language in general use in the community. This is not a necessarily more difficult task than that facing the speaker of a form of standard English, as Labov insists in *The Logic of Non-standard English*,[8] although the task will be made more difficult, in practice, for the child whose teacher has a less than proper regard for his language, and fails to set up learning situations which will allow him to invest in his new task that knowledge of language which he already has.

It is vital that a pupil adds to his linguistic resource the ability to operate in the written medium, because the most important demands in the educational context will be for written language, important if for no other reason than that all the significant judgments about his ability and progress will be based upon his performance in the written medium.

Failure to acquire the ability to operate freely in the written medium, failure that is to become literate, brings with it disadvantages that accumulate with the passage of time, since the further one proceeds in the school system the more pressing become the demands for written work, and the slimmer the chances of achieving literacy if you haven't already done so. Despite a great deal of dedicated work going on in Remedial departments, there has so far been little serious attempt to evolve teaching techniques based upon sound linguistic principles.

Classroom language

The first-former we left on a previous page will move from lesson to lesson, from English, say, to French, to Science, to Music, to Woodwork. . . . In each subject he will be faced with language demands. These will take the form, initially, of a need to understand, and perhaps respond in the form of a question to, the teacher who is setting up the lesson; of having, perhaps, to read instructions, or some form of text; and/or of having to do some writing. It is an illuminating experience to spend a day with a first form in a Secondary School, taking note of the language demands made upon them.

These are extracts from books in use in the first forms of a Secondary School in the subjects mentioned in the last paragraph:

I. ENGLISH

Chapter 1 The Hall by the Tarn

Two figures stood in the darkness, a man and a boy. Behind them the pine woods sighed, as though overcome by a great and unnameable sadness, the melancholy sound made by all ancient forests. As the round moon came from behind a bank of cloud, throwing its silver light over the rough and rocky land below, the two figures peered down into the valley beneath them, their heavy cloaks sweeping away from them in the night-wind that blew towards them from the woods. A great white seabird circled above their heads, crying harshly and pitifully in the moonlight. They shuddered at the sound, looking up in dread. The man's bearded lips moved silently, as though he spoke a charm against the witches of the night. The moon slowly withdrew behind the

138

straggling cloudbank, and for a moment there was utter darkness once more.

Then suddenly, from the valley, came a surge of flame, a great red and orange spurting-up of light. A thick cloud of oily smoke rose above it, into the night air. A flock of birds flew, twittering up from the valley, to the woods. The two watchers drew in their breath as the many wings beat above them in the darkness.

Now the fire-glow spread and its angry light flared out over a black tarn nearby, so that the man and boy saw reflected in the sombre water every shape and hue of the flames.

The Wizard of Earthsea—Ursula Le Guin

2. FRENCH

A. MON ALBUM FRANAÇIS

Start to keep a French scrapbook. Label the cover 'Mon album français' and decorate it in a suitable way, with pictures of France, French stamps, labels or postcards. The scrapbook will be used to collect interesting items and information about France and French-speaking countries. Suggestions will be made for the use of the scrapbook, but you should also try to think of ideas of your own.

Start to keep a list of new items in your scrapbook.

Under suitable headings (e.g. Dans la salle de classe; A la maison) draw pictures of objects whose French names you know, and label them in French. As an alternative to drawing, stick in pictures which you have cut out from magazines.

B. Divide into two teams, 'les Français' and 'les Anglais'.

Ask your opposite number questions such as:
Oú est le professeur?
Qu'est-ce que c'est?
Est-ce que c'est un stylo?
Use only the names of objects which you have already met. Points are gained both for correct questions and correct answers.

Audio-Visual French (Longman)

3. SCIENCE

11 Here are four lists of things:
   a Brass, glass, grass.
   b Daisy, rose, flint, mushroom, wheat, seaweed.
   c Seawood, woodlouse, daffodil, snake, salt, mouse, bracken, crab, whale.
   d Slate, chalk, water, air, aluminium, iron, oil, lead, mercury, asbestos, tadpole, rubber, brick.

Choose one item in each list which you think is the 'odd man out'.
Why do you think so?
Your friends disagree with you, and each other, about all four lists.
Imagine choices for your friends and their reasons.
Is there any reason why one thing in each list must be the right
choice?
Do their reasons make you change your mind? Do your reasons
change theirs?

Nuffield Combined Science, Book 1

4. MUSIC

11 THE KNIGHTS OF THURINGIA

The Story

Most people have heard of the troubadours and trouvères,
nobly-born poets and song-writers who lived in France during the
twelfth and thirteenth centuries. Sometimes they sang their own
works in courtly circles; sometimes they paid professional min-
strels to do so. King Richard the Lion-Heart was a troubadour,
and Blondel was his faithful minstrel.

About the time of the troubadours the German-speaking
countries had their Minnesingers, chief of whom were the knights
Walter von der Vogelweide, Wolfram von Eschenbach, and
Tannhäuser. Like the troubadours, they had a strict code of
rules governing their art and their personal conduct, and they
met periodically to hold friendly tournaments of song in the castle
of the Wartburg in Thuringia.

The Wartburg is one of the most romantic places in Europe.
In later years it became the refuge of Martin Luther, where he
translated the New Testament into German. Long before that
time, however, and even before the coming of the Minnesingers,
it was believed that the goddess Holda, whose worship gradually
became confused with that of the Roman goddess Venus, reigned
beneath a neighbouring mountain.

Legends in Music—John Horton

5. WOODWORK

3   Plans and Elevations

The main purpose of making drawings is to give us a small
picture on a flat (or two-dimensional) drawing paper, which we
can easily carry about, of a large solid (or three-dimensional)
object.

To see how this is done.let us investigate how a solid rectangular
prism resting on a flat level plane is represented in a two-dimensional diagram.

140

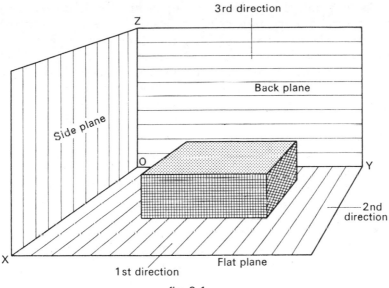

3rd direction

Z

Back plane

Side plane

O

Y

2nd direction

X

1st direction

Flat plane

fig. 3.1

Fig. 3.1 shows the prism resting on the flat plane

Technical Drawing

A fairly rapid glance will reveal that very different kinds of meaning are involved.

'Behind them, the pine woods sighed, as though overcome by a great and unnameable sadness, the melancholy sound made by all ancient forests.'

'The scrapbook will be used to collect interesting items and information about France and French-speaking countries.'

'd   Slate, chalk, water, air, aluminium, iron, oil, lead, mercury, asbestos, tadpole, rubber, brick.

Choose one item in each list which you think is the 'odd man out'.

'Like the troubadours they had a strict code of rules governing their art and their personal conduct, and they met periodically to hold friendly tournaments of song in the castle of the Wartburg in Thuringia.'

'The main purpose of making drawings is to give us a small picture on a flat (or two-dimensional) drawing paper, which we can easily carry about, of a large solid (or three-dimensional) object.'

As he reads, the reader draws upon his linguistic resource to try to reach the meaning of what he sees on the page, a page in this case, where pine woods 'sigh as though overcome by a great and unnameable sadness', where there are such entities as 'French-speaking countries', where 'lead, mercury, asbestos' lie side by side with a 'tadpole', where troubadours have a 'strict code of rules governing their art', and where we can easily carry about 'a small "two-dimensional" picture of a "large solid (or three-dimensional) object".'

All that the reader of this book has to do, as he proceeds down the page, is to reach the meanings of the extracts, see how they differ, and appreciate the point in the argument. For the pupil, however, reaching the meaning is merely the entry qualification to some further activity.

Let us suppose that this further activity is written work, which we will call an assignment. This assignment might take one of several forms. It could be a piece of continuous writing, an essay, perhaps, 'Describe......', 'Give an account of ......', 'Why are/did/were ......?', 'What were the reasons for ......', or some 'creative writing'. It might be in the form of notes, in 'English', on troubadours, for example, or in the form of answers to questions, such as those posed in extract 3 ('Why do you think so?') or as a so-called Comprehension Test to extract 1.

The pupil now has to draw upon his resource to language meaning in the written medium, and in a form of the written medium which has its own conventions. What these conventions are, as they apply to style, setting out, etc, must, if he is to take account of them, form part of his resource as knowledge about language, and how it is to be used in a particular context.

A Comprehension Test based upon passage 1 might be presented to the pupil like this:

1. Why does the author say that the pine woods 'sighed'?
2. What does 'melancholy' mean?
3. What other word could the author have used for 'peered'?
4. Why do you think they looked up at the bird 'in dread'?
5. What does 'as though he spoke a charm against the witches of the night' mean?
6. Why does the author call the cloudbank 'straggling'?
7. Put into your own words 'reflected in the sombre water every shape and hue of the flames'.
8. Give two examples of metaphors used in the passage.

Are answers to questions 1 and 2 to be given as 'one-word'

answers? Or are they required in the form of sentences? The pupil must possess knowledge such as this before he can begin to deal with the 'Comprehension Test' itself, that is to say, to play about with the bits and pieces of language of which the Test consists. What in fact his attempts to answer the questions will reveal of his understanding of the passage in question is doubtful. And what this kind of dabbling in language in such a narrow context subject to such rigid constraints can be expected to reveal of any general capacity is even more doubtful.

The questions on the 'four lists of things' in the extract from the Science book were put in a form which was the result of a deliberate attempt to make the style more informal, to shift it nearer to 'everyday language'. This obviously begs certain questions about the relationship of spoken to written language, and about the relationship of the functional language of everyday to the language of scientific questions. Nevertheless, it does represent an attempt to shift the language of the assignment nearer to the language of the pupil, although trying to 'Imagine choices for your friends and their reasons' is quite a formidable task.

Pupils, then, are expected to know the rules of so many games: to know what an 'essay' or 'composition' is; to know what features of writing make it, in the eyes of the teacher, especially 'creative'; how to set down answers in tests; how to make notes, whether for private, revisionary purposes or for being marked as an accurate record of what has been reduced to note form. All such knowledge *about* language must form part of linguistic resource if, out of that resource, demands are to be adequately met. And if they are to become part of linguistic resource, then opportunity must be given for this to happen. Opportunity and time.

Early language learning takes place with almost unbelievable speed. Later language learning, or, rather, extension of linguistic resource, takes time, time to allow new possibilities of making meanings, and languaging them, to be added to the potential that one already possesses. This may be particularly the case if the meaning, and the language which is to carry it, is remote from one's experience. And time is, so it seems, always at a premium in school, where syllabuses have to be got through, or examinations prepared for. 'You should have finished by now.' But for those who haven't finished there is rarely going to be another opportunity, because the next lesson may bring something new, some fresh demands on capacity for meaning. Once again, it is those furthest away from making contact with the desired meaning

143

who suffer, and whose performance in the classroom is written off.

It is true, of course, that pupils do not spend all their time in classrooms with specialist teachers who make highly specialised demands on their language. Of the time spent in school, from nine to four, five days a week, for some forty weeks a year, some is spent in breaks, lunch-hours, and in what are sometimes called 'out-of-school activities', mixing with and relating to peers and teachers. Nevertheless, position within the school, as a pupil, is essentially based upon performance in the classroom, and, within that context, upon ability to handle written language. Most school reports consist of comments made by subject teachers, with space allocated at the bottom for the comments of form-masters, house-masters, or others responsible for the 'pastoral' side. Many Parents' Evenings consist of meetings with, and reports from, subject teachers.

All this adds up to the fact that public judgments on a pupil's achievement within the school may be made upon a comparatively limited part of his endeavour, that part, perhaps, in which he finds most difficulty in performing adequately. The effect must be to make the rest, in comparison, seem irrelevant.

7 How are pupils expected to learn how to mean?

'I've found a very squashed map of Great Britain.'
'It's like a tree with a bird on it and the bird flying down off it.'
'Mine's shaped like an oak leaf.'
'A bit like . . . very small ice flakes. . . .'

These snippets of language were recorded during a lesson in which some 11-year-old girls were looking into a microscope and trying to describe what they could see. What they were looking at were slides made by rubbing a finger inside the cheek, and then drawing the finger across a glass slide. They were, in fact, looking at, and trying to describe, what the biologist would call cells.

The lesson was of a kind that has become familiar in Nuffield Science, whereby the pupils must discover for themselves, with the teacher acting as a guide rather than an instructor. The pupils in the lesson in question tried hard, and sometimes colourfully, but without success, to find a language that their teacher would accept.

Their predicament was like that of anybody faced with a specific demand to make new meanings out of his language. You bring to the situation your linguistic resource, and endeavour to draw upon it, as best you can within the constraints of the situation, for a response that you hope will prove adequate.

These pupils discovered that their response was not adequate because their teacher would not accept their attempts to describe what they saw. '. . . a very squashed map of Great Britain' is not the language into which you put meaning in Biology. Nor is, 'It's like a tree with a bird on it and the bird flying down off it.' Creative writing, perhaps. Biology, no.

The important question for these pupils is, then, what chance are they going to be given to acquire the ability to use language—that is, to make meaning—in biology lessons in a way that will satisfy their teacher? Put like this, it is, of course, seen to be the important question for all pupils faced with unfamiliar demands upon their linguistic resource.

We will assume, for the time being, that movement towards increased ability to make new meanings will typically start with spoken language, probably with the teacher talking and the pupil trying to reach the meaning of what the teacher is putting into language. This may not be easy, especially if the teacher is introducing an area of meaning that is wholly unfamiliar.

What, in effect, the pupil is being asked to do is to take in what the teacher is saying, and try to match it to what he already knows, to see if he can reach its meaning. The operation may take time, more time than is allowed, because there is a lesson plan to be carried through in forty minutes.

Some recent work, including particularly that of Douglas Barnes,[13] has focused on the nature of linguistic interaction in the classroom, interaction, that is, between teacher and pupil. The investigations have thrown some light on the opportunities given to pupils, in typical classroom situations, to talk their way, as Barnes puts it, 'into understanding' or 'into new meanings'. The findings are not very hopeful.

Many so-called discussion lessons consist of talk by the teacher (it is said that the average lesson begins with fifteen minutes uninterrupted talk by the teacher) followed by a teacher-dominated pattern of interaction. Questions are asked, and elicit short, perhaps one-word, answers. Pupils pursuing their own attempts to make meanings often get little encouragement. Their answers may not be accepted because they don't happen to be the 'right one', or they may apparently be accepted but re-phrased by the teacher in his language. In fact, what often happens (and pupils themselves have pointed this out) is that a kind of guessing game ensues, with the pupil trying to guess what is in the teacher's mind. As always, those who guess quickest find the most favour.

Moreover, the fact that one pupil has guessed the right answer, and has thereby shown that he has reached at least part of the teacher's meaning, may be taken as evidence that others (perhaps most of the class) are similarly within reach. This, of course, may be a complete misconception. Many may be in the situation described by the second-former who confided, in a moment of candour, to the mature student on teaching practice who was taking them for English, 'Most of us don't know what the bloody hell you're talking about.'

146

Such a misconception will have the effect of excluding, perhaps permanently, those who are wrongly assumed to have reached a certain stage of participation in meaning. This exclusion may be reinforced by the teacher who has little sympathy for those who take time to understand, the kind of teacher of whom it was once said, 'You were all right if you knew what she was talking about. She had no time for you if you didn't.' Such an attitude not only places responsibility for reaching meaning where it is least able to be assumed, on the pupil. It operates, inevitably, to the disadvantage of those who are farthest away from the meanings which it is desired they should gain access to.

The process of gaining understanding will at some stage be accompanied by demands for written language, of various sorts. Some have already been mentioned, like essays, compositions, descriptions, notes and tests. The list could be extended to include the writing up of scientific experiments, the drawing of diagrams in which language and diagram operate together to make meaning, the doing of various kinds of exercise. (*Language in Use*,[14] especially the units in Themes A and G, gives examples of a large number of highly context-specific uses of language.)

If the process is as we have described it, then what productive opportunities can the pupil expect to be given to extend his resource to meet such demands for written language as are made of him?

Can he, for example, expect to be given opportunities to re-hearse what he wants to mean, either in speech or writing, to make mistakes, to try again, before he, at length, hopefully, comes to a reasonably adequate attempt? Or will he be expected to discharge his assignment in a once-for-all attempt, something that not even the most experienced writer, faced with an unfamiliar (or even a familiar!) demand, would expect to make do with?

Can he expect that, when he has produced an attempt to meet the teacher's demands, it will be the subject of informed comment and encouragement? Or can he expect that it will receive what Angus McIntosh, in *Language and Style*,[15] referred to as 'little more than a series of red lights or warnings' about particular points of usage?

Too often, the criteria on which these 'warnings' are based are misconceived or inappropriate or inconsistent, and their effect is to mislead or to confuse. Attention may be drawn to grammatical 'solecisms' like 'split infinitives' or reduced forms such as 'haven't' or 'aren't', which in the context of an attempt to make

147

meaning may be comparatively trivial considerations. Comments like 'Never use slang' may be written in the margin of an essay where, indeed, certain kinds of slang expressions may be inappropriate, as though slang were a kind of linguistic offence which no self-respecting language user ever resorted to. The pupil, if he knows what slang is, knows also that this is not true, because he hears it used, as it is in appropriate contexts, every day, including by his teachers.

Moreover, the criteria applied to the marking of 'creative writing' in English, to essays in English, to writing in other subjects, where, for example, the regard paid to such features of the writing system as spelling and punctuation may differ widely, are liable to drastic variation. The pupil, who may be given little opportunity to discover what criteria are likely to apply, is left in a state of confusion.

He may also be given little opportunity to acquire the ability to satisfy the criteria which are applied, since the language activities that he is asked to engage in, supposedly to help him remedy his defects, suffer the crippling disadvantages of resting upon the same kind of linguistically inadequate foundations that underlie approaches to many other aspects of the learning situation in which he is placed.

'Use the following words in sentences to show clearly that you understand their meaning: antediluvian, belligerent, cynosure, discernment, ephemeral, garrulous, hierarchy, idiosyncrasy, jeopardy, mnemonic, obsequies, panegyric.'

An exercise typical of those set in preparation for certain kinds of examination in English.

Fill in the gaps in the columns.

Masculine	Feminine
Prince	Princess
Nephew	—
—	Spinster
Duke	—
—	Mistress
Manservant	—
—	Vixen
Monk	—
—	Bride
Cock	—

An exercise typical of those which appear in course-books intended for use in English lessons.

148

'After her toilet Molly was —— and ——.
Which of the following words fits into the gaps? (a) frisky;
(b) lazy; (c) contented; (d) grumpy.'

An exercise typical of 'comprehension exercises' to be found in
books in use in Primary Schools. (It should be added, perhaps,
that Molly is a cat!)

If the object of his going to school is to enable the pupil to
increase his ability to make meanings in language, what value
have exercises like these—and others of similar kinds? They are
unrelated to anything of an on-going nature that he might be
doing, and they yield no insights into the nature and function of
language that can subsequently be invested in the task of making
new meanings. The bits of language, usually at a lexical (not even
the lexico-grammatical) level, that pupils are asked to play about
with are randomly chosen. In the example above, spinster, duchess,
mistress, maidservant, vixen, nun, bride and hen, all admittedly
in a category 'feminine', appear together. In what context other
than an exercise in an English course-book would they so appear?

Activities such as these derive from no theory of language and
learning which might lead us to suppose that, by engaging in
them, pupils would be likely to increase their ability to perform
adequately in tasks calling for other uses of written language,
especially extended, connected use of written language. Far more
about the nature and function of language must be taken into
account if activities are to be designed that will enable pupils to
invest in them productively the linguistic resource that they have,
so that they might emerge from them with their meaning potential
enlarged.

The depth of knowledge about language ideally required by
those, teachers and others, who make pupils engage in language
activities which purport to help pupils extend their range of
ability to handle language is well illustrated by Ruqaiya Hasan in
the paper she wrote for the first series of Papers in Linguistics and
English Teaching, called *Grammatical cohesion in spoken and written
English*.[16] Its subject matter can be most easily illustrated by
comparing the following two passages:

'The other day, at my local supermarket, I was in the queue
behind the mother of a young boy. Thick yarn and eye-catching
patterning give these country classics a new look. When working
out plans for a new garden or replanning an old one, you must
think of the years ahead. It has been said, with a little bit of
humour, and a tiny chance of truth, that Health is good for you.'

'In the last resort we cannot evaluate any specimen of language —and deciding whether or not it forms a text is a prerequisite to any further evaluation of it—without knowing something about its subject-matter and its function. We need to know what in linguistics is called its "context of situation", and there are three aspects to the context of situation of a text: its relation to human experience (the 'subject-matter' in the widest sense), its setting (by whom it is addressed, to whom, and in what type of social interaction), and its purpose and scope within that setting.'

(The word 'text' had earlier in the paper been defined as 'any piece of language, spoken or written, of whatever length, that does form an integrated whole.')

The first is a random selection of sentences, assembled by taking the first sentence from each of four features in a magazine. The second is an extract from Hasan's paper itself, a paper which describes the linguistic devices which are used to bind language together, those devices which enable us to tell at a glance that the second passage forms a piece of integrated language, while the first is a mere agglomeration of sentences.

The quotation from Hasan's paper was chosen deliberately to illustrate the factors which the author thought it important to bring into reckoning when introducing her subject. It is significant that when she stresses the importance of taking subject matter and function into account, she regards this as, 'in its widest sense', considering its 'relation to human experience', and that when she proposes to look at its setting, she takes this to include 'what type of social interaction' is involved in the writing. Far from regarding a piece of text as something that is produced, and can be looked at, in isolation, she insists that it must be looked at from a functional viewpoint, as a piece of language produced for a purpose, at a particular time, in a particular place.

Texts produced by pupils in school, in English lessons, in History lessons, in Science lessons, in examinations, or whatever, are in this respect no different from texts produced in other places by other people. They, too, relate ultimately to 'human experience', to that tradition of human experience which has shaped the demand for a certain kind of text, and to the 'human experience' of the pupil asked for the text. The pupil, no less than other producers of texts, is subject to the constraints of the 'social interaction' at the point of production of the text, that between himself and his teacher in the class-room.

If, then, we are to consider the situation of the pupil in the

150

class-room who has been given the task of writing something, with a view to commenting on the adequacy of what he produces, we must consider what chance he has of relating what he has been asked to do to what he already knows. What can he draw upon, in terms of his ability to language meaning, that is relevant to the task in hand? Tasks which are within his range will give him a chance of adequate performance, and the kind of reinforcement that adequate performance brings. Tasks beyond his range will bring inadequate performance, brought home to him, often publicly, by all or some of the usual apparatus of marking, marks, grades, positions in form, examinations, and reports, which, all too often, may have the effect of humiliating, rather than encouraging.

This chapter has put the question, 'How are pupils expected to learn how to mean?' The best way of learning how to mean is by trying, perhaps by only partly succeeding, and trying again until one does succeed.

There are signs that, in some schools, pupils are being given the opportunity to acquire experience in situations. Unfortunately, however, when attempts are made to set up situations in which pupils can gain experience of learning how to mean, some are rendered less than helpful by the ideas about language that inform them, as in the case of the following notes drawn up for the guidance of teachers conducting Mock Interviews for school-leavers in a Secondary School.

MOCK INTERVIEW

TEACHER	Good afternoon, Miss Green. Please sit down.
PUPIL	Thank you. (5 points.)
T	Your name has been sent to me by the Youth Employment Service for a position as a Junior Shorthand Typist. Is that correct?
P	(Yes, Mr. Brown told me to call—5 pts.) (Yes only—2 pts.)
T	Very well. What school did you attend?
P	(Wensum Road Secondary School—5 pts. No pts for any other answer.)
T	So you know Mr. Black, then?
P	(Yes, he is my Headmaster—5 pts.) (Yes only—2 pts.)
T	Indeed, Mr Black has sent me some very good girls in the past. I hope if we appoint you, you will be equally as good.
P	(I hope so—No pts.) (I will do my best—5 pts.)

151

T	What were your best subjects at school?
P	(Maths, English, Shorthand, Typewriting—5 pts.) (Other subjects—No pts.)
T	What are your hobbies?
P	(Reading, dancing, stamp collecting, etc.—5 pts.) (No pts for listening to Pop records, etc.)
T	Do you like reading?
P	(Yes—3 pts.) (Yes, very much—5 pts.)
T	When did you last read a book?
P	(Last week—5 pts.)
T	What was it called?
P	(5 pts for a classic, 3 pts for a schoolgirl's book, no pts for anything else.)
T	Well, that is enough about your hobbies. Do you know what we make here?
P	(5 for a yes, 3 for a no.)
T	We make electrical equipment. Do you think you will like working here?
P	(Yes, very much—5 pts.) (Yes—3 pts.)
T	Have you any questions to ask me?
P	(5 pts for each question about salaries, holidays, etc.)

152

8 What is to be done?

Guidance on Marking of Written Work
These notes have been prepared at the Headmaster's request
(see Staff Bulletin No. 2, 11th September 1968) as a *supplement*
to the section 'Correction of Written Work' of the syllabus
(pp 5–6).

Extract from English Syllabus

There follows a list of aims such as can be found in many English
syllabuses. Such lists are likely to include some or all of the
following:

To draw the pupils' attention to the merits and the short-
comings in the content and mode of expression of their work.

To rectify specific errors in spelling, punctuation, grammar
and usage.

To promote understanding of sentence structure, para-
graphing, punctuation, parts of speech, and grammar, as
required for the improvement of style and the correction of
error, accuracy in spelling and the efficient use of a dictionary.

To avoid mistakes of punctuation, grammar, spelling and
idiom.

To encourage syntactical correctness.

To correct major errors, e.g. misrelated participles, gerunds,
infinitives or elliptical clauses; faulty sentence structure, e.g.
serious lack of unity—Eskimoes are good hunters and they are
few in number, etc.

To keep a remorseless watch for slovenly or lazy English.

The essential weakness of statements of aims like this is that
they wobble from one level to another, without ever beginning
to suggest an existence at the most important level of all, the level
of meaning. There is no explicit recognition that what a writer is

153

trying to do is to put elements and structures together to make meaning; no attempt to define priorities in spotting where there might be weakness. There are no strategies recommended which might be used to encourage a pupil to build on what he can do in order to achieve a more adequate level of performance. 'Short-comings' must be pointed out, errors 'rectified', 'mistakes' avoided. It is a purely penal approach, on a par with the custom of setting essays as impositions.

How could aims such as these be translated into any kind of action that would help the writer of the following?

> doscribe som of the advontages of owning your own bugness and some of the problems you are liney to be faced with otworking a new busoness
>
> The advontages having your owne place of your owne is your are in charing of the place your Slove you tell your staff wont to do. If I had a salon of my oune I wold have a small one but I thike it is too much independependance off yeour slove. Problems you would have to faced, is how people be in your shop and be nice to them if you dont be nice to them you will lose them and lose your bussinesos. If you are having a place of your windows should be desperdy nicely, before I setur a business I woild hove to have lote off money and pople to hlep me start my business. The best may would to Avertis in the paper for hlep for hairting And when I hove hlep I woll pople see the groom. If thay good

The writer is a 16-year-old girl, following a course in Hairdressing at a College of Further Education. She has been asked, according to the title of her piece, to, 'Describe some of the advantages of owning your own business and some of the problems you are likely to be faced with in starting a new business'. She is not fully literate, in the sense in which it was defined on page 54. Her linguistic resource does not include the facility of moving easily from spoken to written language. She is not, on the other hand, wholly illiterate. The meaning of what she has written is accessible, on the whole fairly readily, to anyone who is both literate and sympathetic. How, then, can she be helped to greater literacy, helped to extend her linguistic resource to include the possibility of encoding meaning more successfully in written language?

Perhaps the first point to make is to suggest that any assignment she is given should be more realistic, in at least two ways. It should be more nearly within her reach, so that she will have a chance of performing adequately, with all that that implies about the effects of success. In the second place, assignments should be more closely related to the purpose for which language is actually used. People may think about, and discuss with others, 'the advantages of owning your own business.' If it is remotely possible that they may, indeed, one day own their own business, they will be wise to seek advice on 'some of the problems you are likely to be faced with in starting a new business'. Such advice will be needed not only from those who have already set themselves up in business but from bank managers, estate agents, manufacturers' representatives, and so on. You will certainly have to have interviews, ranging from informal chats to formal requests. You will almost certainly have to write letters asking for advice, appointments, and quotations, and you may have to use language for other functions in the course of setting up your business. But whatever else you do in the course of setting yourself up in business you are unlikely to have to write an essay on the subject—unless you did a course in a department in a College where someone thought it a useful assignment to give you.

Given that the writer of the piece was asked to describe (only) 'some of the advantages . . .' and (only) 'some of the problems . . .'; that this requires a knowledge, and an ability to make meaning, that in her case she quite certainly will not have; that she does not handle the writing system easily, whereas the assignment demands a fairly sophisticated ability—given all this, what kind

155

of attempt did she make? The answer must surely be, 'Not bad at all.'

She begins by wanting to mean something like, 'The advantage of having a place of your own is that you are in charge of the place yourself. You tell your staff what to do.' That is, perhaps, how it would be represented in the writing system, with traditional orthography and conventional punctuation.

The girl herself wrote down two ways of languaging her first bit of meaning: having your own place and having a place of your own. It is a characteristic feature of spoken language that bits of two (or even more) structures come out entwined together. What seems to happen is that, at some point in the languaging-of-meaning process where we are planning how to say what we want to mean, more than one option presents itself. We choose one, but occasionally bits of discarded choices remain embedded in what we actually say.

The same thing can happen when we are writing our meaning; bits of two constructions can appear on the page under our pen. Usually, because we can see what we have done, we realise what has happened and cross out the intruding bits, if not at once then on re-reading. This girl had not done so. The chances are that if she had been asked to-read, given the time to re-read, or asked to read aloud, what she had written she, too, would have realised what she had done.

There are, of course, other ways in which what she wrote differs from what would be generally regarded as acceptable in School or College. There are some idiosyncratic spellings: 'owne' for 'own', what appears to be 'charing' for 'charge', 'slave' for 'self' and 'wont' for 'what'. Some punctuation should also be inserted before 'you tell . . .'

Similar points can be made all the way through. It is seldom difficult to see what she means. The meaning of '. . . . but I think it is too much independance of yourself' is not readily available, nor that carried by the last seven words. They reflect her difficulties in combining words into meaning-carrying structures, just as she sometimes has difficulty in combining letters into words.

How—apart from not giving her tasks that lie too far outside the range of her meaning potential—can she be helped? Only if she is encouraged to exploit the resources she already has.

She displays a promising grasp of fairly complex structures. She can begin, 'If you are having a place of your (own) . . .'

156

and continue, 'windows should be (displayed) nicely.' Something went wrong in the middle, so that she wrote, 'a place of your windows' instead of, presumably, 'a place of your own, your windows. . . .' But the underlying sentence structure is clearly discernible, as it is in 'before I (start) a business I would have to have (lots of) money and (people) to help me start my business.' There is evidence here of potential literacy. The language is there.

Her spelling, too, displays evidence of what she knows and what she can do. In some instances, as in 'slave' for 'self' and 'wont' for 'what' she has attempted a correspondence between sound and symbol that at least has a discernible relationship. She occasionally adds a letter ('owne' for 'own') or misses one out ('pople' for 'people') or transposes two ('hlep' for 'help'). She can put in too many syllables ('independependancc'), and she can get in a tangle with 'despeldy' for 'displayed', or when she runs off the page in the last line but one with what looks as if it might have been 'hairdressers', and with the word under that, which is the only *word* in the piece which causes insuperable difficulty to the reader. But if what she (or anyone else) writes is regarded as evidence of *knowledge*, and hence of resource, or potential, instead of evidence of ignorance, then ways can be devised of helping her to capitalise on what she possesses.[17]

Using criteria like this, what could be said about the following?

(a) I am very sorry, that I made plenty noise in your class, and I know that is my foult. And I am asking that I would not do it any more to upset you and I am very sorry for that is because I mist a fall on the ground. And I want to get on with my typing so I am asking you if you would correct my work please and I promise that I would not go back in your book any more, please I am very sorry.

(b) Dear Sir,
I would like you to bring a hearse and a coffin for my beloved friend P. Rees who passed away on the 21st April in a terrible car accident in which he was split in two and serious head injuries. I am happy to say that he died instantly and felt no pain whatever. I would like the deceased to have a silk lined coffin with brass handles on the side, and I would like the hearse to be one of your best. Please collect the body on the 23rd April from my flat.

(c)

To service a Motor cycle.

Plenty of rags the more the better, chrome cleaner, "gunk", spanners, screwdrivers, buckets of warm soapy water and most important of all plenty, and I mean plenty, of patients are just a few of the things needed when starting such a hard task. Time seems to float past when you are cleaning every nut and bolt holding the motor cycle together. It could take as long as a week to make a real profession -al job. A rusty much rotten heap transformed into a glemming machine to be proud off. A dream that seems further away the longer you work.

The bike in question a Honda 175cc CB 'K' registration, new maybe but it get rusty all the same.

Spanner to the attension, dismantlg the main parts leave only the frame engine and wheels. Spanner one, ten millimeter, remove the two nut locating the exhaust to the cylinder head, no technical names for the simple reason I don't know them myself. Twelve millimeter spanner, holding the exhaust to the frame are two nuts which can be found easily and removed away comes The whole

158

exhaust unit with a gentle push forward to
free the exhaust. from the cylinder head.
Keep the nuts and washers in a safe
place tempers are roubled by missing
pieces. Repeat for the second exhaust
The tank will have to come off, bad
luck if there is any petrol inside a
messey operation. Switch the petrol tap
off remove the two rubber tube leading from
the tank to the twin carburators. The
tube connecting one half of the tank to
the other is the most difficult petrol
pours out have a tin. can ready disconnect
the tube and let the liquid flow
into the 'can' a welcome food, the
tank will now lift off

Language study for teachers

How can pupils and students who produce pieces of writing like
this be put into a position in which they can develop the language
and language experience that they have got, instead of constantly
being put into positions in which they will, inevitably, be condemned for not possessing knowledge and experience they haven't
got?

The answer must be, only when their teachers have an adequate
and relevant knowledge of the nature and function of language,
especially as it plays its part in the learning process.

What is meant here by relevant is described by Dell Hymes, in
his Introduction to *Functions of Language in the Classroom*, like this:

'What is crucial is not so much a better understanding of how

159

language is structured, but a better understanding of how language is usèd; not so much what language is, as what language is for . . . what we need to know goes far beyond how the grammar of English is organized as something to be taught. It has to do with the relationship between a grammar of English and the ways in which English is organized in use by teachers, by children and by the communities from which they come; with the features of intonation, tone of voice, rhythm, style, that escape the usual grammar and enter into the essential meaning of speech; with the meanings of all those means of speech to those who use them and those who hear them, not in the narrow sense of meaning, as in naming objects and stating relationships, but in the fuller sense, as conveying respect or disrespect, concern or indifference, intimacy or distance, seriousness or play, etc; with the appropriateness of one or another means of speech, or way of speaking, to one or another topic, person, situation; in short, with the relation of the structure of language to the structure of speaking.'

Equipped with this kind of understanding, teachers would be better placed to discern potential, better placed to devise learning situations in which pupils can develop their potential.

It is part of the argument of this book that this will entail looking at, and where necessary altering, ways in which schools are organised. It entails examining ways in which all subjects are taught, or, in the terms of the way in which the process has been seen in this book, examining opportunities given to pupils to meet the language demands of this subject or that.

It means, quite certainly, looking again at techniques of assessment and marking, by asking questions like,

'For whose sake are we assessing?'

'What is the point of marking?'

'How will marking help the pupil to perform more adequately next time?'

'Are "errors" and "mistakes" to be regarded as evidence of knowledge, and hence of potential, or as some kind of linguistic sin?'

It entails nothing less than placing at the service of the pupils, in learning situations that the school sets up, all that we can discover about the way in which language actually works that will help them to succeed. In this way we might change a situation in which everything seems to conspire against certain pupils—those pupils whose language is under-valued; those pupils who have had less experience of the kind of language on which the school puts a premium; pupils who are accorded low status in relationships

160

set up ostensibly to promote learning; pupils constantly devalued by the whole apparatus of evaluation; in short, pupils whose efforts are seen, 'at best, as irrelevant to the educational endeavour'.

References

1 (p. 13) Reprinted in Bernstein, B. (ed.), *Class, Codes and Control*, Vol. 1. Theoretical Studies towards a Sociology of Language (Routledge & Kegan Paul).

2 (p. 13) Halliday, M. A. K., *Language and social man* (Papers in Linguistics and English Teaching, series 11, Longman). See also *Learning How To Mean* in this series (Edward Arnold).

3 (p. 13) Hasan, R., 'Code, register and social dialect', in Bernstein, B. (ed.), *Class, Codes and Control*, Vol. 11, Applied Studies towards a Sociology of Language (Routledge & Kegan Paul).

4 (p. 17) Doughty, E. A. and P. S., *Language and Community* in this series (Edward Arnold).

5 (p. 19) Doughty, P. S., Pearce, J. J. and Thornton, G. M., *Exploring Language*, Chapter 1 (Edward Arnold).

6 (p. 20) Byers, P. and H., 'Nonverbal Communication and the Education of Children', in Cazden C., John V. P. and Dell Hymes (ed.), *Functions of Language in the Classroom* (Teachers College Press).

7 (p. 24) Fader, D., *Hooked on Books* (Pergamon Press).

8 (p. 35) Berger, P. L. and Luckmann, T. *The Social Construction of Reality* (Penguin)

9 (p. 38) Gurney, R., *Language, Brain and Interactive Processes*, in this series (Edward Arnold).

10 (p. 44) Labov, W., 'The logic of Non-standard English' in Keddie, N. (ed), *Tinker, Tailor* (Penguin). See also Torrey, J., 'Illiteracy in the Ghetto' in the same volume.

11 (p. 47) Abercrombie, D., 'R.P. and Local Accent' in *Studies in Phonetics and Linguistics* (O.U.P.)

162

12 (p. 55) Joos, M., *The Five Clocks* (Harcourt Brace).
13 (p. 64) Barnes, D., *Language in the Classroom* (Open University Correspondence Text).
From Communication to Curriculum (Penguin).
14 (p. 65) Doughty, P., Pearce, J. J. and Thornton, G. M., *Language in Use* (Edward Arnold).
See also Doughty, E. A. and P.S. *Using 'Language in Use': a teacher's guide to language work in the classroom* (Edward Arnold)
15 (p. 65) McIntosh, A. 'Language and Style', in Pride, J. B., Holmes, J. (ed.), *Sociolinguistics* (Penguin).
16 (p. 67) Hasan, R., 'Grammatical cohesion in spoken and written English, part one' (Papers in Linguistics and English Teaching, Series 1, Longman).
17 (p. 75) See, in this connection, Albrow, K. H., *The English writing system: notes towards a description* (Papers in Linguistics and English Teaching, Series 11, Longman).

163

LANGUAGE AND COMMUNITY
Anne and Peter Doughty

To the Reader

For all those teachers who are willing to go
beyond their own classrooms to seek answers
and particularly for the teachers in Northern
Ireland who asked us to write it all down.

Language and Community is not a research monograph, it is not a
'survey of the literature', it is not a contribution to any one
academic discipline, it is a book which sets out to tell a story,
a story about man's most distinctive attributes, his culture,
the environment which he makes for himself, and his language,
the means by which he makes this environment meaningful. We
say 'a story', because we ask the reader to begin at the beginning
and treat it as he would a continuous narrative, reading on to
discover what comes next, and how this may modify his view of
what has gone before, allowing each episode to add its own contribution on the way, though its full significance may only appear
at the end. We call it a story, because we ask the reader to participate in the action by bringing to the narrative at each stage
his own cumulative experience as a human being who has learnt
successfully to use language in the context of one, or many,
particular communities. We want the reader to test what we say
against the record of his own intuitive knowledge of how language
and community interrelate in the lives of all of us.

What, then, does this story have to say about something as
familiar and commonplace as our experience of using language and
living in communities? Our first step is to persuade the reader to
see that language is not 'out there', like a constructional toy given
to us in appropriate instalments as we grow from infancy to
adulthood, but an intimate part of each one of us. Language is
not like a *commodity* we own, but the outcome of a process of
growth and development, growth and development that involves
the individual child in a continuous interaction with the people
and objects of his world. In learning our language, we do not
simply 'take over' passively the 'elements and structure' of our
mother tongue as they are presented to us in the speech of those

167

around us. We are active participants in the language learning process, because it is essentially a process by which we strive to make the world meaningful to us. M. A. K. Halliday gives a brilliant analysis of this complex process in his volume in this series, called *Learning How to Mean*.

Language, for us, as human beings, however, implies a human environment in which we use our language, and thus the next step is to look at this environment as the context in which the infant learns how to become a *social* being, that is, learn how to make relationships with others and find out what those relationships mean. We use the word 'community' for this specifically human environment of relationships which provides the necessary habitat for man as a social animal. It is through his interaction with others, however, that the child learns language, and thus our use of the word 'community' necessarily refers also to the environment for the specifically human activity of using language. This intimate inter-relationship between the community the child inhabits and the language he learns leads us on to consider how the language we learn shapes so positively the meanings we give to what we experience of the world.

Our story then goes on to consider how the school stands in relation to this intimate interconnection between the language we use and the community we inhabit, and a consideration of school in relation to community raises the question of how human beings accommodate to change. 'Going to school', we would argue, is one of the most fundamental changes the ordinary human being has to face in the normal course of his life, because it is the first time most of us are asked to step out of our own familiar community and into another. A critical feature of this change is that school is not just a new and unfamiliar place, where the child has to learn new ways of behaving, but a new and unfamiliar *language climate*, where he has to learn new ways of using language, and a new medium, writing. In order to understand what we demand of pupils when we ask them to use language as the school requires, we need to see how great a contrast there is between our habitual ways of learning and using language, as members of family and community, and the ways customary in formal education. This brings our story to the point where the next step is to focus upon 'the language climate of schools' and that is where the book ends, for 'the language climate of schools', as we suggest in our postscript, requires a book to itself.

What we hope the reader will gain by following our story to this

168

point is the realization that there is more to the matter of pupils using language to learn than a consideration of what is done in class-rooms. Pupils are individual human beings who have learnt language in the process of learning how to live the life of their communities: the whole process has taken place in the context of the patterns of relationships, habits and values that make up that specifically human environment. If we are to make sense of the pupil's problems and needs when he comes to use the language he has learnt in the context of the school, then we must be very clear about the processes by which he has learnt it, and the human environment in which the learning has taken place.

It remains only for me to do two things: make one brief comment on a linguistic problem of co-authorship, and acknowledge the help we have had in the writing of this book. Co-authors work in many different ways, but we choose to have one of us write the text, while the other acts as stimulus, commentator, critic and devil's advocate. In this case, Anne Doughty wrote the text, while I filled the other available role—hence she is the 'I' of the text. 'We' refers on some occasions to 'both of us' and on other occasions to 'all of us', that is, as human beings, for the reader and his experience is included in much of what we have to say. This difference, we hope, is clearly defined by the context. In this way we have tried to avoid such cumbersome locutions as 'one of the authors' 'my co-author' and so on.

A book of this kind grows out of a cumulative experience of reading and talking over many years. We wish to thank all those teachers we have met in our work together presenting *Language in Use* to audiences up and down the country, audiences whose comments have been so valuable a stimulus to thinking and so rich a source of illustration and representative example. We would also thank the students of Manchester College of Education for all they have let us hear of their personal experiences, experiences which throw so strong a light upon the central theme of this book. Finally, we would like to thank Sister Anne McCarrick and Patricia Bertenshaw, both practising teachers in Northern Ireland, and Janet Ede, our friend from Matlock College of Education, for giving their time and energy to reading our early drafts and commenting so usefully upon them. Their help and encouragement was a critical factor in the finishing of this book.

Peter Doughty

Manchester 1973

1 Language

1. Language is learnt from others

When a human infant is born into any community in any part of the world it has two things in common with any other infant, provided neither of them has been damaged in any way either before or during birth. Firstly, and most obviously, new born children are completely helpless. Apart from a powerful capacity to draw attention to their helplessness by using sound there is nothing the new born child can do to ensure his own survival. Without care from some other human being or beings, be it mother, grandmother, sister, nurse or human group, a child is very unlikely to survive. This helplessness of human infants is in marked contrast with the capacity of many new born animals to get to their feet within minutes of birth and to run with the herd within a few hours. Although young animals are certainly at risk, sometimes for weeks or even months after birth, compared with the human infant they very quickly develop the capacity to fend for themselves. It would seem that this long period of vulnerability is the price that the human species has to pay for the very long learning period which fits man for survival as a species.

It is during this very long period in which the human infant is totally dependent on others that it reveals the second feature which it shares with all other undamaged human infants, a capacity to learn language. For this reason, biologists now suggest that language is 'species specific' to the human race, that is to say, they consider the human infant to be genetically programmed in such a way that it can acquire language. This suggestion implies that just as human beings are designed to see three-dimensionally and in colour, and just as they are designed to stand upright rather than to move on all fours, so they are designed to learn and

171

use language as part of their normal development as well-formed human beings.

Before we proceed we must look at the terms 'well-formed' and 'undamaged' as they have been used in the last paragraphs. There are many human beings who do *not* learn language despite the fact, that, like all other human beings, they are genetically programmed to do so. The reasons for this failure are very varied. At one end of the range there are individuals who have suffered brain damage; at the other, individuals who have suffered severe emotional or psychological damage or deprivation; and in between these two, those who possess physical defects like misshapen articulatory or respiratory organs or total deafness. Any one of these handicaps, or a combination of them, will make language learning difficult, or impossible, for these individuals and therefore what is said in this book cannot be applied to them without a modification appropriate to their condition. When we speak of a 'normal' human being, therefore, we mean no more than one who is not handicapped in ways such as these. This does not mean that the ordinary undamaged individual may not have difficulties, even extreme difficulties, to overcome in order to learn language, but it does mean that these 'difficulties' arise out of the ordinary business of living and do not derive from physical or mental handicaps.

Even if we consider a normal infant genetically programmed to learn language, there is still a further condition that has to be fulfilled before language learning can take place. The infant must be born into a properly constituted human environment. In other words, he must spend the period of physical dependence upon others in an environment where there are adults using language in the course of their day to day life and in the course of their care of the child. The importance of this human environment is critical to the child because the capacity he has to use language is a *capacity* only. In order to *realise* this capacity by the acquisition of the patterns of a natural language he must become part of a language-using group so that there is the substance of a language in use for his capacity to work upon.

An example may help to illustrate this key point in our argument. Most readers of this book can be supposed to possess a latent physical capacity which they could use if they wished to learn how to swim or how to play a musical instrument, but it is highly likely that some readers do not in fact swim, or play a musical instrument, because at a critical point in their development they either did not have access to swimming pools or musical instruments, or they did not feel any particular desire to engage in these activities. The presence of an appropriate context, both physical and cultural, is a key factor in realising human capacity. It may well be that the readers who have not realised their capacity to swim or to play a musical instrument are those who grew up in the years before swimming pools became a feature of most towns and playing musical instruments became a fairly normal part of the activities of schools.

Now, just as it is easier for a potential swimmer to realise his capacity in a town with a swimming pool, swimming clubs and an active interest in swimming, so there are some human contexts which actively encourage language learning while there are others that may severely inhibit the process. The inhibiting capacity of many human contexts is a major theme of this book to be taken up in the later chapters. What must be said here is that for a human being to realise his capacity to language, not only must he be physically undamaged, but also he must have a proper human context in which to exercise his capacity. This context is provided by the human group into which he is born and the community of which that human group is a part.

As far as the child is concerned it is immaterial whether the language used by that community is English or French or Swahili, or whether there is one, or more than one, language being spoken within it. His capacity is a general capacity and can be used on whatever language or languages his community presents to him. A particularly clear example of this general capacity is the fact that all well-formed infants are physically capable of making any of the sounds used by any of the world's natural languages. Indeed, at an early stage in his development, the infant 'practises' a whole range of sounds in the process of focusing upon those that are used by the adults who surround him. Later, however, the sounds that he does not hear spoken in his own environment are 'forgotten' as he comes to master the sound patterns of the language he is learning.

One way of approaching this question of the child's general capacity to learn language is to look, not at what happens in a 'normal' situation, but instead at what can happen in a situation where the child does possess his normal human capacity to learn language, but is *not* given the necessary context of human language activity in which this capacity can be realized. Such situations, where a child is deprived totally of a proper human environment

173

are few but they are now known to exist. In very many countries we have, preserved in myth and legend, accounts of children reared by animals. At the same time, we now have, in addition, authenticated accounts from the nineteenth and twentieth centuries of so-called 'feral' children, that is, children who have spent their formative years growing up in a non-human environment. We can reconstruct something of what must happen in these cases. In the first place, if a child is cared for by an animal it will be in contact with that animal and with other animals in the flock or herd or pack. The sounds and movements, tastes and smells of this animal world are in no way 'strange' to the child, for every child is born into an equally unknown world, whether its home is a high-rise flat in England, a peasant cabin in Central Spain, a long house in Borneo or a wolf's den. No matter where a child is born, it is surrounded by unknowns. The fact that part of the process of learning to be human requires a child to make sense of these unknowns has lead at least one American psychologist, George Kelly, to suggest that 'Man is a problem-solving animal'. This would certainly help to explain how incredibly rapidly human infants learn to make sense of their different environments and to use the patterns of language they discover within them. Kelly's suggestion also helps us to see how a human infant could survive in the context of a wolf-pack by learning rapidly what was required of him as a wolf. We can illustrate this by looking at what would be likely to happen to his general capacity to language, were he to find himself in this non-human environment. He would apply this general capacity to the sounds of the pack which surround him and which do have meaning in that context. He learns to make and use the sounds of the pack just as he would were he working with the speech sounds of a human environment. Just as every child on the road where this book is being written knows the meaning of four off-key notes used by the local ice-cream man to signal his arrival, so the feral child will learn very quickly the meaning of such sounds as danger calls. He will also have the capacity to make these calls when he has learnt both how to make the appropriate sound and how to recognise the appropriate context in which the sound will have meaning. What is happening is that the human child is using his general capacity to acquire language, and to 'problem-solve', but he is using them in a *non-human* environment. What this means, ultimately, is that the human child cannot in fact become fully human, because he has not had a human environment from which

174

to learn the language and behaviours which distinguish human beings from animals. The feral child cannot, because of his situation, become an effective human being, but he can in many senses become a very good wolf!

By focusing on this abnormal situation we have tried to show what we mean when we say that a child is born with a general capacity to acquire language. The environment in which that capacity is able to operate will vary enormously from child to child, but the capacity itself has well-defined characteristics which do not vary. No two human beings are exactly the same, even monozygotic twins, but for every well-formed human being we can quote a list of necessary features; one head, two arms, two legs, two eyes, one nose, one mouth, two ears and so on. There is, in fact, a basic design for human beings carried by the genetic programme for the species. Locally, in response to certain conditions, individual features of the design may be modified. For example, Andean Indians living at high altitudes have a much larger chest capacity than Chileans living at sea-level; some desert dwelling peoples have a thick epicarthic fold over the eyes which acts like a built-in sunshield; some desert-dwelling tribes also have the capacity to store fat in the buttocks, but nevertheless we accept that all human beings have chests, eyebrows and buttocks. Similarly, every child is born with the capacity to learn language and to use the language so acquired in order to make sense of the world into which it is born. How it does this, and with what success, and in what environment, are subject to variation and modification. What is *not* open to modification in a well-formed human being is the actual capacity to do both these things; to learn language and to make sense of the world.

2. Language is not just 'words'

In the last section we suggested that a human infant is genetically equipped to learn language providing that it is not handicapped in any way, either by damage or physical deformity or by extreme deprivation in terms of its experience of a human environment. We were making the fundamental, if obvious, point that language can only be learnt through the child's involvement in an environment where adults are using language in the course of their everyday life. To hear language spoken in the environment is certainly an essential for the developing child, but language is more than words and sounds, it is also *meanings*. Hearing language

175

spoken, of itself, however, is not going to give the child the opportunity either to make meanings or to acquire language.

Let us look at one brief instance of a child learning how meanings and words go together. Some months ago I was visited by an eighteen-month-old girl and her mother. I offered the little girl some orange juice and while her mother used the telephone I suggested that she come with me to the kitchen to fetch it. The little girl began to follow me, but on the way she stopped short at a waste paper basket containing among other things the previous day's newspaper. This she carefully picked out and spread over a large area of carpet. When satisfied with her work she sat down in the middle of the papered area and said with a questioning tone 'Orange juice?'. I was so interested in what she was doing that I had forgotten all about the orange juice. At this point Victoria's mother explained to me that as they had moved into a new house with new carpets six months after Victoria was born, spreading a newspaper was a standard procedure before orange juice. For Victoria, 'orange juice', 'drink' and 'newspaper' were all known elements in a situation which had occurred many, many times even in her brief eighteen months' experience of living. She had learnt not only to make the sounds which others would identify as 'orange juice' but she had learnt also that these sounds signified the drink she wished for, and, more than that, by pronouncing them she could cause others to produce the drink. Victoria had learnt two crucial things; that objects have names and that the correct saying of a name is a form of action. She had both seen and touched and drunk 'orange juice' and discovered that these sounds would produce the drink. In other words, her learning what those words mean was a function of experience, involving the active deployment of the words themselves and her accurate observation of their effects upon others. In addition to this, Victoria had learnt implicitly an important piece of information about the behaviour of people in her community. Her mother's insistence on spreading a newspaper before eating or drinking had made available to her in a concrete form the abstract idea of 'cleanliness' without there being any need for her to meet the abstract noun itself.

It would be quite splendid if at this point we could devise a situation in which the reader divested himself of the enormous experience he has of making sense of the world, so that he could see how it is that a human infant has to be involved in *using* the language he experiences in the course of daily life if he is to 'make

176

meanings' successfully out of what he hears about him. We cannot do this, of course, but what we can do is ask the reader to imagine situations in which he, as an experienced adult, might well have difficulty in using language. This would bring him a little closer to the world of the child, a world where at first *everything* is an unknown and is to be made sense of. The most obvious situation for the adult analogous to that of the child is the adult's experience of a context in which the language used is entirely unknown to him. Let us imagine, for example, the average Englishman travelling in Greece or India or China. What is interesting here is to observe *where* the difficulties arise. If, for example, we send our Englishman to buy vegetables in a market he may well do quite an effective job, despite his inability to speak Greek or Hindi or Cantonese. Because he is an adult with experience of his own community, he does have a knowledge of a wide range of *contexts*. All Englishmen have some knowledge of buying and selling, of money and goods, and the ideas of exchange and value. Many Englishmen perhaps could make good use of one part of the interaction going on in the marketplace, for whereas they would not understand the verbal part of the interaction, they might well be able to make sense of the non-verbal part, the gestures, the pointing, the shrugging of shoulders, the shaking of heads, the walking away. Thus, by using his knowledge of buying and selling *in his own community* together with what he knows about the way human beings behave, our Englishman could probably cope quite well with this situation even though he does not have access to the language in question. He would be using for this, however, experience which a child simply does not have. The cumulative experience of buying and selling, of value and exchange, as well as his experience of interpreting the non-verbal behaviour which invariably accompanies face-to-face language activity, all of which is taken for granted by the adult, *is not available to the child*. In a comparable situation, the child has to work to master the whole of this complex interrelationship of language, concept and action. What for the adult is 'obvious' is, for the child, the product of years of hard work.

Assuming that our adult has been successful in the market place we might interview him to find out a little more about *how* he managed. It is likely that in this context an Englishman would comment on the 'excitability' of the Greeks or the 'inscrutability' of the Chinese. What this information leads us to focus upon is the idea that, though certain elements of non-verbal behaviour were recognised by our Englishman, he did not consider them as being 'the same' as those he was accustomed to in his own community. To him the exuberant way the Greeks use their hands, arms and shoulders when bargaining would seem very much more demonstrative than his own limited use of his hands to convey meaning. Similarly he might well find the limited use of facial expression by the Chinese was so much *less* than his own use of facial movements as to seem to him devoid of any 'expression' at all. There is as wide a variation between communities in the patterns of their non-verbal behaviour as there is between the patterns of the individual languages those communities speak. Moreover, these differences in the patterns of non-verbal behaviour emphasise the fact that what the child does learn is very closely tied to the community in which he must learn it.

At this point, let us return to our Englishman abroad. Having coped fairly successfully with the activities of the market place, let us now imagine him seated at a formal lecture on agricultural methods. Here he is not required to participate, merely to listen. Virtually the entire language activity of the situation is *linguistic*, that is, the language activity provides minimal clues to its meaning beyond the patterns of the language itself, patterns which are wholly unavailable to the listener in this case. Even if there are photographs of yams and mounds, rice plants and paddy fields, tobacco leaves and drying racks, how can he make the connections between these things and the sounds the lecturer utters? One might go a stage further and submit this adult to a lecture on company law, or Marxism, or predestination, subjects where little by way of visual aid could be provided. At this point, our adult would have one thing in common with the human infant, the meaning of the language activity in its entirety would be inaccessible to him. Only from the repetition and demonstration which is a part of everyday life in a normal human environment can the child start to make some kind of sense from a whole series of related unknowns. It is through experiencing the pattern and repetition of events around him, and in being drawn into these events, that a child can begin to make sense of the relationship between these events and the language activity that occurs in conjunction with them. Only in this way can an abstract idea like 'cleanliness' be conveyed to a very young child through newspapers and orange juice. A half hour's explanation, however well meant, would fail with the child, just as a lecture in a foreign language fails for an adult who does not have access to the particular set of meanings which we call a language.

178

3. 'He didn't say a word'

In the second section of this chapter we said something about the immense task which confronts every child in the course of learning language. By asking the reader to imagine situations where his accumulated knowledge of his own language and his experience of its use was only marginally useful to him, we hoped to show the scale of the task the child undertakes. What is involved goes far beyond a mere facility to reproduce the sounds and patterns of sounds that the child continuously hears about him. These patterns of sounds must be related to patterns of 'meanings' and it is only by a child's involvement in the language activity of concrete situations that he can make for himself the crucial connection between sounds and meanings. Even the patterns of non-verbal behaviour, the varied movements and gestures of face and body that are so essential an element in the total pattern of 'meanings' our language creates, have to be learnt by the child.

If we accept that language learning is indeed a complex activity, and if we also accept and admire the great success of the majority of children in coming to terms with it, then it is not unreasonable for us to ask why it is that children who have performed quite remarkable feats of learning can on occasions discover that they are unable to find language. It is upon this inability to find language to meet particular situations that this last section is focused.

If we are to consider why a system fails to operate we must consider first of all how the system operates in the first place. In this case what we must look at is the way in which human beings process their experience of the world, because their knowledge of how to use language in any particular situation derives from their total experience of the world.

Let us begin by looking again at the world which the human infant encounters at birth. It is a world full of tastes, sounds, shapes, feelings, people and objects. As we said earlier, none of these things are known to the child, he has to 'make meanings' from them and for them. We might almost say that the child has to start making a vast card index system without actually knowing what to write on the cards. There is no doubt that the child does something with all the information he receives from the moment of birth and if to some readers the analogy of a 'card index system' sounds 'inhuman' or 'mechanical', then perhaps we should look briefly at the kind of information given us in recent years by

179

research into the functioning of the brain. In his book, *The Machinery of the Brain*, Dean Wooldridge shows some sympathy towards those who find the idea of the brain as a machine rather an unpleasant one. He says:

'In former times the idea that the heart is no more than a complicated pump, which would one day be replaced by a man-made device during a lengthy surgical operation would have seemed as shocking to most people as the modern discoveries that the brain, too, operates in accordance with the physical laws of nature.'

Wooldridge then goes on to describe how the human brain resembles in some respects the electronic digital computer. He says that what is so important about the computer is that 'complex computational and logical operations can be broken down into steps that can be handled by very simple processing elements'. Another way of putting this is to say that a complex end result can be achieved by a very large number of relatively simple steps.

Most readers of this book will be familiar with the idea that computers can handle vast quantities of information very quickly. What is perhaps not so generally known is that the actual calculations performed by computers are very simple. The impressive end-results produced by the computer are impressive because of the multiplicity of simple actions which the computer can perform very, very quickly. Consider now the enormous volume of information about the world, about people and actions and things, which the child's early years present to him through his membership of a human community. From this continuous flow of experience, at first wholly new and then, frequently, a bewildering mixture of new and old, unfamiliar and familiar, puzzling and certain, he takes what he needs to build up for himself the complex pattern of meanings we imply when we speak of our ability to understand, or to make sense of, the world about us. Only if we assume a truly remarkable capacity upon the part of the brain for recording, sifting, relating and storing the information this experience presents to us can we account for the rapidity with which the child reveals his capacity to interpret his experience accurately.

In itself, this activity upon the part of the child should astonish us, but there is a further point which has to be taken into account when we think of these early years, a point which adds considerable force to the analogy we have drawn between the brain and
180

the computer. Parallel with this process of making 'meanings' out of the information provided by his experience, and intimately bound up with it, the child has been using his capacity to learn language. Indeed, we would suggest that the making of meanings and the learning of language are so closely connected with each other that we ought not to think of two distinct processes, one concerned with meaning and the other with language, but rather one single process in which there is a continuous interplay between meanings and language. The traditional idea that language exists so that we can put our thoughts into words, that language is the dress of, or vehicle for, thought, too readily encourages the parallel idea that language itself is empty of meaning, and that meanings, or thoughts are unmodified by the process of languaging them.

If, then, we accept that the child's learning of his language and his learning to make sense of his experience are but two aspects of one inter-related process, then we can stress the degree to which the growth of this process is absolutely central to the child's activities in his early years. The capacity to interpret the world and to relate to others is dependent upon its successful growth and this capacity is the basis of man's survival as man. As we have suggested, this capacity derives from the way in which the brain possesses a spectacular power to process new information and to store it in significant order for future use. It is for this reason that we suggest that the activity of the young child, in interacting with his experience, results in his creating for himself a marvellously subtle computer-based card index system. What the analogy points to is *how* the child is able to deal with the sheer volume of data experience offers him for processing: needless to say, the analogy does not define *what* he does with the data once he has processed it.

It would be a great help to the argument, if, at this point, the reader would bring to the discussion a very valuable body of research material: the recollection of any occasion on which he or she found it impossible to find the language the situation demanded. It is likely that any reader will be able to recall some such occasion, for the inability to use language in a certain situation is, as we hope to show, a normal feature of the way in which we learn language. The following two examples, taken from my own experience will, I hope, help the reader to make his own list of examples.

On one occasion, some years ago, I was staying with a family in a remote part of Donegal while engaged on some field-work.

Living with the family was an elderly man who had been in poor health for some time. One afternoon as I was getting ready to go out, the daughter of the house, a young woman of about twenty-three, stopped me and asked me to come and look at the old man, whom she thought was not looking well. I followed her into the dark back kitchen, where the old man was sitting by the fire, his pipe in his hand. 'Don't you think he looks paler since yesterday?' she asked. I agreed, but could find nothing else to say, for the old man was dead.

A less terrible situation, but none the less difficult for me, arose when I returned rather late from a whole day outing with a group of fourth-formers. As they gathered their belongings and shouted their 'Goodbye', when the coach stopped outside school, their behaviour was a mixture of high spirits, tiredness and thoughtlessness. Unfortunately, the Headmistress was working late. Next morning, after my own interview with her, I had to deliver a strong reprimand, plus a class detention for their 'unruly behaviour'. At the end of my expostulations a girl appeared at my desk with a large bouquet of flowers and carefully delivered a short vote of thanks for the marvellous outing which they had all enjoyed. The vote of thanks was followed by her request for 'Three cheers'.

Whatever situations the last paragraphs may have recalled for the reader they will all have something in common. Firstly, they will all have involved dealing with other people. Secondly, they will have generated in the reader a feeling that there *was* language available to meet the situation but, at the moment when language was required, it just was not there to hand. One of the most frequent comments made by people who recount experiences such as those I quoted above, is, 'Afterwards, I knew what I should have said'. Another frequent comment is, 'If I had thought of x then I would have said y but it just didn't occur to me *at the time.*'

This last statement provides a clue to one of the key elements in any situation in which we use language. By using this particular form of words, the speaker implies that there was something in the situation he had overlooked, or had not taken into account, or was quite unaware of *as a factor that could affect his choice of what to say.* It points to the quite crucial fact that, before we can decide *what* to say in a given context we must 'read' the situation. 'Reading' situations is an activity which adults come to do automatically. There are **many** common language phrases which reveal that

182

adults do observe and note many features of the behaviour of others and choose what they say in order to take account of the results of their observations. For example, they 'size-up the situation', they 'take the feeling of the meeting', they 'see how the land lies'. To help them in their observations, adults have both a long experience of reading situations and a long experience of choosing language appropriate to a given situation. What happens when a speaker declares that he was speechless is not that all words 'disappear' in the way that a single word can sometimes do, but that the speaker, or would-be speaker, has either not been able to 'read' the situation, or having 'read' it, is unable to find anything in his experience that would be a guide as to what words would meet the occasion. Using our analogy of the card index system, we could say that a card had been fed into the system reading 'Conversation with Headmaster, what action?' and a print-out returned saying, 'Sorry, no data available.' The result is a situation that very many men and women can still remember with a mixture of dismay and wry amusement many, many years later.

We are always likely to know what to say, therefore, if the cards we feed into the system are cards which have been fed in before. When a situation occurs in adult life, it is often a recurrence, hence we are seldom speechless, because experience is available in the system and will provide us with an appropriate 'tag for action'. It is significant that those men and women who tell the proverbial story of their first encounter with the Headmaster or Headmistress do not in fact tell a 'second meeting' or 'third meeting' story. However difficult these meetings may have been, they certainly lacked the total newness of the famous first occasion. These subsequent encounters had something to draw upon, and even if the tag then available for linguistic action was incomplete or inadequate, there was at least a tag available.

What we are trying to show is that language and experience are both necessarily products of the individual's life as a member of a human community. By participating in innumerable social situations a child learns to use language: it also learns to read situations. It cannot use language in vacuo; and if it cannot read the situation, it cannot use language effectively. The result of this is that sooner or later a human being will meet a situation new enough to find him with no relevant experience 'in store', situations like the two incidents which rendered this writer speechless. What it is important to see is that it is not children only, or boys

183

and girls, or 'the less able', or *any* one group of human beings, who encounter occasions when they cannot find the language they need, it is *all* well-formed human beings, regardless of age, or ability, or experience.

If we can accept this 'failure' as a simple fact of life, rather than as a value judgment, or as a source of anxiety, we will be in a position to make use of the valuable information about our capacity to language that this particular facet of human behaviour gives to us. What it shows us is that we can most easily use language in those contexts with which we are totally familiar; and that we can least easily use language in those contexts with which we are totally unfamiliar. It would also seem that the more often we have to cope with the new and the unfamiliar the more adept we become at coping with it 'on our feet'. Who has not said to himself at one time or another, 'Well, I never saw myself coping with that', or 'I had an awful time at the beginning, but now it doesn't bother me at all.' Most readers of this book will have experienced a period of adaptation to a new situation where new ways of speaking were needed, like going to a secondary school or to an institute of higher education. There may well have been 'speechless' occasions to begin with, but ultimately these were probably overcome, because enough time was available for the reader to build up the necessary experience in the contexts concerned. For the writer, the task of presenting an account of my own class-room work with *Language in Use* to audiences of teachers, showed me clearly that years of teaching and lecturing were only of marginal assistance to me when I was asked *for the first time* to talk about my own work. I might well have been 'speechless' had I not had advance warning of this new task or had I not had a number of friends on whom I could 'practise'.

To sum up, then, we can say that, if a child is born into a community in one part of the world at one moment in time, it will learn the ways of speaking and the ways of behaving of that group of people at that time. It will learn to make sense of the world and to learn language simultaneously. The two processes will be intimately related to each other and the whole experience will be stored by the brain, perhaps like a card index system, but certainly in such a way as to make it possible for the individual to make use of the information he has stored in order to meet the needs of the recurrent human situations in which he finds himself called upon to act and to language. What the child has available in this index is the result of its accumulated experience of its own

184

community. The store can be large or small in comparison to what is potentially available in that community, but what it cannot be is all-inclusive. There will always be situations occurring for that child in that community which are 'unknown' to it, that constitute a 'first time ever' in terms of its already existing experience.

For those of us who are concerned with teaching and learning, 'speechlessness' is a major concern. It is one of the main themes of this book to show that, though we may want to control this 'speechlessness', we can only do this by a fuller understanding of how language works, an understanding which has no place for the idea of 'failure' in relation to the child's, or the pupil's, inability to find language appropriate to the demands of the situations we put him in.

2   Community

1. What do we mean by 'community'?

The trouble about the word 'community' is that we all know
what it means, or, more accurately, we can all derive from our
individual experience of our own community a meaning for this
word. It is not surprising that this should be the case, because
'community' is a common language word like 'school' or 'teacher'
or 'kindness' or 'teatime', and the specific 'meaning' any one of us
gives to such words as these arises from the particular experience
we have had. In a society as complex and diverse as ours, these
words can refer to a very wide range of 'meanings'. Before we go
on to discuss 'community', therefore, a word about the relationship
between words and meanings would be helpful to the argument.
To some readers, it may perhaps seem that too great an emphasis
is being laid on the fact that words mean what we have learnt
them to mean. To them, it is 'obvious' that 'house' means 'house'
and 'tree' means 'tree'; and that meaning difficulties only occur
when one is dealing with non-standard language, or with a local
dialect or with an uneducated or unintelligent person. Many
years of field work in different communities, and many years of
teaching in different schools, have lead me to a much less opti-
mistic view of our general ability to share meanings with others.
For example, when a mother says to a child in a working-class
street in Oldham, a nineteenth-century industrial town near
Manchester, 'Go in the house', she is in fact sending the child into
the main room of the dwelling. 'The house' in this case *means*
'living-room' and it is not surprising that infant teachers in Oldham
report that children, when they first come to school 'cannot draw
houses'. Some of these teachers are happy when, some weeks later,
these same infants are drawing detached houses with four windows,
a central door and a tree growing outside, despite the fact that, as
186

one Oldham teacher put it to me, 'They all live in two-windowed terraced houses and there isn't a tree for miles!' What these children have done is to learn a new meaning for 'house', because 'house' at school is different from 'house' at home.

There is a similar tale to tell with 'tree'. Talking to an old man in a desolate part of Western Ireland I said conversationally, 'I suppose it is because of the wind that you have so few trees?' 'Ah, no, miss,' he replied. 'It's the size of the houses. Sure they're so small they have no need of more trees.' He was, in fact, referring to parts of the timber framework of the roof of his house, the only 'trees' with any relevance to his world. Let me offer one final example, one in which it is hoped the reader will participate himself by checking what meaning he himself would give to the chosen words, both now and in his childhood.

Some years ago while I was still teaching in Belfast I was asked to 'cover' an English class for an absent colleague. My instructions were simple; I was to make the group of eleven-year-olds write something. Having asked them what they would like to write about and been told that they didn't like writing because it was too difficult, I decided to try to encourage them by making the writing into a game. We chose three every-day words which they said they could write about and we decided to see at the end of half an hour if they had all written the same thing. The three items chosen were 'tea', 'bun' and 'ticket'. It would not be true to say that we had as many variations as we had eleven-year-olds, but the range of meaning was indeed thought-provoking. 'Tea' to them was everything, from a beverage which some of them did not drink to the name of the main meal of the day, eaten at 6 o'clock in the evening. For some 'tea' was a social occasion which only took place in the context of visiting relatives on Sunday afternoons: for others it was a picnic in the hayfields when they visited country relatives and were given the job of 'taking the men their tea'. My own piece of writing on the life-saving qualities of tea at the end of school was not paralleled by anyone else, even though many of them did in fact have a cup of tea when they arrived home from school. 'Ticket' and 'bun' both produced a similar kind of variation; for some 'ticket' was a necessary feature of getting to school by bus, for others it meant entertainment of every kind from football to ballet, for one it meant her father's parking problems.

It was, however, 'bun' that produced the variation that intrigued the class most. Many of them wrote as I did, about the

187

various kinds of small cakes that are a fairly standard feature of home-baking in Northern Ireland, but one girl baffled the class by saying that she often had a bun with ham in it for supper. She was the only girl in the room who was not born in Northern Ireland and for her 'bun' was a flat bread cake which could be split and filled to make a savoury snack. Had I been engaged in a social survey, the meanings provided by thirty eleven-year-olds would have given me a wealth of information about socio-economic groupings, use of leisure, patterns of eating and social relationships. As it was, it sharpened my awareness of the effect community can have in mediating between a word and its meaning. It is for this reason that throughout this book we will try to be explicit about what we mean, for only by doing this can we give the reader the opportunity to test for himself whether what is being said makes sense.

We begin with a straightforward definition of 'community': a community is a group of people who live in geographical proximity to each other and who, through their work, or worship, or way of life, or any combination of these three, feel a sense of 'us-ness' when they compare themselves with any other group of people. If we break down our definition phrase by phrase we can look more closely at its different elements and see how they fit together. What can we say about geographical proximity? It certainly seems reasonable that if people live near enough to be in daily contact with each other, then they have the opportunity to share a whole range of common experience. There is no doubt that in many areas where community feeling is very well developed, people do in fact live very close to each other in this sense. This is particularly the case in some of the urban, industrial housing areas where a group of tightly packed streets will correspond with a close-knit community life. A recent outstanding account of community life of this kind is to be found in Robert Roberts' account of Salford, Manchester, at the turn of the century, *The Classic Slum* (Penguin). However, if we ask the question, 'Does proximity alone generate community?' the evidence we have would seem to say 'No'. Many British sociologists are concerned with the way people respond to geographical proximity and among these the work of Ruth Durrant is particularly interesting. Ruth Durrant has studied some of the large new housing estates in Britain, where people have been brought together from all parts of the country by the availability of house and jobs. What she says is that, unless there is some common objective, like the

188

improvement of living conditions, or the avoidance of increased rents, then there is no incentive for these people to act together and they do not make contact with each other. On the other hand, where people who already have an active community life are moved to a new estate, as with the London East Enders moved to North London, they will make every effort to maintain their contacts, despite the fact that distances between individuals on the new estates may be much greater than in the previous environment. Much of the unhappiness caused by resettlement has grown from the different meanings of 'nearness', as understood in the community of the people being resettled, and as assumed 'obvious' by the planners.

Why then does proximity not automatically generate community? The answer lies in the other phrases of our definition. Indeed, we would suggest that sharing a geographical location is much less important in terms of human relationships than sharing even the simplest activity or idea. Let us look then at 'work or worship or way of life'.

There is no doubt that some of the most clearly distinguishable communities in Britain grow out of the context of shared work. If we look at the mining villages of Durham or South Wales, at the textile areas of some of the big cities like Manchester or Leeds, at the farming communities, or the small fishing ports, we can see a very strong sense of 'us-ness' at work in them. It is not surprising that a group of people whose life is focused on a mine, a mill, a farm or a boat will share a whole range of activities with those similarly occupied. In particular the traditions of miners are often pointed to as a group expression of the anxieties of a difficult and dangerous activity, where co-operation is an essential part of life. The miner can best share his feelings with another miner, his stories will mean more to another miner, his jokes, his ways of speaking, his view of the world will all make more immediate sense to another miner than to a textile worker, a farmer or a fisherman. It is because of this shared activity that a shared way of thinking about the world, a shared body of assumptions and attitudes towards every aspect of living, develops, and it is the lack of any real basis for shared activity that keeps the housing estate dwellers from making contact with their neighbours.

At this point it is difficult to continue without asking a prior question, 'And how is it that men carry on this shared activity that supports the shared thinking that is the basis of community?'

189

This is an enormous question. For the moment we will offer one part of the answer only in the form of a single remark from the anthropologist, Malinowski:

'*Language* is the link in concerted human activity.'

In this one sentence, Malinowski requires us to focus unambiguously upon one crucial, and obvious, aspect of community: that man's activities as a social being are possible only because he has language. Moreover, this view of the social function of language is not confined to the more apparent forms of collective activity like mining, fishing or textile working. It also embraces the collective action that expresses our shared feeling with others just as much as our shared work. Perhaps the most immediate example of this is the part religious belief can play in creating the basis of a communities shared experience of the world.

From this point of view, it does not matter whether we consider Jews, Hindus, Catholics, Moslems, Presbyterians, Anglicans, Mormons, or any other of the thousands of named religious groups we have in the world. The common factor in all of them is that those who share a system of belief share also a body of common experience which they do not share with anyone else. We can put it this way: there is a great deal more to religious belief than the joint performance of religious rites, such as we associate with church, mosque, or synagogue. This is because a system of belief, like a religion, is concerned not only with the practice of certain rites but with the events of everyday life. A Jewish woman from a wealthy home, will, if she is a practising Jew, be infinitely easier in the kitchen of a very poor Jewish woman than in the kitchen of a wealthy non-Jewish person. The reason is that in a non-Jewish home she is unlikely to find the two sets of saucepans, without which she cannot observe the Jewish food law which requires that the utensils for preparing milk and meat be kept separate from each other. Similarly, a Free Presbyterian farmer from the Scottish Isles is going to be very upset by the gaiety of Sunday visitors to his island where a particular kind of solemnity is observed on that day. The reader will certainly be able to supply his own examples, but, whatever the belief concerned, it will show that 'belief' involves individuals in sharing a whole range of attitudes and assumptions about everyday life, that is, the life of the community, and that whether the belief involves the purdah of women, the sacredness of all forms of life, or the sinfulness of eating beans, it is providing a fundamental basis for '. . . con-
190

certed human activity' in the same way as the work of the mine, the mill, the farm or the boat.

Finally, we come to 'way of life'. What we must focus on here is the fact that there are communities in existence in Britain where one can find a very wide range of employment and an equally wide range of beliefs or lack of beliefs, and still apply the term 'community', because the 'us-ness' of our definition is felt by the people concerned. What we have here is something which we might not have been able to find a hundred years ago in Britain: people who have worked out how they want to live their life, what sort of house they want, what facilities they want, what kind of surroundings they want, and they have sought out a place which meets all these requirements. They have chosen to live where they live for reasons which, we can say, form part of their belief system, their basis for taking one view of the world rather than another. For this reason the people they live beside share the same beliefs, because they too have come for the same reasons. There are many examples of this kind of community in the more expensive housing developments in the commuter belts to the north and south of London. In most cases, these communities are uniformly what we can call crudely 'middle-class', partly because they attract people from this socio-economic group and partly because newcomers who choose to come, and who have the requisite economic base to do so, quickly adopt the ways of behaving and the values of the existing community. So instead of sharing work, or religious belief, these people share a body of secular views about how one should live, how one's children should be educated, how one should spend leisure, what sort of possessions one should value, and so on; and this provides that feeling of 'us-ness' which is a defining characteristic of community. These people, like those who share work, or who share belief, will have more in common with each other at a fundamental level than with any other group

So far in this section we have shown that community exists where there is sharing of *either* work or worship or way of life. The extent of what is shared differs widely between communities and there are some communities, perhaps the most close-knit of all, that certainly share *all* the possibilities we have mentioned. Consider, for example, the Scottish, Hebridean, Presbyterian fishermen who share not only their work, and their religious views, but also their small and relatively isolated geographical location, their long history as a sea-faring community, their tradition of story-telling and their hard and demanding way of life, as well as many of the individual features of day to day living, even as detailed as the the stitches used by each fisherman's wife when knitting his heavy wool sweaters, or the custom of offering non-alcoholic drinks to low status visitors and alcoholic drinks to high-status visitors.

This last example leads us to an extension of our original definition of community in order to accommodate the fact that what human beings can share with each other is diverse and complex; and that crucial as is 'work, worship and way of life', in creating human communities, there is much more to be said about the detailed patterning of that context. What the sociologist or anthropologist would say is that a community exists when it is possible to point to a group of people and say that they share a common 'culture'. 'Culture' is another word like 'community' which can be used to mean different things. The sense in which we use it here has been very clearly defined by Sir Edward Tyler, the British anthropologist. He suggests that:

'Culture is that complex whole that includes morals, art, laws, knowledge, belief, custom and any other habits acquired by man.'

Given this definition we can see what an enormous scope for variety this will present from community to community.

Consider two communities we might find in Great Britain. One is a peasant-farming, Catholic, conservative, Irish speaking matriarchal, close-knit community with a tradition now of playing hurley, remaining teetotal and agitating for the increase of hill-farm subsidies. The other is a Methodist, Labour-voting, Welsh-speaking, patriarchal, loose-knit community, occupied with a variety of light industries and much given to drinking, lay-preaching and singing in choirs. Both these communities are invention, but all the elements which go to make them up are real elements which do exist in actual existing communities: what the invention does is show the potential for variation.

It is with this variation in mind that I would now ask the reader to think back to the last part of Chapter 1. We had been talking about the fact that however well-developed a person's capacity to use language might be in one particular context, he might still encounter 'speechlessness' when presented with a 'first time ever' experience in which he was required to use language. What I actually said in Chapter 1 was:

'What a child has available in this index is the result of its accumulated experience of its own community. The store can be

192

large or small in comparison to what is potentially available in that community, but what it cannot be is all-inclusive. There will always be situations occurring for the child in that community which are "unknown" to it, that constitute a "first time ever" in terms of existing experience.'

What I would now want to add to that statement in Chapter 1 is a further comment, a comment which the theme of this first part of Chapter 2 has tried to clarify. It is:

and what will meet the child's needs for living and working in *one* community may have little relevance to meeting the needs of living and working in another.

Much more will be said about this particular question. What we must now go on to consider in the next section is how it is that a group of people, living in a particular place, at a particular time, create by their constant interaction with each other, and with the world outside, a way of seeing, a way of thinking, and a way of languaging that is so intimate and personal to that community that an outsider can meet the linguistic demands of the situations he encounters in that community only with difficulty and practice, even though he possesses the same mother tongue, and indeed inhabits the same city or town or village.

2. Learning to be a member of your own community.

'No, John, don't hit Helen, she's your sister. No, John, don't hit Stephen he's smaller than you. John, let Stephen play with your truck, you mustn't be selfish. No. Don't load it up with mud. You'll get all dirty. Helen, put that gun away. Little girls don't play with guns. Where is your doll's pram?'

Most readers will be able to place fairly easily the context in which the foregoing piece of monologue was recorded. A 'middle-class' mother in a suburban garden is intervening in the play of three children under five. What this mother is *doing* is something which is done by every adult who regulates the behaviour of a child, whether that adult is an East European 'babuska', a Samoan mother, an aborigine father, or a children's nurse from any country the reader may choose to name. What the mother is *saying* is a very different matter and we shall consider that a little later on.

At this point in our discussion, it is quite impossible to separate 'language' from our thinking about 'community', even temporarily, because it is through the use of language by adults that a child both learns his language and 'learns his community'. The adults in a child's environment provide him with a constant supply of information as they go about their everyday affairs. They already exist in a group with established relationships and ways of speaking and they draw the child into this world by interacting with him. The word 'interact' is not here used as another way of saying 'talk to'. If children were only 'talked to', they would remain very much in the position of the adult in the last chapter who attended the lecture on agricultural methods delivered in a foreign language. 'Interact' means a great deal more than this for it insists that we treat *all* language activity between people, face-to-face, as activity which involves a two-way process. Here, it implies that we must see the child involved in a dialogue in the course of normal everyday events where he is encouraged to respond, and where his response is listened to or observed. The encouragement to respond may indeed come in the form of the kisses and cuddles of the baby-books, but it is just as likely to involve impatience, or irritation, or sharp command. What is important for the child is that these responses should be made available to him so that he can experience them in the context of his own actions. It would be fair to say that the really deprived child is not the one who has to tolerate a high degree of fairly harsh regulation, but the child who is ignored, left alone, tidied away, for this child is the one deprived of that constant stream of feed-back upon his own words and actions which adults alone can supply in the course of their interaction with him.

The extract with which I began this section is an example of using language to regulate behaviour. It relates to one mother in one particular community, but it is at the same time representative of that 'constant stream of feed-back' that adults supply to children in' *all* communities. It is from the information this feed-back supplies that the child not only learns his language in terms of its semantics, grammar and phonology, but learns also the values of the community in which he lives, because these values are embedded in the language.

How can this be so? How can a language carry the values of a community in such a way that learning a language automatically involves learning a set of values? Let us look now at what the middle-class mother was *saying* as she regulated the play of the three children and take each sequence in turn.

'No John don't hit Helen, she's your sister. No John, don't hit Stephen, he's smaller than you.'

This mother is expressing the view that there should not be discord between brothers and sisters; and that hitting someone smaller than yourself is unacceptable behaviour. We have to say that here, in however simple a form, she is expressing a moral view about the use of physical violence against others and the possible recipients of such violence. John will have to find out on another occasion whether he can, in fact, hit someone who is (*a*) the same size as he is; (*b*) bigger than he is; (*c*) a girl, but not his sister.

'No don't load it up with mud, you'll get all dirty.'

Here the mother is expressing a view regarding what is appropriate and what is not. One might draw from her words the simple conclusion that dirty clothes mean more work for mothers. However, in an age of washing machines and anthropological studies of the symbolic meaning of everyday things this seems too simple a view. As far as we know, no human community is without its taboos on dirt, although what constitutes 'dirt' varies from community to community. One might hazard a guess that this particular mother associates dirty hands and faces with a social group with which she does not want to be associated through the actions of her children. All that we wish to do here is to show that a commonplace command about getting dirty may carry much more symbolic significance for the speaker, and hence have a much deeper meaning for the child, than the mere surface sense of the words spoken might suggest.

'Helen put that gun away. Little girls don't play with guns. Where is your doll's pram?'

In this final comment the mother expresses another view of 'rightness'. In her world, boys play with guns, girls play with doll's prams, just as in a very different community girls concern themselves with digging sticks and boys with bows and arrows. 'Gun' for this mother must have a powerful meaning to provoke such an immediate response. It might be fair to suggest that gun/doll's pram represents concretely for this mother a much deeper categorisation of feelings and emotions than simply what John and Stephen and Helen can play with. In her value system little girls should be 'tender', 'sensitive', 'soft' or 'made of sugar and spice and all things nice' perhaps, as the nursery rhyme and the main stream of woman's magazines would have it. They should not demonstrate aggressiveness, forcefulness, or strong control over others for these are the attributes of little boys. In this context, the gun is a symbol for the mother of all those ways of behaving that her culture leads her to assess as proper for males. So she reacts to 'gun' and substitutes 'doll's pram', for 'doll's pram' in its turn is an objective correlative for those values which this mother wishes her daughter to acquire in forming her view of herself as a female in this same culture.

In this action our South Manchester, suburban, middle-class mother is behaving as any other mother in the same social group might behave. She might well be surprised to find that her action would be fully understood and sympathised with by adults in vastly different communities. For example, there are many hunting tribes where a girl-child touching any object connected with hunting requires an elaborate ritual for avoiding the bad luck that is believed to follow from such an action. This is not the place to explore further why it is that all human groups make the kind of categorisations represented by the gun and the doll's pram in this instance. The universality of this connection between rules and meanings, however, is what we need to recognise, because such rules and their meanings are perpetuated by being passed on through the language used to control each succeeding generation. In this way each adult participates actively in perpetuating the values of the community to which he belongs.

If we take another extract, one which is far removed, geographically and socially, from the one we have been using we can illustrate this similarity of adult action, a similarity that can well be concealed by the vast dissimilarity in what the two adults are actually saying. The following extract was recorded in an area of run-down nineteenth-century housing near the Belfast school where I used to teach.

'What's wrong with you then, whinging there in the house, away out and play—who hit you—Willie Taggart indeed—well why didn't you hit him a kick, yer as big as he is—stand up for yerself and be a man—d'ye want everyone to think yer a wee girl?'

From what this mother says to her child we can in fact work out that she responds to violence quite differently from the mother in our earlier example. For this mother, the use of violence towards others is a defining characteristic of 'being a man'. In fact, we can go so far as to say that she makes it obligatory for her son to demonstrate his manliness by 'hitting Willie Taggart a kick'. Failure to do this will make him into a 'a wee girl', an object of derision in his family, in the street, and in the community at large. By implication, it also tells us something about the relative status of men and women in that community, judged merely as male and female. The pressure on the child to accept this norm for his behaviour is overwhelming and it is difficult for the writer, so familiar with the widespread occurrence of this attitude to violence not to point to the Belfast of the early 1970s as an example of the terrifying effectiveness of patterns of language in shaping subsequent patterns of action.

However, whatever one may feel about the values being presented by the two mothers I have quoted, what is important to the argument is to see that the two mothers are indeed *doing* the same thing. They are teaching their children to behave in a way that will identify them as members of the group into which they have been born and they are doing this by using words and phrases that express concretely the values their community has attached to them. Intuitively, both mothers will try to eliminate behaviour that does not 'fit' the values of their community, for the more fully the child learns and accepts the values of the community the more easily will he be accepted as fully a member of it.

All human communities, therefore, find it necessary to use language in this way in order to bring children into the group. In some communities, it is the mother who performs the largest part of the task and it so happens that the examples used above do both focus upon the mother. This situation, however, is not universal. Patterns of child care vary from community to community and in some cases the mother is of little significance; grandmother, aunt or nurse being the key figure. Whatever the actual local situation might be, however, it is important to see that *all* the adults with whom the child has contact contribute to his understanding of the world by demonstrating their attitudes to the events of everyday life. In some groups, the process of bringing children into the community is carried out intuitively by adults. They treat the children in the way that they were themselves treated as children, because this is the 'obvious' or 'natural' or 'only' way to treat them. This is not the case, however, with many of the social groups which exist in the advanced industrial countries like Britain or the U.S.A. In these countries, many adults are well aware of what membership of a particular social group involves and they may go to extreme lengths to ensure that their children identify themselves with the community concerned. This has been a marked feature of many of the immigrant groups

197

from Europe who have established a new home in the U.S.A. It is also demonstrated by the great expense incurred by English middle and upper class parents to ensure that their children's education will give them the 'right' accent, and the 'proper' way of speaking so that there is no danger of them being identified with any group other than their own.

This whole process of bringing the newcomer into the community, this need to ensure that he is taught the rules and meanings by which a community expresses its collective identity, is the process to which contemporary sociology has given the name 'socialisation'. As we have seen, from the point of view of the relationship between language and community, it is a quite crucial process. 'Socialisation' means, literally, 'the making social of', where 'social' means, not 'friendly' or 'sociable', as in the common language, but rather 'able to act in the society of other human beings', or 'able to function in a social context'. Socialisation, from the point of view of John, Stephen and Helen and the nameless victim of Willie Taggart means that they know what is acceptable and unacceptable in the course of their every-day life. They know that 'selfish' is not sharing with others; they know that you do not load mud into a dumper truck when wearing the shoes called 'best'; they know what they should do when faced with the question of using physical force towards others. The process of socialisation has provided them with the capacity to act in the everyday situations which form part of their world. It will be clear to the reader that the more fully informed the child is about the ways of behaving in his community, or, put another way, the more successfully he has been socialised, the easier life will be both for the child and for the community of which he is a member. On the other hand, the more closely a child is socialised into one community the more likely he is to encounter difficulty in adjusting to living in any community other than his own.

It might seem to some readers that the last two sentences constitute part of an argument 'for' or 'against' socialisation. This is not the case As far as this book is concerned socialisation is a fact of life, a fact similar in kind to the failure to meet linguistic needs we spoke of in the last chapter. Socialisation describes an inescapable part of the process of learning to be human, because it describes the consequences of the necessary interaction between the growing child and his only source of explicit information about the world, the adults who surround him and make his survival possible. It is for this reason, therefore, that we must try

198

to understand how socialisation works and what its effects are. If we have any doubts about the importance of the part it plays in the development of the young human being then we have only to consider the sad plight of the autistic child to see what happens if a child is unable to enter into the socialising process.

3. Seeing as the community sees

In the first section of this chapter we focused upon the idea of 'community' and looked at the way in which communities can be so very different from each other while at the same time functioning in such very similar ways. A key concept in this section was the idea that members of a community share a common culture. In the second section we focused upon the way in which newcomers are socialised, thereby ensuring the continuity of the community and its culture.

This final section shows, therefore, how it is that the process of socialisation not only gives the child access to the set of meanings which we call language but also provides him with a set of values, what we might describe as the 'meanings' which realise the culture of the community in terms of possible ways of behaving. Let us begin by focusing again on the process of socialisation.

What makes the task of understanding the process and effect of socialisation so difficult is that we all, both writers and readers, have been socialised, and so understanding this process involves our focusing upon something which is not 'out there', but something which both intimately affects each one of us and of which we may be relatively unaware. For the present writer, one small incident, recurring regularly, helps to remind me of the power of early socialisation. As a child, brought up in the shadow of a strict Scottish Presbyterian, Sunday observance, I was forbidden to manicure my nails on a Sunday. Now, many years later, I still find myself pausing to remember the day when I pick up a nail file or emery board. When such a trivial incident as this can still convey a whole set of meanings after twenty years, what other deeply held notions persist without my full awareness? Perhaps the reader will test this for himself by considering for a few moments some small consequences of his own socialisation. The following questions may be a useful prompt in helping the reader to assess his own experience from this point of view. Those questions that seem quite irrelevant will at least serve the purpose of indicating what was *not* important or significant in his community.

199

Who did you play with as a child? With all children or with some? If you played with some, why not others? Were they too dirty/too snobbish/too far away/not like us/too old/too badly-spoken? Did you play equally with boys and girls? If not, why was this so?
Were you allowed to play every day?
Who were you permitted to hit?
Were you permitted to lend or borrow possessions?
Were you permitted to cry, to talk when you felt like talking, to get dirty, to kiss, to refrain from kissing?

The answers to these, and to many thousands of such questions, will be available to the reader, or certainly were available to him in childhood, for without a long, long, list of answers a child would not be able to cope with even the most seemingly 'simple' and 'obvious' events of everyday life.

Consider, for example the problem of this three year old. While shopping with her mother in a large supermarket, she is offered a peeled banana by a smiling man in a white coat. Mother is pre-occupied with soap-powders and the little girl is quite baffled. The fact that she likes bananas does not help her to assess this situation. Her knowledge of 'taking things' is not adequate for this occasion. Fortunately, at the critical moment, the information supply returns: 'Say, "Thank you" to Mr Jones, Lisa', is accompanied by friendly smiles all round which tell Lisa that this person is acceptable and that bananas may be accepted from him. On the next encounter she will not have to recourse to toe-scuffing shyness in order to cover her dilemma. Like all children, Lisa is dependent for her answers on the language used by adults in her presence: it is from this language, item by item, piece by piece, that she must extract the information she needs, both to master the language for herself and at the same time to master the complexities of social action in her own community. What Lisa must do is build up her knowledge of the culture. Yet we have defined culture as a complex whole that includes morals, art, law, knowledge, belief, and custom—and it may seem to the reader an impossibly long way from a three-year-old's dilemma over a banana in a supermarket to a definition of culture such as this. I must try, however, to show that complex cultural attitudes are involved even in such a 'simple' everyday situation. For example, in the particular community we have been speaking of, the giving of gifts is part of a reciprocal system. A gift may be given in return for a favour of some kind where money would be considered an

200

inappropriate way of acknowledging the debt. A mother may give flowers or chocolates to someone who has looked after the children but who is not a recognised 'baby-sitter': a man might give a bottle of whisky to a friend who had 'spoken' for him in finding a job or a house. But for anything given, there is the implicit idea of an appropriate return. Now, a person giving a banana to a child he knows has his return in the response of the child and of its mother. The gift reinforces the mutual exchange of friendly gestures between the adults concerned. But what of the stranger? His gift to the child would cause anxiety in this community, because, as he does not know the mother, there cannot be the same exchange of friendly gestures. The view of reciprocity held by the community and acquired concretely by the child will raise the question 'What does he want from me in return?' Perhaps we can put it more sharply by asking the reader to work out, from the information given above, what the response would be in this community if a male stranger were to give a gift to this child's attractive mother? So we see that the apparently simple act of giving a banana to a child is in fact an action governed by the morals, beliefs and customs of the community.

Let us try to sum up the significance of this example. We are saying that a child must learn his culture if he is to function successfully in the social situations that make up his active experience of his community. Elsewhere, Tyler suggests that we can think of all the rules and meanings by which a culture is made concrete for the members of a particular community as 'the habits of the tribe'. We can extend this remark and think of an advanced industrial society like our own as a 'tribe of tribes', so that a child has the initial task of learning the habits of his own tribe, or community. At some stage, however, often very early, he is made aware of the fact that 'they' exist: 'they' being the verbal embodiment in his local and particular world of the 'morals, art, law, knowledge etc.' of the larger world of the society of which his own community is but one 'tribe'. At this point, we must recognise the limitations of space and the scope of this book. We cannot go on to show how all the elements in Tyler's definition might be realised concretely in the child's immediate experience and how this would show up in the language activity associated with his learning his culture. Instead we must use the remaining space in this chapter to consider how the sharing of a common culture can affect the members of a community in their contact with the outside world. Let us consider the following.

'Course 'e beats 'is wife, she's 'is wife ain't she? S'only natchral.'

'But my dear, positively no-one goes into town without a hat. It just isn't done.'

'No, now you can't do that at all. Shure isn't that the west side? Whoever heard of anyone building on the west side?'

Here we have three utterances expressing the views of three different speakers on the subject of wife-beating, hat-wearing and house-extending. What the three speakers have in common is a supreme confidence in the truth of what they are saying. The first speaker does not doubt that beating one's wife is appropriate behaviour any more than the second speaker doubts that wearing a hat is appropriate behaviour. The third speaker is similarly convinced that extending a house on the west side is quite unthinkable. It is highly likely that readers of this book may doubt the 'truth' of one or all of these statements, because their own 'truth' is different from what these three have said. What concerns us here, however, is why the speakers express the view that they do and why they are so confident that their view is the only possible one. The answer lies in their communities. All three speakers come from close-knit communities where the view recorded here is shared by everyone. In this case, 'everyone' must be noted as 'everyone in the community', just as 'no-one' must refer to people who are not members of the community. It is palpably untrue that 'no-one' is ever seen in a British town or city without a hat, but it is equally true that there was a time when 'no-one' of a particular social group would indeed allow herself to be seen hatless in the West End of London. If everyone in a community holds the same view, then this view becomes for them the relevant 'truth', because they 'can't conceive' of any alternative mode of action.

In the writer's own culture there is a saying that 'what you never have you never miss'. Basically, the sense of this saying is that, if you have not experienced something you do not miss it, or feel the lack of it. It would seem that the absence of any alternative view of a subject is not missed, indeed not even suspected, by members of a community, and so their view of the case takes on the lineaments of an unquestionable rightness. For example, when the third speaker, a peasant farmer in Western Ireland, wanted to build an extra bedroom on his two-roomed house, he did not even consider building on the west side. Having assured me that 'nobody ever builds on the west side', it took a lot of tactful questioning to reveal that in this community there is a belief that fairy paths always avoided houses by passing on the west side; and that to build across a fairy path would bring bad luck on the whole dwelling. Despite the fact that this farmer also said he did not believe in fairies, he still refused to build on the west side, because it 'just wouldn't be right'.

All adults necessarily hold at least some deeply held views similar to the three views we have quoted above, but children as young as two or three years old already hold well-formed views of the same kind. Indeed, if they did not, they would be quite at a loss in relating themselves to the intimate world of the family around them. Because they cannot yet handle their language well enough to express these views in a way that an adult can easily recognise is not to be taken as a sign that they do not possess the cultural information which is the basis of social decision making. For those of us concerned with teaching and learning, it is not enough to guess at what view a child may be taking of the situations which it encounters in our presence. If we cannot find out from the child himself how he views what we are trying to do, what he considers 'right' or 'natural' or 'obvious', then we must go beyond the class-room and seek the information we need in the child's community. From his community, the child derives the culture upon which he bases his view of the world. If we remain ignorant of that view, our alternative view, especially perhaps our alternative view of school and learning, will defeat all our best endeavours to understand, or to teach, a child who comes from any community other than the one we know most intimately—our own.

3 Language, the individual and his view of the world

1. How we 'see' our world

It is a commonplace of our everyday experience that 'No two people think alike' and an equally common experience that no two people view an event in exactly the same way. Yet here we are maintaining successfully a vast range of 'concerted human activity', living and working in the context of communities that can exist only in so far as we are able to think like each other and to view events from a common standpoint. What we want to explore in this chapter is the apparent contradiction revealed by these two familiar experiences. If we take the first of these experiences and press it too far, we find we have to insist that language is a very poor means of conveying meanings from one person to another. This is a position adopted by a number of contemporary writers, in particular, Samuel Beckett. We are then left with the problem of accounting for, or arguing away, the apparent success with which human beings *do* manage to reach common agreement, time after time, about a multitude of everyday events. On the other hand, if we insist upon language as a means of communication, and take a rather simple view of the meanings involved in that activity, we may well seem to present a picture of language activity so simple that there is no room for our common experience of misunderstanding, or misinterpreting, the words of others. If we are to understand the part language plays in community, and community in maintaining language, then we must offer an account of language as both the means, and the product, of concerted human activity, an account which avoids both the nihilism of the contemporary writer and the glib optimism of the communications engineer.

Let us begin by taking the commonest of examples, one that every reader will be able to match only too well from his own experience. Let us say there has been a fight in the playground and two boys arrive to give their views as to what has happened:

'He came up and shoved me, sir!'
'No I didn't. I just somehow bumped into him and he hit me.'
'I didn't hit him, sir. I just shoved back.'

And so on. Let us say that no question of dishonesty or deceit is involved. Neither of the lads are trouble-makers and they genuinely want to tell the truth *as they see it*. The first and obvious point is that they use different key terms, 'bump' and 'shove'. Both of them accept implicitly that violent physical contact has to be accounted for, but, while they both accept that 'shove' is an aggressive act, justifying retaliation, it looks as if this is the only interpretation the boy who speaks first has available for violent contact of this kind. To him, it must be intentional, therefore aggressive. To the other boy, however, there is an alternative possibility: that collision in a crowded playground can be accidental, and therefore is not culpable. We could say that his ability to choose between 'bump' and 'shove' in accounting for his actions opens up to him an alternative way of seeing the events not available to the other. Had we more text to consider, we might be able to show that this incident implied a deep difference in the way in which the two boys see the world, a difference ultimately related to their different experience of community. We could suggest that the first boy's experience of violent physical contact was such that he 'could not conceive' of its being other than intentional, while the second boy's experience might well suggest that contact of this kind was to be construed as unintentional until proved otherwise.

When we consider the varying reports one reads of a road accident, a political speech, a new film or play, it certainly seems that there is more to 'seeing' than a matter of eyesight or lighting conditions. Even if it were a question of vision in the literal sense we must remember how much of our ability to interpret visual perceptions is a matter of learning *what* to see. It is not the eye that 'sees' but the brain, and the brain has to learn how to see. People, blind from birth, who have had their eyesight restored by surgery cannot in fact 'see'. They have to be taught to make sense of the unrelated shapes and colours which for them do not have meaning. In some sad cases, they have finally been unable to do this. For those of us who do have sight, what we 'see' does have meaning, but that meaning has been learnt in the course of our growing up. Meaning is something which we create by using language to interpret our experience of the world. How we 'see' the things around us, therefore, is very much a product of our using the language that others already use in the environment in which we find ourselves. When we 'see' things, the 'seeing' is a product of our own experience, hence one boy's long experience of shoving and being shoved leads him to see a particular event as a shove, while the other boy, with a different body of experience to draw upon sees it as a bump.

We can also say that our 'reading' of a situation will be affected by our experience, just as our seeing is so affected. 'Reading' a situation is something we all do, but we are not always conscious of doing it much as we are not always conscious of what it is we are doing when we report that we 'see'. Only if subsequently we have to recount an incident are we really aware of what we have been doing, as with the following account recently overheard on a London bus.

'Oh yes, poor old dear, all alone she was, must have gone off in her sleep. Oh such a time as we had with her son and the police and all. You see I saw her milk-bottle on Monday, and I says to myself, I says, "Old Mrs Smith's having a bit of a lie in this morning, she is." Well the milk was still there in the evening and I says to Elsie, "I reckon Mrs Smith's gone off to 'er sister for the day", for she sometimes does, you know, sudden like, for 'er sister's been poorly. Well, then Tuesday comes and I'm going out on the early shift and there it still is, and I thinks to myself, "Ron, there's something wrong here", and I goes back and tells Elsie to phone 'er son for we didn't have a key—and sure enough when I gets back its all over—poor old dear.'

Ron has read the situation represented to him by the presence of an uncollected bottle of milk outside the flat of an elderly lady. Because of his previous experience, the milk bottle has meaning. He reads the meaning on Monday morning as 'Mrs Smith's having a bit of a lie in'; on Monday evening, he reads the changed meaning as 'Mrs Smith's gone to her sister's for the day'; and then on Tuesday, he reads a new and serious meaning in the continued presence of the milk-bottle outside the flat and makes the prediction that all is not well. His reading of the situation, based on his previous experience of the old lady's habits, enables him to make a prediction which proves to be quite correct. We can say then that both what we 'see' and what we 'read' are based on our use of our previous experience in a particular way; and

206

that our expectations will help us to shape what we do see and read. For example, a bank manager presented with the barrel of a gun, a masked man and a demand for money, will expect an attempt at robbery; he is unlikely to expect either a student rag-day joke or a police-sponsored test of his security arrangements. Similarly a teacher, presented with a 'stupid' child, will expect its silence to indicate an incapacity to answer rather than a capacity to think.

George Kelly, the American psychologist we spoke of in Chapter 1, has a great deal to say about these 'expectations' which we form. He puts forward the idea that man is 'a problem-solving animal'; that day-to-day living involves us in a process of continuous problem solving at every level, from the most trivial to the most serious. As the reader reads this book he may solve the problem of bodily stiffness by changing position or stretching his legs: he may solve the problem of mental tiredness by pausing to look out of the window, or going to make a cup of coffee. These actions are not thought about in any detail, because they have been used before by the reader to solve similar problems. If a cup of coffee, or a break, has in the past refreshed a particular reader, then he predicts that this action will fulfill his needs again should he encounter a similar situation. Kelly suggests that man is in business to make sense of the world around him; and that his major task is to test the sense he has formulated against the events he encounters. It is as if man is continually 'reaching out and beating the world to the punch': his need is to be able to anticipate what is going to happen next so that he can have a plan for action, already prepared, according to his predictions of the likely outcome.

This idea would certainly seem to fit some of the illustrations we have already used in this book. Victoria in Chapter 1, page 18, at the age of eighteen months, predicts that the spreading of news-paper will facilitate the production of orange drink. Earlier in this chapter, the man on the bus, Ron, makes a series of predictions which he tests against real events. Because he has made relevant predictions, he has also formulated a plan of action which leads to his decision on Tuesday morning to contact the old lady's son.

So one major feature of our ability to read situations in which we find ourselves is our ability to make predictions about the behaviour of others, based upon our previous experience of like situations. This leads us to consider a further aspect of this ability to beat the world to the punch. Kelly suggests that one thing which is 'basic to our making sense of our world and of our lives is our continual detection of repeating themes'. This raises the question as to how we do, in fact, detect repeating themes. What we suggest is that the key to our recognising repeating themes in the world is our use of language, both the way we observe its use by others and the way we use it ourselves, when we 'work things out' inside our heads. For example, the children playing in Chapter 2 are very likely to have experienced repeating themes in the instruction of the adult who was intervening in their play. The individual 'do's' and 'don'ts' themselves were very varied, and the criteria used to judge each action particular to it, but this variation obscures the presence of at least two consistent repeating themes which the children would have picked up from the stream of comment regulating their actions: that relationships with others involve a basic distinction between actions that one is allowed to do and actions that one is forbidden to do; and that what actions are, and are not, do-able in particular circumstances is determined by rules which you cannot work out for yourself from the actions themselves. From the first of these two repeating themes, a child comes to predict that all actions must fall into one of two categories 'do-able' and 'not do-able'. In Kelly's terms, the child will develop a 'construct' based on its observance of this repeating theme in its experience. We have to think of a 'construct' as a working hypothesis which is tested against new experience, but, as in science, testing a hypothesis leads us to look for positive evidence that will verify our predictions. Hence the tester is predisposed to look for things which will confirm his view. This is not to say that he will always overlook negative evidence but the presence of a pre-existing 'construct' is likely to predispose him to 'see', or 'read', new events in terms that will verify or confirm, rather than falsify, his predictions. In this way, we can account for the commonplace that we can so easily 'mistake' the new and interpret it as something familiar to us already. We might add that the ability to accept willingly evidence that falsifies our predictions, that is, asks us to change our minds, is a relatively sophisticated ability. No doubt most readers will be familiar with some version of the story about the eminent member of parliament who said, in reply to a statement of evidence counter to his own opinion, 'Don't confuse me with facts, I've made up my mind'.

Consider for instance what would happen if you, the reader, were to wake up tomorrow morning in total darkness. Assuming

208

that you do not live north of the Arctic Circle and are reading this book in winter, and that you do believe that the sun will rise tomorrow, what would your reactions be? Might you first consider the possibility of your watch or clock misleading you so that it really is still night? Might you consider a solar eclipse, or would you assume *at first waking* that the sun had not risen at its predicted time? In relation to experience of this kind, Kelly considers that we must see ourselves as individuals who

'anticipate events by construing their replication',

so that the reader, waking in total darkness, will draw on his past experiences of waking in darkness and make use of these experiences as the basis for his prediction rather than rely upon the new experience of the sun failing to rise.

If we now take what Kelly has said and relate it to the child learning to be a member of his community we can see that the values, attitudes and assumptions of the community constitute 'repeated themes' for the child. Once he has detected these repeated themes, the child can then use them to develop his own system of constructs, his own way of making satisfactory pre-dictions about the events of his world. It is the child, therefore, who 'reads' the meaning of the themes as they repeat themselves in the language and the actions of others: and it is the child who has to build his own system of constructs, based upon his 'reading' of his experience. It is the community, however, which provides the language and the actions of others, the substance of this experience he abstracts from in his building. To refer back for a moment to our opening paragraph, we can now suggest that 'No two people think alike', because each has built his own system of constructs with which to read the people and events of his ex-perience: but that we have no difficulty in creating and maintain-ing all our concerted human activity, because the substance out of which we build is shared in common with everyone else who shares a community with us.

The community, through making language available to the child, makes shapes and objects, people and relationships, into 'knowable' things, things which have meaning and can be talked about. Consider any occasion when a group of children or adults have to make sense of some unfamiliar object, be it a geranium or a generator. Notice their relief when someone offers them a name for the object. They do not so much want an account of the work-ings of the generator, or the structure of the geranium, as a name for a set of recognisable characteristics which can be stored. Once the name is given, 'generatorlikeness' or 'geraniumlikeness' can be added to their repertoire for use on some other occasion when these qualities turn up again in their experience. If a community were to see a similarity between generators and geraniums, because both of these objects were red, then this common feature would come to the children of that community through the way in which the adults joined them together in the language they used for talking about their similarity, rather than their difference.

What, then, would happen if a child who lived in this community which emphasised the similarity between generators and geraniums were to move to another community where generators belonged to the category 'machinery' and geranium to the category of 'plant'? The child's construct would lead him to make predictions about generators and geraniums which would be falsified, because his construct is 'non-transferable'. In Kelly's terms 'a construct has a limited range of convenience', and beyond a certain context it will not hold, that is, any predictions based upon it will be systematically falsified when tested against real events in contexts outside its range of convenience. The first boy in our example at the beginning of this section successfully illustrates this point. He can only construe violent contact as aggressive: in a social context where violence to the person is unthinkable, and such contact can only be accidental, he would find himself operating beyond the 'range of convenience' of his construct. His predictions about the meaning of such contact would be continually falsified by the 'polite' response of others whenever it occurred.

Applying a construct beyond its range of convenience is a major preoccupation of Johnson Abercrombie in her book *An Anatomy of Judgement*. She illustrates the difficulties which arise by quoting the case of a group of medical students who were learning how to read X-ray plates. When the students were told that the X-ray plates were those of tuberculosis patients, the students 'saw' shadows on the plates consistent with this diagnosis, even though the plates were, in fact, entirely clear of such shadows. On the other hand, when they were not given such information about the medical condition of the patients whose plates they viewed, they failed to 'see' shadows which an experienced eye could read very clearly. From her own long experience of situations of this kind Abercrombie develops the idea of 'pre-existing schemata', what the individual brings to the situation in terms of an already worked
210

out scheme or plan of interpretation for the events it contains. Abercrombie's 'schemata', and Kelly's 'constructs' are two ways of approaching the same thing. What they contribute to our present discussion is the idea that human beings do not come to a situation 'fresh', or 'open-minded', or devoid of 'preconceptions', but rather with a well-ordered body of experience from which they derive predictions about anything that relates to it.

That the ordering of this body of experience has to be done through language, and that the language available to the child for this activity will be the language of a particular community, demonstrates the degree to which 'our' view of the world is only 'ours' in a very special sense.

2. Seeing what we expect to see

In the last section, we explored the way in which we build up for ourselves a body of ordered information about the world, derived from our cumulative experience of people, actions and things, a body of information that we then use in order to make predictions about the likely meaning of what happens to us. Clearly, the fact that we do make predictions of this kind certainly does not mean that our predictions are always confirmed by the truth of the events to which we apply them. If all the predictions we made were as 'correct' as their basis in our experience was 'well-ordered', then we would not have in our language a range of expressions like 'dropping a clanger', 'making a boob', 'making a faux-pas', or 'putting one's foot in it'.

Consider the following situation. In the 1930's, a European agriculturalist was employed by a Central African missionary group with a particular concern for the improvement of village agriculture. The expert visited a series of yam-growing villages and noted with horror that the yams were planted in great mounds of earth which had become covered with weeds, because the technique of hoeing was not known. The yield of yams per acre was limited, because mounds were used rather than ridges and furrows. The presence of weeds indicated to the expert, not only a lack of care on the part of the villagers, but also a potential diminution in the fertility of the soil on which the yams were dependent.

With the aid of a team of helpers, the expert organised the weeding and demolition of the inefficient mounds. New crops were planted in parallel rows and hoeing was introduced to keep away

211

weeds. Some weeks later, the first rainstorm of the season produced three inches of rain in as many hours. The furrows between the ridges became small gulleys which eroded the ridges, exposing the newly planted yams, while at the same time carrying off all the carefully loosened top soil to the nearest river.

At one level, the expert is not to be blamed for reading the luxuriant plant growth of the old yam mounds as 'weeds', for it is true that they were not classifiable as food producing plants. What these plants did so very successfully, however, was to reduce erosion by holding the soil together with their roots and by breaking the force of the large raindrops with their foliage. Similarly, the 'inefficient' mound, which reduced the density of plants per acre, was not 'read' by the expert as a conservation device which allowed the villagers to collect what soil was displaced from the top of the mounds from the vegetation traps on their bases and sides and simply return it to the top, a process which was quite impossible when they were faced with hundreds of furrows and ridges and the soil already on its way down river!

We can probably agree that agricultural experts working in Africa ought to make a full study of climatic conditions before 'improving' agriculture, but what concerns us here is to try to see how and why this expert 'got it wrong'. If we consider his 'failure' in terms of what we have said about the work of both Kelly and Abercrombie, we can compare it with the situation we outlined in Chapter 1, when we were considering why, in certain situations, a speaker cannot find the language he needs to meet the demands of a particular situation. We suggested that in many cases this happens to us because we have not had the necessary prior experience of other situations similar to the one in question. Our failure to find the language we need in a situation of this kind is not a sign that we lack some basic capacity to cope with the activity of languaging, therefore, but an indication that, however competent the speaker, there are likely to be new situations occurring for him that will find him 'speechless'. Broadly, we need to accept that well-formed human beings can make sense of what they *have* experienced, certainly in terms of the activities of day-to-day living, so that a failure to do so ought *first* to be considered in terms of the possible newness or unfamiliarity of the experience rather than the weakness or inadequacy of the person concerned.

Our agricultural expert did not 'fail' any more than the children who 'didn't say a word'. It would be more accurate to say that he had made sense of the problem within the conceptual framework

212

provided by his experience of European agriculture: that is to say, he had built a set of constructs relevant to problem-solving in the field of crop cultivation. What had happened was that he then made use of this set of constructs 'beyond their range of convenience', and with correspondingly disastrous results. Had the agriculturalist had the kind of information now available in Europe about local variations in unfamiliar climatic regimes, he might well have modified his set of constructs to accommodate this information: in the absence of such information, however, he could only use what was available to him, his own experience of mid-latitude agriculture. Obviously, we need to distinguish between a possible deficiency in the information available to the construct maker and any conceptual limitations in the ability of the construct maker.

What we are concerned with at this point, however, is just such deficiencies in the information available and their effects upon our ability to build for ourselves a set of constructs that meet the needs of the case. Considered from this point of view, we may better understand the mediaeval natural philosophers when they argued that the sun moved round the earth, for the information which would have led to the modification of this construct had been lost in the centuries following the break-up of the Roman Empire and did not again become available till the end of the fifteenth century. Similarly, it would be somewhat unfair to blame a hill farmer who, finding a fell-walker suffering from exposure, brings him into a warm room and gives him hot drinks or a hot bath. Only recently has research into diathermia shown that this common treatment for exposure can be fatal and that a more appropriate course of action is, in fact, to put the unfortunate person into a bath containing water only one degree higher than the exposed person's body temperature. In severe cases, this may mean that the 'bath' has to be stone cold!

By using his language both to observe and to record and to classify all that goes on around him, a human being develops a way of looking at the world that is intimately related to his own particular experiences. When he encounters new situations, he draws upon his stored experience in order to interpret them. Sometimes his experience is of such a kind that the new situation can be read in the same way as familiar old situations, but sometimes this is not the case. Then we get the mis-readings whose results range from the merely amusing or embarrassing to the unfortunate or even the quite disastrous. Into this first category comes the following story told me by my driving instructor. On one occasion he was proceeding along a quiet road with a pupil whom he considered fairly competent. A roundabout appeared in the distance, so he said, 'When you get to the roundabout, go straight across'. It was fortunate that the roundabout was only about six inches high, for that is exactly what the pupil did. Her 'mistake' was based on the fact that 'straight across' in the past had been confined to crossing roads, not roundabouts. A further factor may have been that she was employing a construct such as 'Instructors say what they mean' or 'Instructors must know what they are doing'.

Unfortunately, misreadings of this kind are often far from amusing and recently a number of tragic accidents, which have made headlines in British newspapers, have pointed to the very high possibility of human misreading as their most likely cause. In June 1972, a Trident aircraft crashed at Staines killing 118 people on board. The lengthy public enquiry which followed this crash established clearly the technical causes of the crash, in this case the premature retraction of the wing leading droops, but what the enquiry was unable to establish was why a number of safety precautions were overridden by the crew and why appropriate recovery procedures were not mobilised in time to prevent the crash. The report suggests that in fact the crew did not 'read' the seriousness of their position. In particular it suggests that the Second Officer whose task was to monitor speed must have assumed that the pilot knew what he was doing. This was a reasonable assumption, given that the Captain was a very experienced pilot, *but* on this occasion the pilot was suffering from an abnormal heart condition which was causing a lack of concentration and impaired judgment. So often did the possibility of mis-reading, rather than mechanical failure, arise in the course of the enquiry that it is not surprising to find among the recommendations made in the report the installation of cockpit voice recorders. What a playback of a cockpit tape from this crash might well have revealed is why no member of the crew read any of the many warning signs that something was amiss and whether, as suggested at the enquiry, there may have been a misreading relatively similar to the pupil's misreading of the driving instructor's 'Go straight across'.

When we consider how easily such situations as these can occur within our own culture it is not surprising that very serious misreadings can occur when we are dealing with the assumptions, attitudes and values of a culture very different from our own,

214

should people continue to read the new situation in terms of what they are already familiar with.

Reading the new in terms of the old is a theme which we shall want to return to in both of the subsequent chapters, particularly when we want to consider the difficulties children may encounter at school, because their reading of the school situation is based on an experience of a community that does not necessarily share a common culture with that of the school. For the moment we must end this chapter by explaining why it is that we lay such an emphasis on the way we read situations, particularly new situations. This, then, is the subject of the final section.

3. 'Seeing' in a changing world

In another context one of the present writers sums up an account of the possible future for the children in our schools in the 1970's by saying that:

'The very least that we can say is that the world in which they celebrate their 65th birthday, the world of the 2020's, will be even more unlike our own world than our own world is unlike the world of 1900. What has happened is that the rate of change has increased out of all proportion to anything men have known in earlier periods. It has reached a point where change grows upon itself, so that we are creating a society in which the *normal* state of that society is one of change.'

Language Study, the teacher and the learner

If we accept that 'we are creating a society in which the *normal* state of that society is one of change', then one might consider what this implies for an individual who has a strong potential tendency to interpret his experience of the world by reading new situations in terms of old. When change was infrequent and very much confined to the sort of changes in the life history of the individual, such as birth, marriage, death, change of activity or occupation, for which an appropriate and public recognised ritual could be provided, then individuals were both alerted to significant change in their lives and helped to come to terms with it by the collective expression of 'the habits of the tribe'. A special effort could be made to 'adjust', and, the adjustment having been made, life could 'go back to normal' in the sense that special effort was no longer required. This was particularly easy to do when the community in which one was having to adjust to change in one's own life did not itself appear to change. Events that did

215

change the life of the community, such as war, plague, or the devastations of natural disasters, were, by definition, not 'change', but aberrations, 'acts of God', discontinuities in the accepted order of things. But what happens, then, when change is not merely personal, but involves the community as well as the individual and is continuous against a background of change. What kind of demand will this put upon the resources of the individual? How can he meet them and what would happen if he fails to do so?

Let us begin by translating this idea of a situation of continuous change into the terms we have been using in this chapter to describe how individual human beings cope with their experience of the world. For the individual we can say that this situation puts him in a position where he is faced with a continuous need to perform his problem-solving in contexts and situations that are marginally or wholly new to him. Now, we have implied that his major resource for interpreting new situations lies in his ability to bring language to bear upon the problems of interpretation they present to him. In particular, by using language in interaction with ourselves, by 'talking to ourselves', exploring the problem inside our own heads, we can think through and test against our previous experience possible solutions. One of the best examples of this is the way we 'rehearse' in our heads, perhaps for days, a difficult letter we are required to write. By using language in interaction with others, however, we can consult with them: we can seek further information and we can use the printed page to extend our own resources. Our capacity to solve our problems, therefore, is directly linked to our capacity to bring language to bear upon them; and our capacity to use language is a function of our experience of using language, an experience immediately relatable to the ways of using language, the attitudes towards, and assumptions about, its use current in our own community.

Consider, for example, the implication of the following comment, made by a man of twenty-seven, a mature student at a College of Education:

'When I first came to College I thought everyone was picking on me. I would say what I thought was right and they would say "No, it's not like that", and then tell me a whole lot of things that I hadn't known about. Sometimes I just said nothing more. Sometimes I lost my temper and just said the first thing that came into my head, usually nasty. But then I began to see that people were still friendly after these arguments and I realised that you
216

could disagree with a person's argument without disagreeing with them as a person. I saw too that even if you thought talking about something got you nowhere, somehow it seemed clearer to you afterwards, even if you still thought the same thing.'

This student read the situation at college in terms of his previous experience. He saw fellow students and lecturers as 'picking on him', because they did not immediately accept the truth of what he said. As this man came from the kind of close-knit community where everyone held the same views on many of the key matters of life, comment in that community would be by definition hostile, for, if it were not, then comment as such would not have been necessary. All that would be required would be a gesture or a word of confirmation. Coming to college, this student reads the presenting of an alternative view as an attack upon himself as it would most certainly have been in his own community had he presented a view different from the one expected of him in the circumstances. It is only because he recognises the friendliness of people, following what he has construed as 'an attack', that he questions his first reading of the situation and, as a result, replaces the construct 'To disagree with what I say is to attack me personally', by the construct, 'To disagree with what I say is to offer an alternative view of the case'. The reader will see that when this student stops using 'picking on me' and starts talking about 'arguing with me', he is not 'being euphemistic', 'speaking properly', or 'talking posh'. Although his contemporaries in his own community might describe his changed behaviour in these terms, he is in fact revealing a basic change in his construct system by his choice of this alternative mode of expression. He does not forget the words 'picking on me', nor does he abandon the construct which guides his use of them. As they no longer fit his view of what happens in his new environment, however, we could say that he has learnt the limits of the range of convenience of the construct concerned and has developed an additional construct to cope with his altered reading of the situation.

The student also makes the point that he used to think 'talking about it got you nowhere'. Most readers of this book will have used talk both personally and professionally to think through their problems, but for this student the idea that talk achieved something was quite new. Having decided that this was the case, however, he was forced to reconsider the relationship between language and action. Like many others in our society, his own

217

community held firmly to the view that language does not, of itself, constitute action. Consider how many phrases in the common language express an underlying sense that language is somehow unrelatable to what actually happens in our own experience. Many of us believe that 'Talking gets you nowhere', or dismiss some comment as 'mere talk', or insist that what is needed is 'Action, not words', or declare that 'There's no good to be done in talking about it'. Perhaps it is fair to say that our student's new experience now puts him in a better position to see what Malinowski really meant when he said that: 'Words are part of actions and they are equivalent to action.' He would also probably be able to see why it is that the writers of this book regard the 'words' used by the two mothers in Chapter 2, as 'actions', actions which have a very powerful effect in shaping events.

This student's view of the world was clearly reflected in his habitual way of speaking. As he changed his way of looking at the world, so he had to find a new way of speaking to express both to himself and to others the new meanings he had made. At the same time, finding this new way of speaking alerted him to new possibilities and prompted him to reconsider other ways of speaking and ways of seeing which he had previously considered 'natural', or 'obvious', and therefore no subject for serious enquiry.

If we accept that the world we live in is in a state of continuous change, change which is unlikely to lessen as time goes on; and if we accept that the ability to utilise the resources of our language in order to make sense of the world and our relationships with other people is our major resource for coping with the problems this situation will create for us; then it would seem to us that understanding how we use language to live is a necessary part of the equipment of every adult and, consequently, the special responsibility of all of us who are concerned with the education of both children and adults in this ever more demanding world.

4 Language in community and school

In the first three chapters of this book we have tried to build up a picture of the way in which the young human being learns to make sense of the world and, in the process, learns both a language and a culture. This complex three-way process brings our child into a specific relationship with the human environment about him, that is, with his community. Providing a child has had continuous contact with such a human environment, by the age of four or five he will have mastered the rules and meanings that make up his language and he will have worked out concretely the rules and meanings that make up the culture of his community. Together, these two sets of rules and meanings, intimately inter-connected as they are, and grounded in his cumulative experience of the world, provide him with a set of constructs that he uses to interpret the continuous inflow of experience which he encounters in his life as a normal human being. What he has achieved in these early years of life is a massive organisation of information about the world. How this organisation is carried out is something that we can only make reasonable guesses at in the present state of our knowledge. What we can be certain about, however, is that it has taken place. There is no other way in which we can account for the enormous success with which the five-year old functions in relation both to the immediate world of its experience and in its use of language in interaction with others. We can also say something about the information itself, what it is that the child organises in those early years, because the substance of much of this information about the world is provided by the language and culture of the child's own community. We may be uncertain as to *how* the child actually acquires the rules and meanings concerned, but we can point to *what* these rules and meanings look like in terms

219

of their practical realisation in the linguistic and social behaviour of communities.

We have now reached the point in our argument where, for the first time in normal circumstances, a child will move outside its community of birth in those countries with a formal education system. By 'going to school' a child enters a new community, and necessarily he is exposed to new ways of seeing, new and different information about the world, new ways of using language and all the unknown situations of a new culture. To some readers, this may seem too extreme a statement, an over-dramatised view of what is a perfectly 'natural' step in the life of every individual. We would ask those readers to suspend judgment for a little and accept that a very strong statement of this kind is necessary just where we do face a situation that so many of us have come to regard as 'natural'. It was not always so, even in our society, as the records of the fierce resistance to compulsory schooling show, and it is not so even now for rather more children in our society than perhaps we are ready to admit. What this chapter is concerned with, therefore, is the justification for so strong a statement about the impact of school upon the child coming new to it.

1. The relationship between school and community

Those readers who are uneasy about the idea that a child moves outside its community of birth for the first time in going to school may have in mind the children who go to the village school, or the children who go to school at the end of their own street, or on their own housing estate. In Britain, at any rate, only a small proportion of primary age children travel long distances to school, in rural areas where schools are not available or in urban areas where parental choice of a particular school make a journey necessary. The point we would make, however, is that geographical distance is not the most important criterion for assessing a change of community. If community is based on shared values, then what we must look at is not the geographical distance between the child's home and the child's school, but the experiential distance between the attitudes and assumptions familiar to the child in his home and those attitudes and assumptions which he will meet in school.

It would seem likely that a child going to a local school, taught by teachers who have been born in the home area, would find them offering him a very similar view of the world to his own, but we have to ask if this would necessarily be so. Firstly, it is unlikely that the child will find 'local' teachers in his school. Teachers are a highly mobile group who work away from their home areas for many reasons. Many infant and junior teachers are married women who move around the country as their husbands move. Another large group of teachers travel away from their home area in order to do the particular work in teaching that appeals to them. A new factor, which has recently contributed to this mobility, is the variation in house prices across the country. The steady outflow of young teachers from the very high-cost areas of London is causing great concern to the local education authorities. The recruitment of more experienced teachers to these areas is also proving increasingly more difficult for the same reason. What these three commonplace factors indicate is the degree to which we are becoming a society where movement is normal and the person who grows up, lives and works in the same locality becomes the exception.

Nevertheless, there are schools where many of the staff are themselves products of the same community as the children they teach. Yet can these staff be said to be 'local' when the cars in the school car-park and the address list in the school office indicate that few, if any, actually live in the area immediately adjacent to the school? This is not an argument for saying that 'teachers ought to live where their pupils live'; it is simply an observation of what seems to be the case for the majority of schools where the writers have either worked or visited. The reason is not mysterious. For social and economic reasons the majority of teachers do not choose to live where their pupils live. Often, indeed, they could not do so even if they wanted to, for few teachers are eligible for the council houses and flats which house a large proportion of Britain's school children.

Beyond all this, however, there is the unavoidable fact that the majority of those who become teachers are changed in the process. They no longer find that they can identify with the values, the attitudes and assumptions, of the pupils they teach, even though those pupils may well be the children of men and women they grew up with.

The reasons for such a radical change in one's view of the world as this are many and complex, but what stands out is the effect of a divergent choice of occupation upon our sense of shared values. At the age of sixteen, the would-be teacher chooses, first,

221

to stay on at school for two years to take A-level and then to continue in full-time formal education for another three or four years. Meanwhile, his contemporaries from his own local community choose to leave at sixteen, take whatever job is available, or go into a job where any further education was in relation to a trade or skill, set in the context of industry or commerce. From his first decision to stay on at school, the teacher no longer leads the same life as his contemporaries, so it becomes increasingly unlikely that he will continue to share their values, even if he believes that he does. This is the case whether his friends work on the shop floors of industrial estates, in the offices of the city centre, or function as executives in any business or industry in Britain. Simply by choosing to become a teacher an individual exposes himself to experiences which are not shareable with his contemporaries. This is also true for doctors or nurses or accountants or surveyors, but the special position of the teacher means that the values he embodies in his view of the world are quite crucial for the basis of his work as a teacher is an assessment of the needs of others, his pupils. If we are to understand how conflict arises in this situation we must first of all see why it is that the teacher so often presents to the pupil, whatever his geographical proximity, or however sympathetic the relationship, a set of values that differ from those the pupil has already developed in the context of his family and his community.

This point has been made at some length, not only because it is important to see that pupils are most likely to encounter different values when they go to school, but also because most readers of this book will be familiar with the arguments put forward in Britain in the last ten years which would explain conflict between pupils and teachers as the expression of a clash between the 'middle-class' values of the teacher and the 'working-class' values of the pupils. This is a very large topic and one which we cannot develop in this present volume, but two points at least must be made. Firstly, it would seem from the ideas implicit in these arguments that there are two, and only two, sets of values at issue; and that the superior virtues of 'working-class', as opposed to 'middle-class' values is self-evident. Secondly, it would seem that these two sets are completely separate from, and diametrically opposed to, each other. It is difficult indeed to accommodate such a view with what we know about the way communities function. If the reader considers the variety of community with which he is familiar, and the success with which communities

222

perform the initial task of socialising their newcomers, then it does seem that adopting a crude dichotomy between middle-class/working class is likely to obscure many of our problems rather than help us to make sense of them by looking at both teachers and pupils in terms of their respective experiences, amongst which their experience of, or sense of, 'class' is certainly very important. If we insist upon a simple two-term system for describing the shared experience of over fifty million people we may indeed be guilty of over-simplification in the cause of ideology.

Let us consider for a moment, a single example of a 'conflict-producing value', one which is shared by all teachers regardless of how they might choose to identify with the values of a particular social class. Most teachers feel that they have 'a responsibility towards their pupils'; that they have some specific role to play in their pupil's development; that when they go into a classroom, they are there to 'do' something. Now this view of the teacher's role finds its realisation in patterns of class-room activity that differ very widely from teacher to teacher. It is realised in one way by the teacher who said to us, 'After all's said and done, they don't know anything until I teach them it, now do they?' and then instructed his student teacher to 'Ram some grammar into them'. It is realised quite differently by the teacher who said, 'Well, it's our job to turn them out able to do a good day's work isn't it?'; or the teacher who said to me, 'We must start where the pupil is and lead him on from there'. Even the teacher who said, 'I just want to create an environment where each individual child can find himself', is offering a version of this role.

Now these four teachers are saying very different things; and indeed, they are very different people with quite diametrically opposed views as to how pupils learn and how, therefore, they should be taught. They have one thing in common, however, They are all committed to changing their pupils. They want to move them from where they are now to a somewhere that they judge their pupils must be in the future. At one level, there is no difference between the objective of the first teacher, who sees 'ramming some grammar into them' as one step towards making them less ignorant; and the objective of the fourth teacher, who wants to exert change through creating an environment where pupils will move from the state they are in at present to a different state, one of 'finding himself', a notion the pupil probably does

223

not have, until this teacher gives it to him. What matters, therefore, is not whether these teachers and their pupils are 'middle-class' or 'working-class', but whether the idea of 'changing', to which all teachers are committed, is understood by their pupils and accepted as one consequence of being at school. Certainly, given what we know about their internal organisation, it is possible that pupils from 'working-class' communities may be more resistant to the idea of 'changing' as such, and less open to the idea that this might be a consequence of going to school, than pupils from 'middle-class' communities. There are very many possible reasons why a human being cannot, will not, dare not, or simply does not want to, change from the position where he or she is at one moment in time to the point where we would like him to be. Because this is the case, we must turn aside from the main theme of this chapter, so that we can look more closely at 'change' in biological and psychological terms before returning to our school-going pupil.

2. A necessary digression

'The key to understanding the significance of the activities of plants, mammals, and men is the recognition of their homeostatic nature, and the fact that they tend to preserve the continuity of life.'

J. Z. Young

'A person anticipates events by construing their replications.'

George Kelly

These two quotations, one from a biologist, one from a psychologist, give us our point of departure, for they remind us of the fact that there are many ways of looking at man, each one of which may add something valuable to the total picture we are interested in building. No one of us can ever experience all the possible ways of looking or seeing for ourselves but we can make use of the 'seeing' of others by testing them out against our own experience of the world. This is what we shall try to do with these two ways of seeing.

In 1932 the word 'homeostasis' was used for the first time. It was used by a physiologist who was writing about a tendency observed in mammals to maintain constant the composition of their blood in spite of changes in their environment. 'Homeostasis' means literally a 'steady standing', a state of equilibrium

224

or balance relative to the surrounding environment. Its importance for our argument derives from the fact that, since the concept was formed in 1932, it has been used and tested by biologists and found to hold good for so many circumstances in the life of organisms, from plants to man, that they are prepared to affirm it as a fundamental organising principle of life itself. Related specifically to man, the concept of homeostasis allows us to suggest that man is designed to keep himself in a state of balance with his immediate environment, and that this involves, not only a balance in terms of his function as a living organism, like his need to keep constant the composition of his own blood, but also in terms of his existence as a social and cultural being, a thinking self.

Contrary to one popular view of their activities, many contemporary biologists do concern themselves with all those aspects of men which to us, as men, seem overwhelmingly important. Though they may find in their work little to support traditional distinctions between 'mind' and 'body', or 'reason' and 'emotion', their view of man does not exclude the behaviour which we associate with our use of these words. What they offer us is a view of man that embraces both his biological continuity with all other living things, and his distinctiveness as a species which has learnt how to emancipate itself from subjection to the constraints of the natural environment by using its brain to create its own environment. In other words, what makes man man is the fact that he has created for himself a social and cultural context which is, for him, his 'natural' environment, that is to say, the environment without which he cannot survive as an individual or as a species. If we now relate the fundamental notion of homeostasis to man as a species whose 'natural' environment is social and cultural, then we can suggest that the individual maintains himself in equilibrium through his control over his relationship to that social and cultural environment.

If, then, we accept that man is unique as a species in that the principle of homeostasis means for him both continuous monitoring of his relationship to the natural environment and to the made environment of society and culture, we can ask what this might imply for him once that made environment was subject to radical change.

Firstly, it might be more accurate if we said that *man must make those adjustments necessary to ensure his own homeostasis*, rather than saying that man changed, or did not change. Now these

225

'adjustments' could be described in a variety of ways. Depending on one's own personal reading of the situation, they might appear as change, or as resistance to change. Whatever our own personal view of the case, however, we must realise that the adjustment the individual does make is necessary *to him* at the time when he makes it. It is not that he is doing what he *wants* to do necessarily, but what he sees he *has* to do if he is to maintain in equilibrium his relationship to the world about him. He has to maintain himself, because if he does not, he is put at risk. We might say 'he has to be able to live with himself', or 'he has to learn to live with it', or 'he has to come to terms with it'. Perhaps we are very conscious now in our own times that the consequences of failure can be so severe that they destroy the individual concerned.

Let us try to give an example of what we mean by this. A divorced woman has an only son of whom she is extremely proud. She boasts of his doings to her neighbours, telling them how intelligent he is and what her hopes are for him when he grows up. When the child goes to school, difficulties arise. The child seems unable to cope with learning to read and write and the school suggests that special help may be needed. The mother refuses. She is convinced that her son is being misunderstood by his teachers and that his inability to cope with reading and writing is due to his unhappiness with their treatment of him. She continues to refuse special help for her child and continues to tell her neighbours stories about her son's achievements. It is obvious to everyone, except the mother, that the child is in difficulties and needs help, but the mother cannot see this. Some people might say she was 'blind', some 'stupid', some 'neurotic'. What view they took would depend on a variety of circumstances, but in terms of homeostasis, we might say that this mother had made the adjustments necessary to her to maintain her equilibrium. Because of her emotional dependence on her son, she could not face up to the fact that his ability would not fulfill her predictions. In particular, she may not have been able to cope with the imagined reactions of the neighbours to whom she had formerly boasted. It was essential to this woman's well-being that she did not change her view of her son, for changing her view of him meant a whole range of other changes she could not face up to. It was therefore necessary to her to adjust her view of her son's teachers or of his school.

The question of how human beings maintain their steady
226

state in an environment of change is an important one, particularly if the reader accepts the argument that all teachers are committed to creating an environment in which their pupils are asked
to change.

Let us now relate what we have been saying about the
individual's need to be in equilibrium with his total environment
to what we said in Section 1 of Chapter 3 about the individual's
use of his construct system to, '. . . anticipate events by construing their replication'. As the argument proceeds, we want
the reader to remember the implications of what we have just
said about the class-room and the school as an environment in
which change is continuously demanded of the pupil, because the
substance of what he is asked to do there involves so much that
is necessarily new to his experience. We would also point out that
this newness extends from mental processes to social relationships.

It seems to us that what the biologist, Young, describes as the
individual human being's commitment to maintaining a steady
state in relation to his physical, his social and his cultural
environment, the psychologist, Kelly, describes as the individual
human being seeking always to anticipate events by predicting
that they are about to happen once more, exactly as they have
been known to happen before. If we do indeed cope with our
experience of the world by assuming that it will continue to take
the form that we expect it to take, then we have to accept that,
ordinarily, we go about our daily business of living with a very
low *expectation of change*. We can draw upon strategies for action,
worked out on previous occasions, continuously and unthinkingly,
because we anticipate that events will replicate themselves, so
that the majority of our responses can be 'automatic'.

We are familiar enough with such patterns of 'automatic'
behaviour in our command of commonplace activities like riding
a bicycle, driving a car, knitting a sweater, or playing a game of
tennis. Let us go one stage further, however. How many of us
who drive have a 'normal' route out of our district and how
many of us, on some occasion, have found ourselves happily
driving along this 'normal' route when our journey on this
occasion really required us to set off in the opposite direction?
Similarly, how many of us, after some domestic rearrangement,
say, of books or tools or kitchen equipment find ourselves, for
days, reaching to the old place, the former home of dictionary,
screwdriver or wooden spoon? The next stage is to consider how
often we have gone to take a third or fourth form in September,

227

expecting them to offer a particular pattern of 'difficult' behaviour, even though this form will be composed of between thirty and forty individual pupils who have never been third or fourth formers before? Perhaps the fact that they do so often oblige by giving us the behaviour we predict of them might lead us to ask what part our predictions play in eliciting such behaviour, and what part the local 'habits of the tribe' passed down from one generation of pupils to the next. What we are suggesting then is that the events of our normal day, the routine of rising, the journeys to and from work, the activities of the working day, including even a high proportion of those acts we consciously describe as decisions, we cope with according to well-tested routines.

From both a biological and a psychological point of view, then, we are indeed designed to be, and operate best as, 'creatures of habit'. Were we not so, we would not be able to cope with the sheer volume of continuous problem-solving our encounter with the world thrusts upon us every moment of our working lives. Imagine for example what it would be like if driving to work took as much effort as the very first drives one did when learning to drive, or imagine how the morning schedule would be affected if shaving or making up were not a well-tested routine. In order to cope the better with our immediate and accustomed environment, moreover, very many of the constructs we build have this 'limited range of convenience'. One could say that, in maintaining our steady state successfully, we lose efficiency if we see too many sides of the case. It is interesting to consider how well some familiar aspects of contemporary society recognise this fact. Liam Hudson has suggested that those do best in examinations like the traditional O-level who see only a limited range of possibilities in a question: many firms in the 1960's discovered that graduates were often slower to reach decisions than non-graduates, because they took account of a much wider range of circumstances in the process.

So we come now to the ordinary child, the pupil in front of us, an individual human being who has learnt how to maintain himself in a steady state with his total environment; who has built up a system of personal constructs in the process to enable him to interpret his immediate experience, an experience largely shaped by the social and cultural life of a particular community; and a high proportion of whose existing constructs, therefore, are likely to have a 'limited range of convenience'. What now

228

happens when he comes into this new environment of the school? How is he to maintain himself in equilibrium by adjusting to this new social and cultural environment? What does he do when he has to operate outside the range of convenience of so many of his constructs? Part of the answer is that constructs can be modified, though this takes time, often a very long time. Part of the answer is that it is more efficient for a human being to be able to use initially the constructs it has whatever the immediate consequences of their limited range of convenience than to try to develop a large number of new constructs all at once. As we build our constructs by testing our predictions against real events, we have to be able to experience the *falsification of our predictions*, not once only, but often many times, before we can accept a modification to the construct concerned. There is a sense in which it is proper to say that a construct has to fail before it can be modified. As the construct system is a vital part of the individual human being, however, every prediction falsified by events is a threat to his homeostasis. He must adjust to the new situation to survive, but how this adjustment is made will depend on how he reads the situation. If he reads the new-ness of the situation as a total threat to his integrity as a person, he may react very violently or withdraw completely within himself in order to keep that self safe from what he construes as an attack.

For some teachers, perhaps, the idea that what they see as 'lethargy', 'stupidity', 'rowdiness' or 'rudeness' in their pupils could be explained in terms of the way a human being is designed to function, may be difficult to accept, but it may be more profitable in the long run.

3. 'On becoming a pupil'

'Stand up properly when you speak to me—take your hands out of your pockets, don't mumble. What was that? You mustn't tell tales you know. He took what? Your work book. Well what was it doing lying around? You mustn't leave things lying around must you?'

This should sound familiar to the reader, for the similarity with our earlier example is deliberate. Once again we have a young human being in a situation where his behaviour is being regulated by adults. This pupil is being presented with a constant stream of information about how he should stand and how he should

229

speak; what he may say and what he may not say; and what attitudes are appropriate towards his own property. The sociologist would call this process 'secondary socialisation' to distinguish it from the 'primary socialisation' we discussed in Chapter 2, Section 2, and we shall see subsequently the importance of this distinction. One common factor, however, in both primary and secondary socialisation, is the use of language to exercise control over others. Just as it was through the language used by adults that the young child learnt to use language itself and learnt the ways of behaving in use in his community, so it is through the language used by a different set of adults, his teachers, in the different environment of the school that the school-age child meets new ways of behaving, new do's and don'ts.

Up to this point, it may seem that we have talked about socialisation as if it were an inevitable one-way process which leaves the child no option but to accept all the values, attitudes and assumptions presented to it by the adults who regulate its world. This was not our intention, for all readers will be only too familiar with the kind of protest a young child can produce when parental control conflicts with the child's immediate interests. On the other hand, it is fair to say that the younger a child the less real possibility it has for rejecting the values presented to it by the adults who control its environment. Until the point where we start to think of the school-going child and even for the majority of those, perhaps, for long after, we are dealing with children who are likely to be deeply affected by the threat of disapproval. For them, the withdrawal of toys, sweets or playmates is a serious matter: the withdrawal of love, affection and sympathy is a disaster to be avoided at all costs. While the child is so vulnerable protest can rarely be sustained for long, but as the child develops towards the young person this situation inevitably changes. As the child comes to handle its language more competently, so it can express its feelings more clearly. As it meets and talks to other children, visits other homes, compares experiences, it sees the possibility of alternatives. Once a child can see the possibility of alternatives to the view of things it has derived from its experience of primary socialisation, there are aspects of that experience which it is capable of reviewing and thus ultimately changing. It has to be said, however, that some authorities would insist that such changes are only ever concerned with relatively unimportant matters and that we carry the marks of our primary socialisation with us to the grave.

230

Protest in a wide variety of forms, however, is a fundamental response of the individual human being to the pressures exerted upon him by the efforts of others to regulate his behaviour, whether he has only the yells of the new-born child as means or the hardware of the urban guerilla. For this reason, it is not surprising that all communities see protest as a threat, and that they have well-tried and tested ways of bringing the views of the individual into line with the view of the community concerned. The pressure to conform is most clearly seen in very close-knit communities, particularly peasant communities, where a divergent member is even more of a threat than in a loose-knit community because his behaviour will be seen by all and will be read as 'a bad example' by the guardians of the community. During the time I spent working in Western Ireland and in Greece I saw many examples of the very strong pressure which the local community could exert upon an individual member. For example, on one occasion I found that one of the two shopkeepers in a small, nearby village was associating with a married woman. In a strongly Catholic and family-centred community, this was a very serious affair. The community succeeded in breaking up the affair by ceasing to patronise the shop of the offending member who was then forced out of business and had to leave the district in order to find work. While the affair was going on, the woman involved was isolated by the women of the community, but after the departure of the shopkeeper she was accepted back into their circle, partly for the sake of her husband and children, and partly because the departure of the shopkeeper gave the community the opportunity to lay blame on him and so avoid the inconvenience of maintaining sanctions against the woman.

The closer-knit the community, the easier it is for the community to function as one and this isolates the offending individual. The sanctions applied range from extreme physical violence such as the killing of a seducer by an avenging brother, still not uncommon in rural areas of Greece, to a beating up meted out to a young man who is thought to have 'got above himself'. Sanctions can also be economic, as with the shopkeeper, but the most familiar sanction of all, practised at every level of society and in every community, is the demonstration of disapproval through the use of certain ways of speaking, or often, *not* speaking, that anyone who has lived in the community will immediately recognise. This demonstration takes a wide variety of forms from the 'raised eyebrow' or the 'cold shoulder' to the total isolation of 'sending to Coventry'. We could say that the language used in interaction with individuals so disapproved of is emptied of all the elements we use to signal responsiveness to the other as a person. It is as if, linguistically, we chose to treat him as an object, even to the point of talking as if he were not present at all.

Given that human-beings have a great need for companionship and social contact, especially in relation to familiar faces, then social pressure of this kind is perhaps the most powerful pressure of all. It is, therefore, social pressure of this kind which is employed when the value system of a group is threatened by the actions or opinions of a newcomer. What particular actions or opinions a community will see as a threat will obviously depend on the community, but, in general terms, what threatens a community is what it really fears and what it really fears is anything that seems to strike at the cohesiveness which gives it its identity. What it is most likely to fear, therefore, is different ways of seeing, different ways of behaving and, of course, the different ways of speaking that make these underlying differences clear, that is, anything which offers an alternative view to the one it embraces for itself.

Now a school is *not* a community, in the full sense of our definition of chapter two. However, like all institutions with an active life of their own, a school does create for the newcomer the conditions we have described as secondary socialisation. In so far as it does socialise those who enter its life, then we can think of it as a particular kind of community. Indeed, there is a long tradition in this country that values the life of the school as a community above its function in imparting knowledge. What we have said so far in this section about the individual in his own community, therefore, we can now apply to the pupil within the 'community' of the school. He joins an institution with a well-developed set of values, attitudes and assumptions. What happens if he protests at their implications for his own activities? What happens if the school does not like his values, his attitudes and assumptions; or his ways of behaving and his ways of using language?

Where schools differ radically from communities is that schools are socialising individuals *who do already have a value system of their own*. This is why the distinction between primary and secondary socialisation is so very important. A community under-

232

takes the primary socialisation of a member who enters it possessing neither language, nor an organised way of looking at the world, while a school creates the conditions for the secondary socialisation of an individual who already has a language and a culture of his own. Unfortunately some schools and some teachers persist in regarding their pupils as 'empty vessels' or 'blank sheets' wanting only the imparting of particular bodies of information in order that their initial ignorance be transformed into later knowledge. To them, all that is relevant is that pupils are ignorant, until instructed in things which the school values as knowledge. If they fail to learn, the fault lies in them. They remain ignorant, because they do not have the ability to become knowledgeable. Failure of this kind in the context of the community of the school, however, is so often read by the school as a global failure of the pupil *as a person*. His success in living the life of his own community is irrelevant, yet to the individual pupil this success is necessarily the basis of his integrity as a person. If pupils are thus presented with such a clash, a clash one could reasonably call a clash between cultures, or ways of evaluating experience, then it is not all that surprising to find deep conflict between pupil and school, and an often violent rejection of the culture of the school.

From all that we have said about primary and secondary socialisation we must accept that a conflict between alternative cultures is extremely likely to arise when a child goes to school. When we consider the capacity of a child to cope with the world, however, conflicting views are not in themselves a threat. If man is a problem-solving animal, then the divergence between alternative views of the world is 'a problem' which could be resolved by each individual child. It is the child's ability to cope with the conflict of views that he meets which would seem to us of real importance, not the mere occurrence of conflict itself. Ultimately, if a child is unable to work out a solution to a problem of this kind, it experiences a kind of frustration which we may not yet fully understand, but whose results we are only too familiar with in terms of a total rejection of all we try to offer in the class-room. How then can we help the child to resolve problems of this kind when it goes to school? Let us ask first how the child would use its natural capabilities as a well-informed human being to set about the problem for itself. It applies its resources to the problem: the language it already possesses, the ways of seeing it has available, and its previous experience of the

233

world which it can draw upon by using language 'inside its head'. All of this, however, the child brings with him from his life in the community. What a child comes to school with is both a language and a culture, each closely bound up with his experience of the other, but it is this language that he must use for learning to be a pupil and for acquiring the 'language for learning' that the school will use throughout the pupil's years of education.

4 'Language for living' and 'language for learning'

What this section is about is how pupils come to see possibilities for using language in different ways. In order to talk about this, we need to be able to focus on what a pupil already possesses when he comes to school and the kind of development which must take place if school is to be both a profitable and enjoyable experience for him. 'Language for living' and 'language for learning' are two terms which will help us to consider this development.

In the first four chapters of this book we have built up a picture of the ways in which a child learns his language and his culture by becoming part of an already established community. He begins this process at birth with the help of a genetic potential to learn language and a capacity to order experience which enables him, through language, to interpret, evaluate and store all his experiences. By being involved in the life of a family and a community the child realises this potential both to learn language and to order his experience of the world, so that he builds up a system of personal constructs which form the basis of the decisions he makes about people, actions and things. The result of this period of intensive ordering and storing is that by school age, say five years old, a normal child has a good command of his language and can use it in a wide variety of ways in the course of his everyday life. It is to this total capacity for using language in everyday life that we give the label 'language for living'. The name itself reflects the basic idea that without language there can be no community, no shared activity, no shared experience; one might say, indeed, no 'living', in the terms that we understand it.

Now the content of any one child's 'language for living' is something that we could work out, if we had enough information about his community and his immediate surroundings. What we can say about *every* child's 'language for living', however, is

234

that it will be intimately related to the ways of speaking of a particular family and a particular social group. What we have tried to stress throughout this book is that a child can only make use of the ways of speaking that are available to him; and if he lives in a community where children have little scope for meeting new situations, and adults, even parents, have little time or inclination for talking with young children, his repertoire of different ways of using language will be limited. If, similarly, a child has accepted the view of a community which thinks that 'children should be seen and not heard'; or that 'children should speak when they are spoken to', then the child's 'language for living' will be markedly different from that of a child who has been encouraged to talk when he has something to say; or to explain what he has been doing; or to express preferences, or to ask questions.

In most cases, whatever our evaluation of the child's 'language for living', it has proved adequate for his needs in his own community. There are two reasons for this. Firstly, the child's language is learnt in that community; hence it is particularly suited to the needs and interests of that community. Secondly, while a child lives exclusively in his own community, that is, while he is below school age, allowances are made for any difficulties he encounters. When the child goes to school, however, there is a radical change. He enters a world, which will be significantly different from his familiar world of home and community. An enormous demand is made upon his linguistic resources for he has to find new ways of speaking to match the new ways of behaving school requires of him. Moreover, this remains fundamentally true however far we may go to meet him by creating conditions in Nursery and Infant school that reflect continuity with his life outside school.

This social aspect of school in itself severely taxes the capacity of many children, but this is far from being the only demand school makes upon them. Schools, even nursery schools, are places where 'learning' takes place and in order to participate in the activities the school provides the child must use language in ways which fit the needs of these activities. It is most likely that, for the majority of children in this country, these ways of using language will be new, or certainly very different from those habitually used in their life outside school. 'Language for learning' is the label we can use to refer to all those ways of speaking which are required by the activities and processes of formal

235

education, and which may or may not already be a part of a child's 'language for living'.

'Tell me what happened in the story'; 'Tell me about the picture'; 'Why did you paint a picture of a rocket?'

From his earliest days in school, the child is expected to meet a whole series of such linguistic demands. He is being asked to use language in ways in which he may never have used it before and, unlike the situation he found himself in as a young child, where adults expected him to have difficulties, 'because he is only a child', it is often now assumed that he can manage 'if only he tries', because he shows he can use some sorts of language very fluently. Because the child has a good command of 'language for living' in his own community, or in the social context of the school environment, it does not mean that he can necessarily cope with 'language for learning'. Some children, of course, do develop some 'language for learning' as part of the total 'language for living' that they take to school with them. For these children, questioning and explaining and finding out about things have already been part of their experience. They will not need to sit silent, as some infant classes do, when a teacher says, 'Tell me about this picture', for they will know that it is the content of the picture, the objects or the people portrayed in it that is being referred to. They will not, as some children do, decide that there is nothing sayable about pictures apart from whom they belong to.

Whatever the variations in the proportion of the language for learning which children bring to the school context, there is one way of using language for learning that very few children bring with them, the ability to use the written language. Throughout this book we have focused on ways of using spoken language, because we have been speaking of pre-school children, but once we talk of school-going children we must add this new way of using language, a way which is entirely different and separate from any of the ways of using language which have previously been mastered. Apart from a possible request to 'write his name', the vast majority of children never meet a situation in their own family and community where they are expected to come to terms with the writing system. For most children, in fact, 'learning to read and write and do sums' is what you go to school for, because this is the view of the school's function they have derived from parents and community.

236

What we must now do is to see how a pupil acquires the language for learning required by his new environment. In the course of this discussion we must keep in mind one basic question; 'Why is it that any child who has successfully developed language for living in his family and community finds himself unable to go on to develop language for learning in the context of school and formal education? The 'answer', if one can properly speak of an 'answer' to so complex a question, will lie somewhere in the intimate interrelationship of language, community and school. Just as a pupil may come to school with a set of values that may be seriously different from the set of values he encounters at school, so a pupil may also come to school with an established set of ways of using language. Some, or even all, of these ways may limit, or inhibit, or totally prevent, his developing the ways of speaking, and especially perhaps the ways of writing, which are as essential to his every day life in the context of school, as is his language to his life in the context of his community.

5 Family, community and the idea of 'language-climate'

At the end of chapter four we suggested that if we are to understand how an individual acquires language for learning then we must look again at the language for living he acquires in his own community. There are two reasons for this. Firstly, if human beings have both a tendency to see new situations in terms of old, and also a tendency to resist any change that may affect their homeostasis, then it follows that his initial learning of language will have a very profound affect upon his attitude to any future learning of language that he may have to do. The way in which he learns to use language initially, and the attitudes he develops towards the use of language at that time, will shape his approach to learning other ways of using language, not only in the school context, but throughout adult life. Secondly, the rapidity with which social and cultural change occurs in our world puts a premium upon the individual's capacity to find language for coping with the new, but this capacity can be limited by his view of how he can use language both for living and for learning. For both these reasons, therefore, we must look again at family and community, and ask ourselves how their structure might affect the way in which their members come to view the possible uses of language.

1. 'Personal' and 'positional' families

The two terms 'personal' and 'positional' have been used by sociologists to describe two opposite ways in which families can create for themselves the internal cohesion which gives them separate identity. These terms will help us focus on the fact that families do differ from each other in the way they see their individual members and in the ways in which these individual

238

members relate to each other within the family. In these terms, 'positional' families are those in which individuals relate to each other in terms of their relative positions. Father is father, youngest child is youngest child, and the behaviour expected of each is related to this role and its status. Youngest child may not sit in the chair by the fire, because that is father's chair: father may not bath youngest child, because that is the job of mother. The rights and obligations of each member of the family are clear and unambiguous by demonstration, but reasons for these rights and obligations do not have to be given because they are 'understood'. Things are as they are, because that *is* the way they are: the young child makes his way by being told what he must do or must not do, but he is never told why this is the case. In contrast, in a 'personal' family; members relate to each other as fully differentiated individuals. Children, as well as adults, are seen as individual people, as Jean or George or Mary, not as 'eldest son', or 'youngest girl', or 'baby'. Much of what happens in the family is, therefore, the result of negotiation and common agreement, because it is accepted implicitly that all its members have rights *as individuals*, but there is a corresponding obligation to consider the needs of the other members. If this view of the workings of a family seems hard to grasp, consider for a moment this example. What does it tell us about a family if we hear on the one hand a mother say, 'Stop yer noise, you'll wake yer father', and on the other, 'If you make all that noise you'll wake your father, and that's hardly fair when he's been up all night, now is it?' In the personal family things do not happen automatically, because that is the way they always happen, the needs of the individual and of the group are open to discussion and the young child makes his way by being told what he may and may not do, and *why* he may or may not do it.

Now it might be difficult, indeed impossible, to find any one family that will fit either of the simplified descriptions I have given above, but the great value of these two terms is that they allow us to refer easily to common ways of behaving which we have all observed. We can, in fact, make a kind of scale with 'most positional' families at one extreme end and 'most personal' families at the other end. Perhaps the value of these terms as a way of looking at families can best be demonstrated if the reader will pause for a few moments to reflect upon his own family and to try to decide where on our scale his family might come. There are two ways in which the reader can approach this task: either

239

he can try to remember whether there were clear cut rules and regulations for the ways in which the members of his family were expected to behave, or he can try to remember the ways in which language was used to relate to other members of the family. The reason that *either* of these approaches can help the reader to make his assessment is that 'positional' is strongly associated with one set of ways of using language, and 'personal' with another.

In some of the most positional families, families like those I encountered in the remoter parts of Western Ireland, so much of everyday life is governed by long-established rules of behaviour that a whole range of situations which might cause discussion in the personal family simply do not arise. For example, if the division of domestic duties between males and females is specified by the culture, that is, accepted as wholly given, then there is never any question as to who is to do what, or when it has to be done. Moreover, the language used in these circumstances would involve simple assertion: 'I'll be cutting the top field this morning', or a statement of the expected, 'Five o'clock, time to put the meal on'; or an injunction which assumes knowledge of the appropriate action upon the part of the recipient, as with 'Jenny, its five o'clock', where Jenny, as the youngest girl, knows that is her job, and only her job to lay the table for the evening meal. In the context of the personal family, however, any domestic task might be done by any member of the family who was competent to do it, so that the use of language for considering possibilities, making alternative suggestions, planning what has been agreed, or justifying a particular plan by offering evidence in support of it, would be involved. We must emphasise, however, that what is characterised here is two alternative *styles* of organising one's life, not two absolutely exclusive *modes of using language*. What the *style* of living does is to make the need for one or other *mode of using language* more or less likely.

What we are trying to indicate by using this extreme example of personal and positional families, is that the way a family is organised in terms of who can do and say what things to which people is crucial to the child's understanding of what it can do with language. Clearly, a positional style of organising the life of family or community does limit the options open to the child for finding out what he can do by using language in different ways.

240

'Don't speak to me like that.'
'Don't answer me back.'
'Do it when I say so and don't ask questions.'

These three commands can be looked at in terms of the relationship between speaker and hearer, or they can be considered in terms of the linguistic options they leave open to the recipient. Possible responses are fairly limited for this particular recipient: he must speak in an acceptable way, acceptable that is, to the controlling adult: he must not offer an alternative view of the case to that presented by this adult, whether or not he knows why he must do so, because he is forbidden to ask questions. One wonders if there is any linguistic alternative at all open to this hearer other than silence. Perhaps, even, this was the intended consequence of the speakers choice of words. In terms of relationship, we could say that instructions such as these are a recurrent feature of the life style of positional families, where there is a strong focus on status, and a sharp dichotomy, therefore, between the relative status of adults and children. It is the sharp distinction between child and adult, between younger and older adult, between male and female, that makes so many ways of speaking unacceptable. It is in this way, therefore, that the pattern of family relationships can directly affect the linguistic options open to its members. If a whole range of linguistic options is closed to a child, it may well be that it includes options which form part of the language for learning that the school requires from the child.

Let us take a specific example. Many teachers in both primary and secondary schools require from their pupils a willingness and an ability to take part in class discussions, to participate in what we can call *exploratory talk*. This kind of talk is familiar to all readers of this book: it occurs whenever a group of people get together to consider a course of action, whether the action is choosing a day's outing, or deciding the content of next term's courses. Exploratory talk is characterised by the opportunity it gives for us to test out half-formed or tentative ideas. Each participant considers the contributions of others and accepts that the object of the talk is to make the best sense of the matter in hand, given the information that is available. Now what is the position of the pupil who has never heard this kind of talk? What is there in his experience that he can draw upon in order to take part in the talk as he is bidden?

We could put this rather differently by asking what constructs he could draw upon to help him solve his problem (see page 50).

241

If the child comes from a family and a community where he has never heard exploratory talk the range of convenience of the constructs he has formed to help him interpret the use of language face-to-face will be too limited for his present needs. What this limitation looks like and how it affects the reading of a new situation is well illustrated by the following comment, a comment made by a mature student at a College of Education about his own experience.

'When I first came to College what I couldn't stand was all the arguing. The lecturer would stand up and say something and someone would start to argue with him and it would go on and on and I would think, "We're never going to get anything done here". It seemed to me that they were just bickering instead of getting on with it, though the lecturer didn't seem to mind. I suppose really it was because of my father. He couldn't stand arguments. If you ever started to disagree with anything he said, he would just lose his temper and say "I'm telling you, there's no two ways about it", and off he'd go. I suppose when I first came to College I saw discussion as argument. I couldn't see any point in it. After all, the lecturer knew and we didn't, so it was up to him to talk and us to listen.'

This comment, together with the example provided by another student in Chapter 3, page 58, gives us some idea of how exploratory talk must look to the individual who has never experienced this kind of talk before. Some interpretation has to be found for what is going on and if the only constructs available in the individual's experience involve 'picking on me', 'bickering' and 'argument' then these terms will be used, however unfortunate their connotations in the context of exploratory discussion. Later in this chapter we shall look at how these two students came to develop new constructs related to the exploratory talk which they now had access to, but for the moment let us look again at what this student is revealing about the attitudes to language he has acquired in the process of learning his language in the context of his own family.

In his family, the relationship between father and son was such that whatever father said had to be accepted. It is not considered appropriate behaviour for a son to argue with his father. If the father holds the view that 'There are no two ways about' any subject, then the putting forward of *any* alternative view of the case, or any qualification of the position the father has asserted, will be construed as 'argument'. A further element in the student's

242

experience of learning is revealed by his assumption that those who 'know' have a right to speak and those who don't ought to be silent. It is very likely that his father would insist upon his status (*a*) as male, (*b*) as father, that is, titular head of the family, (*c*) as adult, in insisting on the rightness of his views when 'arguing' with his son. His son, therefore, has come to accept a link, on the one hand, between status and 'having the right to speak' and, on the other, between authority and knowledge. That a class of mature students, sharing a wide and rich experience of the world, might indeed 'know more' than their lecturer on many occasions, and that their lecturer might be wise enough to see this, is beyond the range of convenience of the constructs about talking, about knowing and about learning that this student has brought with him from his early experience of these things in the context of his own socialisation.

In this one short comment, this student reveals a great deal about the way language could be used in his family. He also gives some indication of the tightly regulated relationship he has available with his father. What is also revealed is the potential for continuity which the adoption of these particular attitudes to language would give to a family or to a community. If one eliminates the right of an individual to present alternatives by making all exchange of views, all qualification of another's assertions, 'argument'; if one then makes 'argument' a crime against the authority structure of the family and if one denies the right to speak to anyone who does not 'know' what the family or community 'knows', then any change of attitude or assumption within family or community will be very unlikely, except as a very slow process over generations. One result of this kind of structure is that any strong-minded person who insists on his right to advance his own view of things will either leave the community out of frustration, or be forced out by the weight of hostile opinion. Once again, the net result is to reinforce the perpetuation of the 'likemindedness' of the family or community concerned.

We are not asking at this point whether or not continuity of this kind in communities is 'a good thing' or 'a bad thing'. There are consequences, however, for the individual and the community, when society as a whole is no longer organised as a series of such communities. Just as the student who revealed these attitudes to language had difficulties when he encountered a new situation, so communities who perpetuate these attitudes to language will

243

inevitably have difficulties if they encounter new situations. The possibility of there being a community in this country which can avoid new situations as we move towards the end of the century seems to us very unlikely.

2. 'Language climate' in family and community

Let us begin by using an illustration to help us define exactly what it is that we mean by 'language climate'.

Just before we left London to come to Manchester, we received two separate invitations to spend the evening with senior professional colleagues whose homes we had not previously visited. Our only information about the social situation we would meet on these two occasions was that an evening meal would be provided. In the event we met two very different situations. On the first occasion, we were welcomed to an elegantly furnished house where our hostess, wearing a long velvet skirt, talked about the dreadful weather as she led us to a panelled drawing-room where sherry was being served. Through the double doors leading to the dining-room, we could see a polished oval table, with cut glass and cutlery laid for eight people.

On the second occasion, we found that our host lived in a ground floor flat of a large block of flats. He greeted us at his front door wearing an apron which said 'Keep Britain dry' and carrying his two year old son. He apologised for the temporary absence of his wife who was 'having a fight with the oven', and led us to a small sitting-room where a dozen people were sitting or standing in groups talking, and a table was stacked high with plates, cutlery and paper napkins for a buffet supper.

Now both these situations required from the writers the kind of assessment which the reader will have made many, many times for himself, unthinkingly, when faced, as we were, with a new situation where he was required to interact with a group of people more or less unknown to him. The most immediate thing that the reader would do, as we did, was to make an assessment of the formality or informality of the occasion. In any situation one has to prepare a plan of action before speaking, and assessing the formality or informality of the occasion is a first step in making a whole series of further decisions about what actions might or might not be acceptable in this context. Some of these decisions are decisions about the use of language: to talk or not to talk; to initiate conversation or to let others take the lead; to change the topic of conversation; to listen or to remain silent. One might quickly make up one's mind that certain topics were to be avoided or that certain topics would be appropriate. For example, on the first occasion a remark of the hostess about the sad fate of the local selective school suggested that the subject of comprehensive education would not be an appropriate one. All of the decisions, therefore, which the reader might make in a social setting, be it informal or formal, professional or personal, pleasurable or otherwise, are based on his reading of the situation, his assessment of the total 'atmosphere'. It is to that part of the total atmosphere which influences our decisions concerning our use of language that we give the name 'language-climate'.

Every reader will be able to think of his experience of a whole variety of different language climates. Some of these language climates we might describe as 'hostile': for example, the very formal interview where the reader felt unable to use his habitual ways of speaking, but was forced into ways of speaking where he felt uneasy. This was, indeed, the writer's experience at that very formal dinner party. On the other hand, there are 'supportive' language-climates, the kind which one often finds in the company of old friends, or long standing colleagues, where one need not fear being misunderstood and where one can risk revealing a half-formed idea, or make a spontaneous comment.

As with the terms 'positional' and 'personal' we do not want to focus upon 'ideal' examples of either 'hostile' or 'supportive' climates, we want rather to use the terms in order to point to the particular elements in situations which shape our linguistic response to them. The key feature of the language climate as far as the individual speaker is concerned is his freedom or otherwise to use language in the ways in which he is most happy to use language in expressing his view of the world and his relationship to others, 'hostile' and 'supportive' help us to focus upon this key feature.

We can use the example of the informal supper, and the formal dinner, to illustrate some of the distinctive features of 'hostile' and 'supportive' language-climates. We can only compare them, however, if we consider them in respect of an individual who is *equally familiar* with both formal and informal situations of this kind. There is a sense in which the language-climate of *any* situation is likely to be read as hostile by an individual who has no previous experience of similar situations as our student so read the seminar situation at college.

245

Let us assume then that the reader has experienced occasions similar to the two that we are considering. We can make certain predictions about the linguistic demands which the two evenings would have made upon him. In linguistic terms, the demands of the larger informal gathering in the small sitting-room are far greater than the demands of the formal dinner party. In a setting such as the informal supper party the 'rules' for behaviour, linguistic and otherwise, are more open and flexible than in the formal setting. A great deal more is left to the individual judgment and discretion of the participants. For example, in this situation the reader would have had to decide for himself whether he was entitled to talk to one person all evening because they had found a topic of great mutual interest, or whether he should talk to as many people as possible, restricting himself more or less to social talk in doing so. He will have to decide whether to join in the talk of an existing small group at a particular moment, or whether to wait until the topic under discussion changes. There are also decisions to make as to whether to help with serving supper, whether to offer to help with the washing up, whether to leave when the first guests leave, or whether to stay to the end. This informal situation, by leaving open so many alternative possibilities for action, makes a very great demand upon the individual in selecting from all these possibilities the ones which best relate him to the situation. In meeting this demand, however, the reader would have the freedom to talk or to remain silent, to join a conversation, to change the subject, to assert a point of view, to express his sincerely held convictions, or to ask questions, for the language climate is basically 'supportive'.

At the formal dinner party, the reader would have found very few of these linguistic possibilities open to him. On the other hand, provided that he was familiar with such settings, choice of what to do or say would present very little difficulty just because the options available were so limited. A limited range of options means that linguistic events become highly predictable, so that, once an initial reading of the situation has been made, what follows has little that is 'new' about it. In terms of language climate, therefore, it is proper to say that the formal setting is the more 'hostile', because the only alternative to knowing, and keeping, the rules is silence. We have the seeming paradox, therefore, that the more difficult setting in terms of the demands it makes upon our capacity to language is, in fact, the more 'supportive', while the setting that makes the fewest demands, because it offers virtually no options to the participants, is the more 'hostile'. We can test this by asking ourselves what would be the fate of someone who was equally unfamiliar with both these settings. It is reasonable to suggest that, in the formal setting, he would be virtually excluded from any active participation in the events of the evening, while in the informal setting he would feel able to risk some sort of participation, however tentative, because he would sense that this was one of the options available.

The formality or informality, of relationships would seem to be a key factor in the formation of language climates and indeed the reader may have observed the similarity between what we have said about the language climate of formal and informal settings and what we have said about the relative formality of positional and personal families. For example, in the less strictly regulated personal family individuals generally find they need to use language in a wide variety of ways, and make decisions continuously as to the appropriate thing to say next. In this sense, there is a similarity here with what has been said about the informal supper party. On the other hand, the positional family has a fixed pattern of relationship and correspondingly limited options for using language very similar to the rule-bound nature of the formal dinner party. In the case of both positional family and formal dinner party there are very clear rules governing who can say what to whom and in what manner. The rules are not made explicit, because participants are *expected* to know the rules, and the rules allow only a certain limited range of linguistic options to them.

Once again we must say that it is not our concern to ask whether the limiting of linguistic possibilities is in itself 'a good thing' or 'a bad thing', or what the relationship is between personal and positional families and social structure. What we must ask instead is whether the limiting of linguistic options in the way we have described, and the resulting effect on the individual child, pupil or adult, will enable him to deal more easily or less easily, with the range of situations, familiar and unfamiliar, which he is likely to meet in his everyday life.

So far, we have been talking exclusively about personal and positional families and we have had to point to one key feature of the language climate of the positional family, its limitation on the options it allows its members in their use of language for living. After the age of five, however, a child spends progressively less

247

time exclusively within his own family environment. School becomes a major factor in his life, and friends and playmates provide access to other homes and other families. It might be thought that the child from a positional family would gain access to those ways of speaking which were not part of his own family experience through his contact with other families and with school. The language climate of schools will be the topic of section four of this chapter. What we must do here is to consider the relationship between family and community in terms of their respective language climates.

When we were working towards a definition of community in Chapter 2 we suggested that the most important force in creating communities was the sharing, and perpetuating, of a particular set of values. In particular, we pointed out that factors like geographical proximity were of minor significance in the development of 'us-ness' compared with even the most simple shared value, attitude or assumption. Hence we were led to describe 'positional' and 'personal' as ways of experiencing values, the organising of deeply-held beliefs so that they express themselves in terms of a particular pattern of relationships and a particular pattern of using language. If we find a whole group of families organising their beliefs along similar lines there are two questions we must ask. Firstly, 'Whence came the model for these families to use in organising their beliefs?' If we answer, 'From the community, of course, the repository of the shared values of the culture', then we must ask, 'Is it then reasonable to extend the range of convenience of our terms "positional" and "personal" so that they will refer to the organisation of life within the community as well as within the family?'

These are very difficult questions and anything like a full answer is beyond the scope of this book, but it has to be said that the answers to these questions are far from being of theoretical interest only. From my own fieldwork observations in very different communities, and recent work describing the life of communities in Britain, examined with this perspective in mind, my feeling is that 'positional' in the family is a reflection of 'positional' in the community. If this *is* the case, then the implications are very important indeed, for this means that the child from a positional home is likely to encounter the *same* ways of organising relationships, and the *same* ways of using language, in his dealings with his community, as he experienced in his own family. We could also make the further point, that the more positional a community is,

248

the more intolerant it is of alternative ways of behaving, and hence the more likely that a friendship between a child from a 'positional' family and a child from a 'personal' family will be short-lived.

This leaves the school. What we are likely to find in the schools of a 'positional' community is one of two things. On the one hand, in a fairly small number of cases, there is complete accord between the culture of the community and the culture of the school. so that there is a continuity of language climate between them. On the other hand, in a much larger proportion of schools, there is a gap between the culture of the community and the culture of the school which is so wide that there is a total discontinuity between them. In the first case, the pupil meets little or no opportunity to acquire new ways of using language for living; in the second, he cannot carry home what he finds at school, or use in school what he uses at home. Only the most tough-minded children can tolerate the strain of having to live what amounts to two separate lives. The majority do what one would expect: bow to the ties of home and community and contract out of the culture of the school entirely.

If an individual brought up in a positional family within a positional community spends his life in that community, it would be fair to say that there would be much in his life that he could always take completely for granted. His capacity to construe events by their replication would be very high, because of the relatively limited range of options open to him, and his need to read and interpret new situations would be very low. The language climate of his whole environment would be entirely supportive to him in that only his habitual ways of speaking would be required. What then will happen if the urban area where he lives is declared a slum and clearance begins; or if the mine, or mill, or factory, where he works, closes and there are no alternative jobs in the area, or if a motorway turns his remote village into a commuter's paradise; or if an oil rig turns his fishing village into an oil town; or if industrialised agriculture, reafforestation, or mining, changes the composition of the local population? What happens is that changes will occur that will radically alter the fabric of the community he has known and within which he is able to operate so successfully, and change of this order is the last thing for which the individual from the positional family and positional community is in any way equipped to handle.

249

3. Change: the role of the language climate

Not all individuals will be in such vulnerable positions as those in the situations we suggested at the end of the last section, but if change is something which will inevitably affect every individual alive in the last quarter of the twentieth century then we may well ask how they are going to cope? Although there are many answers to that question, the reader will be able to supply a range of examples of his own which illustrate the different ways in which people already do cope with change. At one end of the 'coping' scale we have the 'non-copers', the people who simply cannot manage to come to terms with whatever change faces them whether it is social, economic, practical or personal and their unhappy stories reach our newspapers daily.

Another group try to cope with change by pretending that it has not occurred There is the Grammar school headmistress who tries to enforce the wearing of gloves by teenagers in the 1970's; the old man who refuses to believe that the motorway really is going to be built through his condemned house; the parents who cannot accept that their children are now adults. Then there are those people who just manage to cope, who do 'get by' or 'muddle through' or 'manage somehow'. Their coping does not make the newspapers, or even the doctor's surgery, so we seldom have any evidence for the time or energy or anxiety that they have expended in order to come to terms with whatever changes have occurred. At the furthest end of the scale, we have those people who find change presents little problem to them. They 'take things in their stride' and adapt to the new situation without any particular visible stress or anxiety. How do they do it?

The answer to this question is unlikely to be simple, but one element is sure to be involved: the part played in their ability to cope by a highly developed capacity to use language 'on their feet'. Let the reader choose any change that he has ever had to cope with and consider what part language played at every stage in the process. Firstly, language will have entered into his initial reading of the situation; then he will have used language to think through the problems involved. Language comes in when we decide to ask for help from friends, to request or gather factual information, to sort and categorise this new information. If there is no stage in reading, assessing, deciding or acting in order to cope with change that does not use language, either internally or

250

externally, then it would seem that the language we bring to bear upon the task is the key factor in our success or failure.

The language any one of us brings to a situation, however, is a product of our experience and of our opportunity both to observe and to practise ways of using language. We have pointed, too, to the limited ways of seeing and behaving and speaking that are characteristics of the positional family and community. This would lead us to the idea that those people who can best cope with change are those whose experience of using language and making decisions embraces a very wide range of different situations, and has frequently required them to cope with the linguistic demands of situations new to them. It would seem that some people have a much greater capacity to 'work things out for themselves' than others. Perhaps we might be in a better position to ask how this necessary process is best developed or accelerated if we could get a clear idea of what 'working things out for themselves' really looks like.

In the course of writing, I have already used comments made by mature students at a College of Education. These comments were recorded after discussions with students about the changes they had encountered in their lives and how they had coped with them. As the students had indeed 'worked things out for themselves' we can use their comments as a starting point.

'When I first went to Grammar School it was like going into a different world. They even spoke so differently that they wouldn't have understood me if I'd spoken the way we spoke at home. I began to feel terribly inferior, because I couldn't express myself. At home no-one ever said very much. Dad was out all day and Mum had four of us to look after, so there didn't seem much to talk about. Then I found I could do languages. I think it was because they taught you from the beginning, not just expected you to know and I decided I wanted to get away. I saw that if I could do things like the others, I could go on to College, so I started to try to say more. It was awful, but I managed because I knew what I wanted.'

'Before I came to College I lived in Exbury, I went to school in Exbury, I worked in Exbury and I married an Exbury man. I couldn't imagine that people really lived any differently, or thought any differently, from the way that I thought. When I came to College I couldn't get used to being with people from different places especially foreigners. I found I could often get on better with the foreigners than with the people who lived only a few miles away from where I lived myself. I never thought that

251

people who lived so close could think so differently, or people who lived so far away could have such similar ideas about certain things. I realised that if you wanted to understand people you had to find out what they thought, not assume that they thought like you.'

Now the experiences which these three students are recounting are different in detail, but there is a common quality in the experience which they have gone through. All of the students began their lives in a situation which limited their experience of the world. They lived, respectively, in a Manchester industrial suburb of nineteenth century back-to-back houses: in a mining village in North Yorkshire and in a high-cost, low density, garden suburb in Cheshire. All three students considered that their homes were 'more positional', and that all three homes made it clear that their own particular way of behaving was the 'right' and 'obvious' way to behave. But what in fact has happened to the students?

In all three cases, they have encountered a new situation, one with which they were quite unfamiliar and one which presents, not just a different, but often an opposite view to the one they themselves hold. Mr A sees the discussions of his first months at College as 'arguments', when people 'pick on him'. Mrs B finds that at Grammar School you are expected to be able to express what you are thinking, while at home it is considered that 'there isn't much to say'. Mrs C discovers that not everyone in the world thinks like she does. This, however, is not the end of the process, but the beginning, for in each case the students observe the new situation. They read what they see happening in discussion, in the classroom, in contact with new people, and they match it with what is familiar to them in their own construct system. Mr A, for example, matches 'discussion' to 'argument' but in fact rejects his own reading when, as he says himself, he saw 'that people were still friendly after one of these arguments'. He is alerted to the fact that the new situation is different and, having seen this, he moves towards it in order to find out more.

One might say that each student moves towards the new situation rather as one might move towards a nearby hill to view one's former position in the hollow. Like moving to a new physical viewpoint, moving to a new mental viewpoint has two effects: it allows one to view at close quarters a new piece of landscape and it allows one to look back at the point from which one has come.

As one student summed up his experience for me: 'Once you've

252

realised that there is more than one way of looking at anything, then you are never the same again, for when you meet something new, you are on the look out for things, you may not know what, but at least you know to look'.

What in fact the students described to me is a process which was observed and written about at length by G. H. Mead, the social psychologist. He calls this process of moving towards the new and reconsidering what has gone before 'reflexiveness'. He sees it as,

'the turning back of the experience of the individual upon himself'.

He also sees it as a process which enables the individual,

'To take the attitude of the other towards himself'.

We could say that reflexiveness gives us the opportunity BOTH to put ourselves in a different position from the one we have always been accustomed to adopt, so that we can experience that position for ourselves, AND to put ourself in a different position, so that we can review our own experience by standing outside and looking in upon what is familiar and habitual to us. We can demonstrate this process by recording what an individual might be thinking at various stages on his journey from a familiar and known perspective to his taking up a new and unfamiliar one.

'Ah—I thought that was obvious, but it isn't.'
'So that's how it affects me, is it?'
'So that's what it means in my life to . . .'
'So that's what it means in life to . . .'

The ability to be reflexive which these mature students have developed, has helped them to adjust to very considerable changes in their lives. It has also given them the confidence to say that, although they may not *welcome* change, they do feel now that they will be able to 'think it through for themselves' and make the relevant decisions. If reflexiveness is indeed a capacity that can be developed to help individuals cope with change, and if schools accept that part of their job is to equip the individual for coping with his life beyond school, then there are two questions we must ask about schools. Firstly, do schools provide the right kind of opportunities for pupils and students to explore ways of thinking and talking alternative to those which have been habitual to them in family and community? Secondly, do schools provide the supportive language climate which will be necessary if the pupil or student is to have the courage to develop the linguistic competence without which he cannot be reflexive?

It may be that there are as many answers to the first of these questions as there are individual schools. Certainly the reader will be able to supply some answers from his own experience. What we must do in the remaining space we have is to consider what the language climate of schools might look like.

4. The language climate of schools

In the first two sections of this chapter we explored the way in which the organisation of relationships in family and community affects the individual by extending or narrowing the options available to him when he uses language. We then considered the implications of this for an individual who was faced with living in an environment of continuous change. We argued that one key factor was his ability to bring language to bear upon the new experience which confronted him, and we suggested that this was linked with his ability to be reflexive about his experience. We went on to say that this reflexiveness could not be fully developed unless opportunities occurred for the individual to extend both his ways of thinking and his ways of speaking. Extending one's ways of speaking is a complex process, for it must involve exposure to new experience and we have already considered at length what difficulties new experience presents to the majority of people. The language climate is also involved in the process and enough has been said about the language climate of different kinds of community for the reader to see that the process of coming to terms with new experience is actively supported by some climates, while many can be neutral, or even entirely hostile to the process. What we must now consider is the language climate in schools. If we accept that extending an individual's linguistic competence is a necessary objective for the school and if we accept that extending this competence is best pursued in a supportive language climate, then we have to recognise that school is the most likely, or even the *only* possible, source of such a climate for the majority of our children at the present time.

Most readers will have been inside a number of schools, whether as pupils, or subsequently as parents and as teachers. Some readers will have experience of very many schools, because of their professional concerns, but all readers will be aware of the differences that are immediately observable when one goes from one school to another. Some schools have a well-cared for appearance with bright wall displays, flowers and pupils' work

254

carefully arranged: some seem uncared for, cheerless and bleak. From school to school, noise levels vary from the silence of the tomb to the hubbub of the marketplace. In some schools, pupils chatter in corridors; in others, file silently from class-room to class-room. For those who visit schools professionally such small individual features have more than superficial meaning For example, a skilled reader of schools can tell from the rules he observes in practice the attitude of the staff towards the pupils: whether they regard pupils as objects to be organised and controlled, or as individuals with the capacity to think for themselves and to make decisions. He can work out from his reading of the 'atmosphere' of the school some of the underlying attitudes which grow and develop when a group of people interact over a period of time. What we want to focus on particularly is how this atmosphere affects the language climate of the school, and therefore the use of language by all those who work there. We must focus upon the cultural climate of the school as a whole and consider which of its assumptions, attitudes and values most immediately contribute to the creation of its language climate. For example, in terms of language climate, it may not matter whether or not there are flowers in the class-room, but it may be critical that talking is forbidden in corridors.

Let us look now at one of the most accessible parts of the culture of the school, its 'rules'. Consider the following:

'Don't talk in class'
'Don't talk in the hall'
'Don't talk in the corridors'
'Don't speak to a teacher like that'
'Don't answer back'

Once again we ask the reader to reconstruct from his own experience the language climate of any school in which he was a pupil. Hopefully, it will not have been like the hostile climate created by the school where these five rules were in use. In that particular school, the linguistic options presented to pupils were so limited that most pupils had taken refuge in apathy, the behavioural equivalent of silence, or absenteeism. If we look closely at the five rules we see that they circumscribe speech between pupils and between teacher and pupil. The only form of verbal exchange between teacher and pupil was the question and answer form. The reciprocal use of language, as in dialogue proper, was simply 'unthinkable' for teacher or pupil. In many cases, the teacher shaped the sentences and required only the appropriate one word reply slotted in to the appropriate space. The spoken language used in learning was thus confined to one simple kind: the other major form of language use was a brusque language of control, which required only compliance on the part of the pupil, or at best a verbal sign of acquiescence such as, 'Yes, miss'. It is such features of this school language climate as these that make it fair to suggest that we have here a climate closely analogous to the one we have already explored when we discussed positional families.

This is an extreme, but not untypical, example of how a climate is created in which pupils have little opportunity to develop their thinking or ways of expressing themselves. It is not surprising that a personnel manager interviewing pupils from this school should complain that not one boy or girl had been able to say two sentences in reply to his questions without using such fillers as 'You know . . .', 'Kind of . . .' 'like'. We would ask when these boys and girls had last been presented with the opportunity to utter a complete sentence without fear of interruption or criticism.

We must now look beyond such an extreme example as this. There are many, many schools where one might say that the cultural climate as a whole was much less hostile to pupils, but where a close examination of the language climate might reveal serious limitations in its capacity to be supportive.

Consider the following 'rules'

'Don't ask questions now, there may be time later.'
'I'm not interested in the experiment being exciting: we only want results and diagrams.'
'Don't sit there reading, you're supposed to be outside.'
'Comics and other magazines must not be brought into school.'
'Juniors always play this side: the Seniors go over there.'

While considerably less abrasive than our first set of rules, these are equally limiting in their effect upon the linguistic options pupils will feel they are able to take up in the environment of the school. They also remind us that if we want to see the full extent of the features which go to make up a language climate we must look in the corridors and in the playground as well as in the classrooms. We should consider what possibilities are open to pupils when they are not in class, but still within the school. What would the reader now make of the following unwritten rule, 'Girls are not permitted to use the Library on dry days', or the injunction of one headmaster to his younger staff that they should not 'fraternise with pupils on the school premises' as this would 'undermine

256

discipline'; or of another that pupils should be discouraged from discussing their school work with their parents.

Let us consider for a moment what the effect might be on a pupil from a 'more positional' family who comes to a school where the language climate is hostile. In his family and community, this pupil will have acquired a set of ideas about what can be done with language. He will be familiar with the idea of language as a means of social control: he is controlled by his parents or elders; in turn he controls younger children by using the same forms. He has developed a 'language for living' which he uses to carry on his life as brother, son, boy-next-door, friend, member of a peer group. In a hostile language climate, he will meet a language of control that is certainly familiar to him in one sense, for it will be peremptory and will not be explicit as to the reasons for its commands. However, it will be exerted, not by members of his own community, but by 'outsiders', outsiders who are putting pressure upon him at the same time to use a 'language for learning' that he has little opportunity to acquire as they do not offer the opportunity to practice. Not surprisingly, this pupil is unwilling to 'get it wrong', by trying a half-formed sentence with a teacher who is likely to say, 'Come along, boy, out with it, I can't stay here all day.'

At the same time, we can ask what opportunity this pupil will have for seeing language used in new ways, ways that are different from any that he knows from his home situation, other than those that are least accessible to him, the ways of using language for learning customary in the context of formal education. Given such a climate, he may well leave school, as the student quoted on page 84, without ever having taken part in discussion, without ever having been asked to consider, to select, to report, to plan or to argue. Far from presenting alternatives his time at school will have offered him only what he was already familiar with, and offered it in such a way as to alienate and antagonise him. On the other hand, were the pupil to find himself in one of the many schools where staff have given their attention to creating conditions in which pupils feel secure and able to 'risk' the hazard of speaking about what they 'don't know', are 'not sure of', or 'have had an idea about', then he would be in a totally different position. In this climate, a condition which we find in many of the best primary schools, particularly those where the teachers have constant contact with each other and a deep knowledge of the community from which their pupils come, our pupil would see and hear pupils and teachers engaging in a kind of talk that he had not experienced at home. By sharing in the activities of the class, he could enter into the talk, at first tentatively, and then more confidently, until ultimately he had added to his ways of speaking the ability to discuss, to plan, to imagine, to speculate and to share all this both with his peers and with his teachers.

From the foregoing, it is clear that a key difference between the hostile and the supportive language climate lies in the relationships which are possible between staff and pupils. The hostile climate is likely to be found where staff/pupil boundaries are strictly maintained:

'Staff corridor—no admission.'
'Say "Sir", when you speak to me.'

A supportive climate is much more likely to be found where staff/ pupil relations are friendly and less formal:

'How would you describe that shape? Anyone got any ideas?'
'Can someone help me with the projector?'

This contrast is not accidental. Formality is a device used in most human communities to limit the terms of some relationships, and to exclude others as 'unthinkable'. Like many other such devices formality makes life much easier for all who participate in those relationships. 'You know where you are', in relation to anyone met with in the community: that is to say, the degree of intimacy is pre-established and what can, and cannot, be a part of the relationship is determined by the degree of intimacy involved. On the other hand, informality allows very wide variations of behaviour within the bounds of a particular relationship. Formality makes predicting future responses very easy: informality requires that we monitor closely the progress of the interaction all the time. For some teachers and some schools, this degree of indeterminacy in the relationship between teacher and pupil is quite unacceptable. The Headmaster who did not want his staff to 'fraternise' with their pupils was no fool: intuitively, he realised that a change in the degree of formality means a change in the terms of the interaction between staff and pupils. Change of this kind is something which neither party may wish to cope with, because it involves the learning of new ways of behaving and new ways of languaging. As this headmaster realised, in the context of a school, new ways of behaving imply new ways of controlling others. A change in the language climate of a school necessarily implies some change in that part of the cultural climate

258

of the school concerned with maintaining 'good order and discipline'.

At this point it is necessary to say again that pupils as much as teachers may resist any change that seems to require an effort from them. For the writer's however, the teacher's situation was summed up for us by one of the teachers who attended the summer school we worked with in Belfast in July 1972. After three days of discussion in which he took little part, this teacher came to us and said: 'I've thought through what you've been saying about developing their language and I think you are right, but I don't know what to do. You see, I teach in a very formal school and I get order by a mixture of being tough and trying to be fair, but what you suggest means changing my whole way of going.'

This teacher could see the need, but he did not feel able to act at that moment. Subsequently he did act, and in spite of a very formal, indeed, rigid situation he did create a change in conditions within his own class-room. What he did in effect was to create what we might call a 'micro-climate', a small area within the general language-climate of the school where conditions were significantly different. Within the confines of his own room he was able to do something to off-set conditions in the school in general.

The pupils' view of change is crystallised for us by the group of fourth formers who, after about five weeks of the autumn term, got up a petition, demanding that the one of us concerned 'get on with teaching us something and stop all this talk'. The general climate of the school was not exactly supportive and most members of staff took a very 'subject content' view of their work. These fourth formers wanted work in English to conform to their expectations of what 'work' in a school context ought to look like. These expectations had no room for the idea that *they* had a positive contribution to make to their learning through their participation in various kinds of shared language activity.

What these two brief illustrations suggest is that the task of modifying the language climate of a school requires a concerted effort upon the part of the staff that may be very difficult to initiate. What they imply, however, is the degree to which any teacher could create for himself and his pupils a 'micro-climate' in the context of his own class-room. Whatever the nature of the language climate prevailing in a school, it is up to every teacher to decide for himself what he might do to modify its manifestations in so far as his own work is concerned.

Postscript

We ended our last chapter by suggesting that every teacher is in a position to consider how he could best enhance his pupils' ability to use the language they have in the context of the school, and to learn the language they need if they are to meet the school's demands in terms of language for learning, because every teacher has a local control over the linguistic micro-climate of his own classroom, however hostile to the linguistic needs of pupils the total climate of the school may be. Easily enough said, the reader may think, but how is it to be done? What kinds of things would create the conditions in the class-room that could lead to a favourable climate for language activity? How could these be reconciled with a prevailing climate that was hostile, or with the dictates of syllabus and public examination? Is it not the case, perhaps, that the curriculum of the secondary school, as we have it at present, creates the most hostile language climate of all for the large majority of secondary school pupils?

These questions are properly asked and point to the seriousness of the problems that face us if we wish to make use of our knowledge of language and community in order to develop a more effective approach to language as the medium of learning in the school context. Moreover, they imply that something major *can* be achieved by working to modify the habitual attitudes towards, and assumptions about, the use of language, both for living and for learning, that we customarily find in schools of all kinds at the present time. It may be in the minds of some readers that there is a body of recent research which has suggested the school counts for so little in relation to the combined weight of home and peer group that, really, nothing very much by way of change can be hoped for through changing the structure and practice of formal education. Throughout this book we have laid particular emphasis

260

upon the critical interrelationship between language and community, in the sense that learning a language is the equivalent of learning a culture, and a culture is an expression for the whole body of values that go to make up a community. Surely, then, if school can do so little to modify the attitudes and assumptions pupils bring with them from their home and community, how likely is it that school will be able to modify the pupil's own language.

Again, this objection is a serious one. If it were true, then there would be little point in attempting more than a holding operation as far as the majority of pupils were concerned, and the relative temper of the language climate of the school would be a very minor matter. However, it seems to us that it is precisely the possibility of modifying pupils' ways of using language that gives the lie to this pessimistic view of the school's potential for change. We would see the language climate of the school as the critical factor in the school's ability to provide those alternative ways of seeing the world out of which changes in the pupils attitudes and assumptions might grow. It is this climate that determines whether or not he will be allowed to use the language he has learnt successfully as a social being in the new context of his formal education, and whether or not he will be given appropriate opportunities to learn the language he now needs, if he is to meet the demands of this formal education, in the only place where these needs can be provided for, *the context of the learning situations that give rise to them.* If the climate excludes from the school the pupil's own ways of using language, then it excludes also the pupil's own ways of looking at the world; and if it does not allow him to present his own ways of looking at the world, then it can scarcely expect to create the conditions in which the pupil might choose to modify them.

So this brings us back to the questions raised in the first paragraph of this Postscript and to the kinds of answers that would substantiate so strong a belief in the possibility of creating a favourable language climate for the school. Perhaps it is significant that the last paragraphs might read rather strangely to someone who works in the more progressive Infant or Junior school. At its best, the contemporary Infant school is an excellent example of how a language climate can be created that leads to continuous positive language learning. Another example is provided by the best work now being done in secondary schools by the English Departments that build their work around the pupil's exploration of his own experience through writing and talking about it in words of his own choosing. Another clue to the creation of a favourable language climate is provided by the approach Professor Stenhouse has developed for the Humanities Curriculum Project where, in effect, he requires the teacher, in the role of chairman, to create such a climate by himself remaining neutral. There is a similar requirement for the creation of a locally favourable climate implicit in the moral education material Peter McPhail has developed for Schools Council under the name of *Lifeline*.

These questions really require a rather different kind of answer, however, which would be directed specifically to the practical problems they raise. Part of this answer would be provided by a sequel to this book which would explore in detail the concept of language climate in the context of education, showing what features of the school situation and the interaction of the class-room are most significant in its formation, and how these affect pupils' and teachers' use of language for learning. This sequel we hope to be able to provide. That lies in the future, however. For the present, we can point to another part of the answer, the provision of practical help for the teacher who wants to try and do something about the language climate of his own class-room. Here he can turn to the resource for work with language called *Language in Use*, where he will find a wide range of suggestions about the ways in which class-room activities can be organised so as to give the maximum opportunities for pupils to develop their command of language, spoken and written.

Language in Use is so designed that the suggestions it offers can be adapted to the needs of any classroom, for it is a resource in the hands of the teacher, not a body of material for the pupil. Hence it is not limited in its application to any one age group or level of ability, nor need it be confined to any one area of the curriculum. It has by now been used in an enormous variety of individual learning situations, embracing as wide a range of language climates, from the most hostile to the most favourable. The cumulative experience of those who have used it suggest that the approaches recommended do succeed in creating a language climate, locally, in individual class-rooms, that enables pupils, *and their teachers*, to modify their ways of thinking about language and its use and, in the process, modify also their ways of using language. How and why this is possible is the subject of *Using 'Language in Use': a guide to language work in the class-room* by the present authors.

262

At this stage in the growth of our understanding of the part played by language in education, we need to develop our thinking along all three lines suggested by this Postscript. We need to know more about the processes by which we learn language, the effect of the context in which we first learn language upon our subsequent ways of using language, and upon our capacity to continue indefinitely the process of learning new ways of using language. We need to know much more about the inter-relationship between the language we use, the community we inhabit and the culture we express through the values we hold. We need to see much more clearly where the school fits into this complex pattern: how it regards pupils' existing capability as successful users of language for living; what demands it makes as a user of language for learning upon the individual's capacity to language, and to learn language; how it relates itself to the community from which it draws its pupils, and to the culture whose values their attitudes and assumptions embody. It is to meet such needs as these that *Explorations in Language Study* was established and *Language and Community* is one part of the process of demonstrating why these matters are so vitally important to everyone involved in education.

At the same time, we need to develop our ways of showing how such explorations as these can be related to day-to-day practice in class-rooms of all kinds with pupils of all ages and levels of ability. We must be able to offer some concrete guidance to the teacher who says, 'Yes, this makes good sense. I see where the old ways won't achieve what I want to achieve. What do I do about it?' We must show that new ideas can lead on into new practice, and that that new practice can then modify the ideas which gave rise to it, so that we can break down and discard, once and for all, the old bad distinction between Theory, the Province of those who wouldn't show how their ideas could work in practice, and Practice, the Province of those who wouldn't admit that ideas could have anything to do with their needs. Titles in the Series like Brian Harrison's *English as a Second and Foreign Language* and Eric Ashworth's *Language in the Junior School*, exemplify the necessary interrelationship between new ideas and new practice, while *Using 'Language in Use': a guide to language work in the class-room* is a detailed account of what a teacher can do to create a favourable language climate and how he can do it.

The third line along which our thinking must develop is a concrete realizing of our answers to the question, 'What do I do?', in terms of resources and materials. It is a sad reflection upon the educational scene that so many teachers are convinced that this is the *only* line that really matters. This view is epitomised by the teacher who rises to his feet after a presentation and says, 'That's all very well, but *what* do I do with 3g, second period on Monday next?', by which he means, regrettably, 'Give me something I can use and don't bother me with questions about the why's and wherefore's of using it.' This is really a plea for something to structure the time teacher and pupil spend together, irrespective of whether or not anything significant *happens* during that time. When we speak of 'resources and materials', we have in mind something very different, something that will enable the teacher to implement successfully the new practice he has decided upon, and not a means by which he can abdicate the responsibility for making decisions of that kind for himself. What we have in mind is exemplified by *Language in Use*, by *Lifeline*, by the Humanities Curriculum Project, where the resource requires the teacher to come to terms with new practice and think it through for himself before he can use it successfully. Each of these resources has great potential for helping a teacher to give concrete expression to his decision that the language climate in which he worked must change. They are not a substitute for that decision, however, and, in the absence of it, are likely to prove a sad disappointment.

We have come a long way from the point at which we began, with the new born infant, helpless and languageless, dependent for survival upon the supportive social context of family and community, and dependent upon the relationships of that human environment for the language without the learning of which survival will become difficult indeed. What we have tried to make plain in this Postscript is that the journey the reader has been asked to undertake does lead from that point right down to the discussion of resources and materials for use in the class-room, and that at no point along the way is it legitimate for him to make a break and say, 'Up to now it has all been very interesting, but this is where the nitty-gritty begins.' Ultimately, our every act in the class-room has to be seen against the broad design of how we use language to live and to learn, because that perspective alone will lead us to make the right choices in our day-to-day decisions, when those decisions involve language in the context of teaching and learning.

264

Notes on further reading

As the reader will imagine there is a vast literature lying behind the themes treated in this book, but we do not propose to shower him with titles, partly because we have a very realistic view of what it is possible for any one reader to find time for, and partly because we feel that lengthy bibliographies are valuable only to those who are already reasonably familiar with the literature of the fields concerned and we have written specifically for those to whom these fields are very new. Full references follow at the end of this section.

Let us begin, therefore, by listing the books which have contributed directly to the thinking that has gone into this book. *An Introduction to the Study of Man* is a very large book, but it has an excellently detailed table of contents, so that anyone who wanted to follow up the ideas we have drawn from it would find it very easy to do so. *Inquiring Man* is the most accessible way of finding out more about the ideas of George Kelly, but it is not an easy book to read, for the ideas it discusses are complex and the writing is very compressed. The most accessible way of finding out more about the social aspects of our argument is to turn to *Language and Social Behaviour*, where again the reader is helped in his search by a very detailed table of contents. Chapter 8, 'Social class and language' and Chapter 9 'Social class, language and socialisation' are particularly relevant to the argument of the book. Chapter 8 contains the most lucid account of Bernstein's work available, but the reader who wants to tackle Bernstein for himself can best do so by turning to *Class, Codes and Control*, and begin by reading Bernstein's own Introduction. He should then read Paper 9, 'Social class, language and socialisation'.

For the view of language we have used, *Exploring Language* provides a first step, especially Chapter 7, 'Command of a language', while Chapters 5 and 6, 'Language and relationships', and 'Language and society' have more to say about our view of how we use language to live. The reader can then turn to the work of M. A. K. Halliday, starting with two papers in *Explorations in the Functions of Language*, 'Relevant models of language' and 'Language in a social perspective'. He should then try 'Learning how to mean', in his volume of the same name.

It is less easy to point to any one source for our thinking about community, though we must say that the situation in Northern Ireland over the last five years has provided a shaping context for it. We have learnt much from the sort of work summarised so ably in *Communities in Britain*, and from original studies of particular human environments such as *Akenfield*, *The Classic Slum* and *The Unprivileged*. Beyond that lies the more formal literature of social science, where we would point to the work of Erving Goffman, especially *The Presentation of Self in Everyday Life*, a highly readable and entertaining book, and Peter Berger, whose work on the concept of social reality is crucial to our thinking. It has to be said, however, that this is formidable territory to enter for the reader who is not familiar with the language of sociological theory.

From the ever-growing literature about pupils, schools and their relationships, we would mention three titles only, each one of which explores from its own position many of the ideas we approach from our linguistic perspective, *Society, Schools and Humanity; Young Teachers and Reluctant Learners* and *Teaching as a Subversive Activity*. The vast bulk of the literature of educational studies is arid indeed, but each of these books is pungent, readable and sharply focused on the needs of pupils and their problems.

Finally, there is the professional aspect of all that we have said in this book, the implication that every teacher, and everyone else who is concerned directly with schools and education, ought to come to terms with what we can now say about the part played by language in education. The first two chapters of *Exploring Language* offer a brief consideration of what is involved, but the reader will find the fully developed argument which underlies the aim of this present book set out in Part I of *Language Study, the Teacher and the Learner*, 'The concept of language study'. Part II of that book, 'A Guide to Reading in Language Study' is there for the reader who is now ready to make his own way into the literature and find out for himself what the exploration of language in education might have to offer him.

An Introduction to the Study of Man, J. Z. Young. Oxford 1971.
Inquiring Man: the Theory of Personal Constructs, D. Bannister and Fay Fransella. Penguin 1971.
Language and Social Behaviour, W. P. Robinson. Penguin 1972.
Class, Codes and Control Vol. I, Basil Bernstein. Routledge and Kegan Paul 1971, and Paladin 1973.
Exploring Language, Peter Doughty, John Pearce and Geoffrey Thornton. Edward Arnold 1972.
Explorations in the Functions of Language, M. A. K. Halliday. Edward Arnold 1973.
Learning How to Mean: Explorations in the Development of Language, M. A. K. Halliday. Edward Arnold 1974.
Communities in Britain, Ronald Frankenberg. Pelican 1966.
Akenfield, Ronald Blythe. Penguin 1972.
The Classic Slum, Robert Roberts. Pelican 1973.
The Unprivileged, Jeremy Seabrook. Longmans Green 1967 and Penguin 1973.
The Presentation of Self in Everyday Life, Erving Goffman. Allen Lane The Penguin Press 1969.
The Social Construction of Reality, Peter Berger and Thomas Luckmann. Allen Lane The Penguin Press 1967 and Penguin University Books 1971.
Society, Schools and Humanity, Douglas Holly. Paladin 1971.
Young Teachers and Reluctant Learners, Charles Hannam, Pat Smyth and Norman Stephenson. Penguin 1971.
Teaching as a Subversive Activity, Neil Postman and Charles Weingartner. Penguin 1971.
Language Study, the Teacher and the Learner, Peter Doughty and Geoffrey Thornton. Edward Arnold 1973.

Resources and materials referred to in the Postcript

Language in Use, Peter Doughty, John Pearce and Geoffrey Thornton. Edward Arnold 1971.
Using 'Language in Use', a teacher's guide to language work in the classroom, Anne and Peter Doughty. Edward Arnold.
Humanities Curriculum Project. Heinemann.
Lifeline. Longman.